Party Government and Regional Representation in Canada

This is Volume 36 in the series of studies commissioned as part of the research program of the Royal Commission on the Economic Union and Development Prospects for Canada.

The studies contained in this volume reflect the views of their authors and do not imply endorsement by the Chairman or Commissioners.

Party Government and Regional Representation in Canada

PETER AUCOIN
Research Coordinator

*Published by the University of Toronto Press in cooperation with
the Royal Commission on the Economic Union and Development
Prospects for Canada and the Canadian Government Publishing
Centre, Supply and Services Canada*

University of Toronto Press
Toronto   Buffalo   London

Grateful acknowledgment is made to the following for permission to reprint previously published and unpublished material: Deneau Publishing & Company Ltd.; Macmillan of Canada; Speaker of the House of Commons.

© Minister of Supply and Services Canada 1985

Printed in Canada
ISBN 0-8020-7280-1
ISSN 0829-2396
Cat. No. Z1-1983/1-41-36E

CANADIAN CATALOGUING IN PUBLICATION DATA

Main entry under title:
Party government and regional representation in Canada

(The Collected research studies / Royal Commission on the Economic Union and Development Prospects for Canada,
ISSN 0829–2396 ; 36)
Includes bibliographical references.
ISBN 0-8020-7280-1

1. Federal government — Canada — Addresses, essays, lectures. 2. Representative government and representation — Canada — Addresses, essays, lectures. 3. Canada. Parliament — Caucuses — Addresses, essays, lectures. 4. Political parties — Canada — Addresses, essays, lectures. I. Aucoin, Peter, 1943–   II. Royal Commission on the Economic Union and Development Prospects for Canada. III. Series: Research studies (Royal Commission on the Economic Union and Development Prospects for Canada); 36.

JL167.P37 1985   320.971   C85-099134-X

PUBLISHING COORDINATION: Ampersand Communications Services Inc.
COVER DESIGN: Will Rueter
INTERIOR DESIGN: Brant Cowie/Artplus Limited

44,813

CONTENTS

FOREWORD

When the members of the Rowell-Sirois Commission began their collective task in 1937, very little was known about the evolution of the Canadian economy. What was known, moreover, had not been extensively analyzed by the slender cadre of social scientists of the day.

When we set out upon our task nearly 50 years later, we enjoyed a substantial advantage over our predecessors; we had a wealth of information. We inherited the work of scholars at universities across Canada and we had the benefit of the work of experts from private research institutes and publicly sponsored organizations such as the Ontario Economic Council and the Economic Council of Canada. Although there were still important gaps, our problem was not a shortage of information; it was to interrelate and integrate — to synthesize — the results of much of the information we already had.

The mandate of this Commission is unusually broad. It encompasses many of the fundamental policy issues expected to confront the people of Canada and their governments for the next several decades. The nature of the mandate also identified, in advance, the subject matter for much of the research and suggested the scope of enquiry and the need for vigorous efforts to interrelate and integrate the research disciplines. The resulting research program, therefore, is particularly noteworthy in three respects: along with original research studies, it includes survey papers which synthesize work already done in specialized fields; it avoids duplication of work which, in the judgment of the Canadian research community, has already been well done; and, considered as a whole, it is the most thorough examination of the Canadian economic, political and legal systems ever undertaken by an independent agency.

The Commission's Research Program was carried out under the joint direction of three prominent and highly respected Canadian scholars: Dr. Ivan Bernier (*Law and Constitutional Issues*), Dr. Alan Cairns (*Politics *and Institutions of Government*) and Dr. David C. Smith (*Economics*).

Dr. Ivan Bernier is Dean of the Faculty of Law at Laval University. Dr. Alan Cairns is former Head of the Department of Political Science at the University of British Columbia and, prior to joining the Commission, was William Lyon Mackenzie King Visiting Professor of Canadian Studies at Harvard University. Dr. David C. Smith, former Head of the Department of Economics at Queen's University in Kingston, is now Principal of that University. When Dr. Smith assumed his new responsibilities at Queen's in September, 1984, he was succeeded by Dr. Kenneth Norrie of the University of Alberta and John Sargent of the federal Department of Finance, who together acted as co-directors of Research for the concluding phase of the Economics research program.

I am confident that the efforts of the Research Directors, research coordinators and authors whose work appears in this and other volumes, have provided the community of Canadian scholars and policymakers with a series of publications that will continue to be of value for many years to come. And I hope that the value of the research program to Canadian scholarship will be enhanced by the fact that Commission research is being made available to interested readers in both English and French.

I extend my personal thanks, and that of my fellow Commissioners, to the Research Directors and those immediately associated with them in the Commission's research program. I also want to thank the members of the many research advisory groups whose counsel contributed so substantially to this undertaking.

DONALD S. MACDONALD

At its most general level, the Royal Commission's research program has examined how the Canadian political economy can better adapt to change. As a basis of enquiry, this question reflects our belief that the future will always take us partly by surprise. Our political, legal and economic institutions should therefore be flexible enough to accommodate surprises and yet solid enough to ensure that they help us meet our future goals. This theme of an adaptive political economy led us to explore the interdependencies between political, legal and economic systems and drew our research efforts in an interdisciplinary direction.

The sheer magnitude of the research output (more than 280 separate studies in 72 volumes) as well as its disciplinary and ideological diversity have, however, made complete integration impossible and, we have concluded, undesirable. The research output as a whole brings varying perspectives and methodologies to the study of common problems and we therefore urge readers to look beyond their particular field of interest and to explore topics across disciplines.

The three research areas, *Law and Constitutional Issues*, under Ivan Bernier, *Politics and Institutions of Government* under Alan Cairns, and *Economics* under David C. Smith (co-directed with Kenneth Norrie and John Sargent for the concluding phase of the research program) — were further divided into 19 sections headed by research coordinators.

The area *Law and Constitutional Issues* has been organized into five major sections headed by the research coordinators identified below.

- Law, Society and the Economy — *Ivan Bernier and Andrée Lajoie*
- The International Legal Environment — *John J. Quinn*
- The Canadian Economic Union — *Mark Krasnick*
- Harmonization of Laws in Canada — *Ronald C.C. Cuming*
- Institutional and Constitutional Arrangements — *Clare F. Beckton and A. Wayne MacKay*

Since law in its numerous manifestations is the most fundamental means of implementing state policy, it was necessary to investigate how and when law could be mobilized most effectively to address the problems raised by the Commission's mandate. Adopting a broad perspective, researchers examined Canada's legal system from the standpoint of how law evolves as a result of social, economic and political changes and how, in turn, law brings about changes in our social, economic and political conduct.

Within *Politics and Institutions of Government*, research has been organized into seven major sections.

- Canada and the International Political Economy — *Denis Stairs and Gilbert Winham*
- State and Society in the Modern Era — *Keith Banting*
- Constitutionalism, Citizenship and Society — *Alan Cairns and Cynthia Williams*
- The Politics of Canadian Federalism — *Richard Simeon*
- Representative Institutions — *Peter Aucoin*
- The Politics of Economic Policy — *G. Bruce Doern*
- Industrial Policy — *André Blais*

This area examines a number of developments which have led Canadians to question their ability to govern themselves wisely and effectively. Many of these developments are not unique to Canada and a number of comparative studies canvass and assess how others have coped with similar problems. Within the context of the Canadian heritage of parliamentary government, federalism, a mixed economy, and a bilingual and multicultural society, the research also explores ways of rearranging the relationships of power and influence among institutions to restore and enhance the fundamental democratic principles of representativeness, responsiveness and accountability.

Economics research was organized into seven major sections.

- Macroeconomics — *John Sargent*
- Federalism and the Economic Union — *Kenneth Norrie*
- Industrial Structure — *Donald G. McFetridge*
- International Trade — *John Whalley*
- Income Distribution and Economic Security — *François Vaillancourt*
- Labour Markets and Labour Relations — *Craig Riddell*
- Economic Ideas and Social Issues — *David Laidler*

Economics research examines the allocation of Canada's human and other resources, how institutions and policies affect this allocation, and the distribution of the gains from their use. It also considers the nature of economic development, the forces that shape our regional and industrial structure, and our economic interdependence with other countries. The thrust of the research in economics is to increase our comprehension of what determines our economic potential and how instruments of economic policy may move us closer to our future goals.

One section from each of the three research areas — The Canadian Economic Union, The Politics of Canadian Federalism, and Federalism and the Economic Union — have been blended into one unified research effort. Consequently, the volumes on Federalism and the Economic Union as well as the volume on The North are the results of an interdisciplinary research effort.

We owe a special debt to the research coordinators. Not only did they organize, assemble and analyze the many research studies and combine their major findings in overviews, but they also made substantial contributions to the Final Report. We wish to thank them for their performance, often under heavy pressure.

Unfortunately, space does not permit us to thank all members of the Commission staff individually. However, we are particularly grateful to the Chairman, The Hon. Donald S. Macdonald, the Commission's Executive Director, Gerald Godsoe, and the Director of Policy, Alan Nymark, all of whom were closely involved with the Research Program and played key roles in the contribution of Research to the Final Report. We wish to express our appreciation to the Commission's Administrative Advisor, Harry Stewart, for his guidance and advice, and to the Director of Publishing, Ed Matheson, who managed the research publication process. A special thanks to Jamie Benidickson, Policy Coordinator and Special Assistant to the Chairman, who played a valuable liaison role between Research and the Chairman and Commissioners. We are also grateful to our office administrator, Donna Stebbing, and to our secretarial staff, Monique Carpentier, Barbara Cowtan, Tina DeLuca, Françoise Guilbault and Marilyn Sheldon.

Finally, a well deserved thank you to our closest assistants, Jacques J.M. Shore, *Law and Constitutional Issues*; Cynthia Williams and her successor Karen Jackson, *Politics and Institutions of Government*; and I. Lilla Connidis, *Economics*. We appreciate not only their individual contribution to each research area, but also their cooperative contribution to the research program and the Commission.

IVAN BERNIER
ALAN CAIRNS
DAVID C. SMITH

PREFACE

Among its terms of reference, the Commission was required to consider "changes in the institutions of national government so as to take better account of the views and needs of all Canadians and regions." The section of the Politics and Political Institutions Research Area entitled "Representative Institutions" had its research program shaped primarily by this particular focus of the Commission's terms of reference.

Nine studies were undertaken within the research program of Representative Institutions. The critical role of political parties as devices of political representation generally, as well as their particular functions within the operation of our system of party government, were central themes in a number of these nine studies. This was to be expected given the constitutional design of parliamentary government and our practice of responsible government.

In the actual design of the research program, two major foci were identified for extensive study. The first was the role of our national political parties as devices for the representation of national and regional interests and their integration into party policy, which for the governing party of course means national government policy. Our objective here was to provide an assessment of the degree to which national political parties serve to integrate our national polity. It was this task that Professor David Smith undertook, and his analysis and assessment provide a carefully developed account of the actual behaviour of our parties in regard to national integration.

The second focus identified for extensive study was the actual and potential capacity of the party caucus to provide for the representation and reconciliation of national and regional interests within the workings of party government. Professor Paul Thomas undertook this assignment and has produced an in-depth look at the basic dynamics of the least well-known of our structures of party government.

The papers by Smith and Thomas, as well as research on related topics, make clear the fundamental role which we have given to political parties within the operation of our national political institutions. In what began as an overview by the research coordinator but ended up as essentially a separate paper, I have explored the crucial link that party provides between the forces of regionalism on the one hand and the functions of our national institutions of government on the other. Contrary to Smith and Thomas, I do argue for extensive reform but, like them, I assume that our national politics is and will continue to be firmly grounded in a system of party politics. It is for this reason that my paper is included in this volume on party government.

PETER AUCOIN

ACKNOWLEDGMENTS

The task of analyzing the complexities of our institutions of national government required the involvement of many people. First of all, I am grateful to all the researchers who undertook studies for the Commission's research section on Representative Institutions. I am honoured to be the coordinator of their published studies.

Alan Cairns, as Director of the Politics and Institutions of Government research program, provided intellectual direction and collegial support that were always appreciated if not always acknowledged. John Hayes, Mark Krasnick, Maurice Pinard, Donald Savoie and Jennifer Smith served as members of my research advisory group and their advice contributed greatly to the research program and its individual studies. In addition, Jennifer Smith's evaluations and suggestions on a number of topics and her succinct and lucid analyses were always helpful and appreciated.

The assistance and advice of Cynthia Williams and Karen Jackson, executive assistants of the research program, were essential to this project. As scholars in their own right, they also added immensely to the intellectual exercise. The detailed comments and suggestions of Richard Simeon, Bruce Doern and David Ablett contributed greatly to the study of a number of topics. The logistical work of Donna Stebbing, the editorial help of Ruth Crow, and the secretarial and administrative assistance of Dawn Riley, Cindy MacDonald and Marilyn Slayter were also greatly appreciated.

P.A.

1

Party Government, Representation and National Integration in Canada

DAVID E. SMITH

Introduction

If there is one constant that emerges from a study of Canada's national political parties since Confederation, it is that they are uniquely placed to accommodate the conflicting demands inherent in a federal system. For much of the country's history, they have acted as the principal conciliators of the society's tensions. In so doing, political parties have commonly been accepted as the sinews of a healthy Canadian federalism. But it is equally obvious that for the past quarter century the governing party in Ottawa has chosen not to play this traditional role. Instead, it has defined the political contest and promoted policies such as language, the Charter and medicare, which overarch the social and territorial divisions of the country. In short, while national parties have the power to court the regions, the Liberal Party in the last two and a half decades has chosen not to do so.

The reasons why the Liberal Party has set nation ahead of region and the effect of this decision on political debate in Canada are crucial to understanding the current state of parties. In fact, until the significance of what has occurred is acknowledged, the present debate over the reform of national political institutions will remain inconclusive. Although a diverse culture and economy limit choice, parties nonetheless are autonomous organizations which consciously select policies within these limits; the choices they make, as much as the institutional environment in which they operate, determine the quality of representation and national integration by which they are judged.

While political parties have scarcely gone unstudied in Canada, their central role in the operation of national political institutions has, surprisingly, escaped the attention it deserves. Two reasons may be suggested for this oversight. First, parties are informal private organizations which, when they are successful in dominating the House of Commons, provide for a time the formal public institution which is government. Except on rare occasions before the 1970s and thereafter mainly for election expense purposes, national parties have stood outside the law. Consequently, they have not been amenable to external reform, and Canadians, who by habit and tradition are institutionalists in their political interests, have left them alone. The nexus between party and government, which it will be argued below is the heart of Canadian politics, remains unexplored in its details and the reciprocating influence of its parts has been underestimated.

A second reason for this condition is the blinkered scholarship which accompanies the prevailing theory of parties. This is the brokerage theory, which is both empirical and prescriptive. It purports to describe how parties actually practise their art and it defends that practice. According to this theory, political parties in Canada are supposed to be agents of consensus, not instruments of choice: they should include, not exclude. Therefore, the attention of scholars and critics is focussed on how well or how poorly national parties accommodate the variety of opinions that characterize modern society. Moreover, the hold of this theory is so strong that where parties are found to be insufficiently national in their appeal (measured in brokerage theory by the bases of their voting support), blame is generally attributed to formal political institutions such as the electoral system, and the utility of the theory itself is not questioned. Avoiding for the time being arguments about the electoral system's relationship to the party system, the fact remains that the influence of brokerage theory is to divert attention once more from what is argued here to be the crucial relationship — the relationship between national political parties and the development of national political institutions.

The primary thesis of this paper is that party government, that is, the system of rule which places a party in government, has determined Canada's political development. It has done this not only because party government results in a remarkably concentrated form of political power, but also because parties must look outside of Parliament to secure the support necessary for dominance in Parliament. Always then, there are the two dimensions to party government: the intra-parliamentary and the extra-parliamentary. Each requires special abilities from the party leader if he is to succeed in dominating his party. Since Confederation, political parties have had to make choices about how they would seek to secure support. Until the First World War they followed what is described in this paper as a local approach, paying heed to constituency factors but often enveloping their appeal in a national or expansive language. After the war a more accommodative approach was favoured in which emphasis was placed on reconciling group interests. This, in turn, gave way after the Second World War to what might be called a centralist or pan-Canadian approach to seeking support, wherein policies were designed to appeal to individual citizens regardless of their geographic location, religion or class.

The origin, study and evolution of party government in Canada are elaborated in the first section of this paper. The second section examines three models of party government and their approaches to winning support, with particular emphasis on the experience of parties in the twentieth century. The final section examines parties as devices for representation and national integration. Among the subjects considered in this section are regional representation within parties, the place of protest parties and the power of appointment as an alternative method to secure regional representation.

Some introductory comments on the perception of national parties are in order here. While the argument about political party development presented in this paper dissents from the more popular attention given institutional explanations, it would be misleading to discuss Canadian parties but ignore the general indictment, if only because it is so prevalent.

The general view is that national political parties in Canada have failed as organizations of representation and accountability. Neither of the old parties, it is said, can still engage the loyalties of voters from all sections of the country, and party discipline in Parliament undermines informed opposition as well as effective expression of constituency interests. Recent attempts at democratizing parties by promoting greater rank-and-file participation in policy formulation appear, even by generous estimate, to have been modest in result. At the same time, organizational changes in the Liberal Party in particular in the last two decades have spawned a professionalism which generates intra-party resistance from the constituencies. The costs, measured by the decline in the relevance of political parties to major issues of the day, are evident on all sides. What was the contribution of political parties to the constitutional debate and settlement of the last decade? Where do parties stand on aboriginal rights? A year after its proclamation, have parties waxed or waned as citizens invoke the Charter of Rights to redress wrongs? The sombre answers to these and similar questions indicate the shrinking relevance of political parties in modern Canada.

These are serious concerns. Even the least astute observer recognizes that party and Parliament are central to Canadian democracy. Parliament is the forum where political parties are most visible, but the report of the Canadian Bar Association's Committee on the Reform of Parliament (1982, p. 22) states that it is "too partisan and largely inefficient." Even if the accusations of failure of the party system are exaggerated, their widespread and repeated expression gives cause for concern and demands a reply. Murray Edelman (1971, pp. 7–10) has written of politics as a metaphor whose "symbols sustain and develop [man] or warp him" and material benefits or deprivation are less important than the "cues" leaders give that they are responding to demands even if the response is negative.

It is here, in the low esteem for national parties as effective instruments of popular expression, that the danger lies.

During the spring and summer of 1983, the Special Joint Committee of the Senate and the House of Commons on Senate Reform heard arguments that the failure of national institutions to integrate Canada was a direct product of political parties which, for a variety of reasons, had ceased to balance regional interests.[1] That claim will be explored below, but its pronouncement is a measure of the disillusion among western Canadians, for instance, whose frustration occasionally echos the old query: What is the constitution to us if we mean nothing to the constitution?

It is tempting to dispute these criticisms by arguing that they arise from an idealized view of party in the past. To some degree, this is true. Probably at no time was either of the old political parties so all-embracing in the territory it claimed to represent or its elected members so independent as adversaries of the executive as modern critics like to suggest. Modern government and the extensive and complicated demands it faces are unprecedented, and historical analogies are at least suspect if not irrelevant. It should also be remembered that in 1867 the Fathers of Confederation did not grant representation the same primacy as either their American counterparts a century before or modern critics of political parties and Parliament a century afterward. The objectives of Confederation were practical: relief from debt, new railways, enlarged financial and credit capacity. The legitimacy of the new federal state rested on these and other purposes of government successfully achieved. Samuel Beer (1978, p. 15) has described the American experiment as "representational federalism"; a more descriptive label for the Canadian experiment would be "purposive federalism."[2]

That being said, the modern perception of party and national political institutions as defective in their ability to represent and to govern does not disappear. The malaise that is said to infect government, broadly defined, remains and requires explanation and analysis. It is the purpose of this paper to do both, beginning with a discussion of the origin and concept of party government.

Party Government

Origin and Concept of Party Government

Canadians live under the misunderstanding that theirs is a young country, when in fact it has enjoyed a comparatively long uninterrupted constitutional development. The major continental powers of Europe have all experimented with several constitutional structures in the period since Canada was formed as a federation. In none of them can it be said, as it can in Canada, that political parties played an instrumental part in their creation. Nineteenth-century party organization, though incomplete by today's standards, predates modern Canada; it was the rudiments of party which converted colonial forms of rule into responsible government.

The achievement of responsible government was the achievement of party government. While every schoolchild learns of the first achievement, the second tends to go unremarked. Because Canadians have been governed nationally for well over a century by one or the other of two political parties, they accept, almost uncritically, the role of party in government. This is not to say that political parties — their leaders or their policies — escape censure. Rather, it means that government in Canada is assumed to mean party government. The adverb "almost" is necessary because once there were the Progressives, who did not accept party government as inevitable, natural or, in light of their experience, desirable.

W.L. Morton (1950) best summarized the Progressives' critique when he wrote:

> The evil [of the governmental system] was found to be in the party system of representative democracy. The elected representatives of the people were elected by the party organizations, which corrupted weak members of the electorate and took advantage of traditional partisanship among the voters. Once elected the representative became the agent not of his electors, but of the party. The party, in its turn, was controlled by the "boss," or by the party caucus, and both by the moneyed interests which has supplied campaign funds and which expected favours of government in return. (pp. 16–17)

The Progressives stand out as critics of party government as much as for the rarity as for the force of their accusations. Canadians accept party government because they are familiar with it. If pressed to give reasons as to why party government is necessary, their answers, though less trenchant perhaps, echo the arguments for responsible government made long ago by reformers like Robert Baldwin and Joseph Howe. That is, that party government secures responsible government, that party government democratizes a constitutional system whose origins are not democratic. They would say, with Disraeli, that "without Party, Parliamentary government is impossible."

The achievement of responsible government conferred on political parties a primacy in the governmental system which can hardly be exaggerated. At the centre there is the "governing party," a telescoped phenomenon between whose parts it is difficult if not impossible to distinguish. Party and government bear on each other: party enhances or limits what government can do; government enhances or limits the ambition of party. The intermingling of party and government and the consequence of that hybrid for Canadian federalism will be discussed below. At this point, the essential feature to note is that party government confers exceptional power on the leader of the legislative party in particular (especially when in government), the legislative members generally, and a handful of notables.

This power allows them to exert control over their extra-legislative parties, that is, over the rank and file, and to use them for electoral purposes.

How the inside party determines to use the outside party depends on many factors, such as ideology, electoral calculations and leadership aspirations, but that the party leaders enjoy an advantage which results from a political system that places them at the very centre of government is the hallmark of Canadian politics.

Studies of Party Government: Leaders and Centralism

It is the nature of Canada's governmental system that explains the extensive but selective literature on the country's political parties. Although there is evidence that it may be changing, scholarship has been more concerned with the constitutional and institutional aspects of the political system than with its actual governing. Studies of leaders have been favoured over studies of the politics, behaviour and policies of their parties. The result is a bias in academic writing which accepts, but does not analyze, the importance of party government.

In the literature on Canadian party politics the study of minor parties came first; the study of major parties came later and in a less comprehensive fashion. For instance, although there are individual works of distinction on the Liberal and Conservative parties, there is no massive analysis comparable to the ten-volume series on Social Credit written between 1950 and 1959.[3] Appearing early in the 1960s were the first large-scale electoral studies, beginning with John Meisel's *The Canadian General Election of 1957* (1962; see also Meisel, 1964). These have continued up to the present as cooperative enterprises (see Penniman, 1975, 1981; Clarke et al., 1977). Since 1950, there has been an explosion of biographies and autobiographies of party leaders in this century who, excluding those of the Co-operative Commonwealth Federation and the New Democratic Party, served also as prime ministers.[4] Mackenzie King heads the list in attention given, but since he tried to a degree,[5] and the others even more so, to set himself apart from day-to-day party matters, especially finances, and since Canadian parties are not driven by doctrine or ideas, these works reveal remarkably little about the dynamics of party politics. They do, however, tell us a great deal about personalities and in so doing reflect as well as encourage the Canadian preoccupation with leaders and leadership. One source of this unidimensional attitude toward politics, and one that sets Canada apart from Britain, is that here few members of cabinet other than the prime minister write memoirs.

In the last three decades, there has been no full-length explanation of the party system in Canada comparable to, say, S.E. Finer (1980), *The Changing British Party System, 1945–1979* or Walter Dean Burnham

(1983), *The Current Crisis in American Politics*, which are only two recent works from a vast selection on the subject in Britain and the United States. The closest approximations would be John McMenemy and Conrad Winn (1976), *Political Parties in Canada*; Hugh G. Thorburn (1979), *Party Politics in Canada*; and M. Janine Brodie and Jane Jenson (1980), *Crisis, Challenge and Change: Party and Class in Canada*. In this literature, discussion not devoted to the party system and leadership selection or federalism or social cleavages usually focuses on Liberal party dominance. Over the last decade, the issues of the *Canadian Journal of Political Science* underscore the selectivity of research interest, while the comparatively modest treatment of political parties in the three standard English-Canadian university textbooks on Canadian politics demonstrates the general paucity of attention. The most recent edition of R. MacGregor Dawson (1970), *The Government of Canada* devotes less than 20 percent of its pages to the subject (that is, 3 of 23 chapters, with the titles "Political Party," "Party Organization" and "Party Activities and Problems"). Richard J. Van Loon and Michael S. Whittington (1981) in their most recent edition of *The Canadian Political System: Environment, Structure and Process* give 10 percent of their pages to the subject, this time in two of 19 chapters titled "Political Parties in the Canadian System" and "The Parties: An Historical Perspective." J.R. Mallory (1984) in his revised version of *The Structure of Canadian Government*, discusses political parties within one chapter ("The Electorate") of the book's 10 chapters, a discussion which occupies less than 6 percent of the volume's 463 pages. The principal work in French on Canadian politics, André Bernard (1977), *La Politique au Canada et au Québec*, deals with political parties in a single chapter of 15 pages, which constitutes 11 percent of the book's pages.

One reply to these comments might be that the influence of the party system, like monuments to great men, is all around us: party infuses our political life and it is impossible (and would result in distortion were it possible) to distill its essence. Another response is that the discussion so far excludes reference to the electoral system or to representation and that these are of immense and growing concern for parties and for national politics. There is substance to both statements, though the first, concerning the pervasiveness of political parties, is justification itself of the need to establish firmly their place in current Canadian politics, while the second, as examination of any index to periodical literature will show, is of recent vintage and indicates that academic fashion parallels (though it may precede) the popular view which equates parties with elections and campaigns.

If, in research, British and American political scientists give more attention to their respective party systems than do Canadian scholars, the explanation possibly lies in the more intense competition between their major parties. Certainly, in the last 20 years, the striking feature (for a Canadian) of politics in those countries is the alternation which takes place between Conservative and Labour governments in Britain and between Democratic and Republican presidents in the United States. In these instances, it should be noted, competition is not linked positively to voter interest. In both Britain and the United States, voter turnout in recent decades has slumped and the effect of this apparent lack of interest on the electoral fortunes of parties who regularly expect to occupy the seat of government is to concentrate academic attention on the condition and operation of the party system.

In Canada, where alternation in government between parties at the federal level is infrequent and where voter interest remains constant (the turnout was the same in 1980 as in 1945), there is understandably less sense of the need to explore a party system whose performance appears anything but unpredictable. In place of this concern Canadian academics have substituted their own, i.e., the effect of federal-provincial governmental tension on the organization and operation of national parties. The focus of research attention thus shifts from how political parties interact, how they govern or how they choose to appeal to the electorate, and turns to questions about intra-party friction between federal and provincial wings of the Liberal, Progressive Conservative or New Democratic parties. Always, too, emphasis on federal-provincial rivalry elevates party politics into a clash of personalities. The product of this research interest is books on the disintegration of national parties or on the travails of party leaders. How party government works or how the party system operates is favoured with less attention. The effect of this contrast in research priorities is to strengthen the predominant characteristics already evident in the politics of each of the three countries: in Britain and the United States, to promote a national focus and in Canada, to fragment it.

In all three countries, however, the study of party theory is shunned. The *ABC Political Science Index*, which lists political science journals from some 30 countries, indicates this differential interest of Western political scientists. For any single year, there may be well over 100 articles cited, but fewer than 10 percent are normally concerned with general theory, the vast remainder being devoted to elections, policies and reforms. In addition, of those devoted to theory, a disproportionate number are published in French, German, Italian and Spanish journals. In short, Anglo-American concern about parties does not extend to abstract speculation. The practical questions of politics seize the attention of scholars just as they pique the interest of the public, and in Anglo-American countries political parties, organized as they are to win power, are eminently practical institutions.

Thus, in Canada and, with different emphasis, in the United States and Britain, interest apes practice in the study of political parties. The description by an American political scientist of parties as "the most diaphanous of institutions" suggests why their enveloping influence often escapes notice and why, when it does not, it is as frequently misperceived

(Clotfelter, 1975, p. 559). The nature of politics is little understood by the public, and parties around which Finer (1980) says "the government system fits . . . as the skin fits the human frame" (p. xi) are perhaps the least understood of all. A paradox is plain in such statements, for parties are the institutions credited with being the principal vehicles of modern democracy by which public opinion is transmitted and governmental responsibility ensured. Academics contribute to the haze by their Manichean-like practice of depicting parties in terms of "opposites": there is the theoretical world of parties, and then there is the real world; there is the active party leader, and there is the passive; there is the professional and the amateur; there are the leaders and the led. None of this is of much help to the public whose suspicion of parties appears endemic.

What is certain is that outside of a general election campaign in each of the three countries mentioned, parties as institutions for electoral or even for legislative purposes are scarcely visible to the average citizen. In their stead are the dozen or so party personalities who dominate media coverage of political events. Cabinet government confers power on a few, and public perception of the political parties who provide the cabinet personnel is similarly concentrated. For this reason, the literature in Canada agrees that "the influence of political parties on the daily experiences of Canadians is not great" (McMenemy and Winn, 1976, p. 152). That judgment extends to the legislative party as well, for it suffers a similar ignominy when party and government are equated. The spotlight of publicity on the front benches of both sides of the House relegates all others to the shadows.

In their study of Parliament, Allan Kornberg and Judith D. Wolfe (1980) reported that "the image that appears is one in which the 'Prime Minister' and 'elections' are Parliament" (p. 50), a characteristic whose source a different set of authors, Clarke et al. (1977), trace to media coverage of campaigns: "Only 15% of news reported during the [1974] campaign had anything to do with anyone other than the party leaders" (p. 279).[6] Not only the campaign, but also the manner in which the election results are initially reported reinforces this singular view. On election night, television and radio report gross party scores with fleeting attention paid to constituency results. Newspapers do scarcely better, only rarely publishing all constitutency returns for the nation. This is the political variant of the more general distortion that accompanies statistical reporting: "statistics [define] issues by the categories employed, the questions asked (and not asked), and the tabulations published" (Social Science Research Council, 1982, p. 30). This social science phenomenon extends beyond the subject of political parties and elections but is one more factor contributing to the "gladiatorial nature of the election" (Finer, 1980, p. 127).[7] The consequence of this is to transform political parties into spectators of the single drama of leadership competition on which attention is fixed even when the contest moves to the parliamentary forum.

Studies of Party Government: Candidates and Localism

Several unhappy consequences derive from this diminished view of political parties. Despite the fact that public, media and scholarly attention focus on leaders, studies of political leadership in Canada are few and, from the perspective of this paper in particular, analysis of the reciprocal influence of party and government on leadership is scant. While it is often taken for granted that government leaders who are also party leaders may use the respective resources of each office to pursue a variety of goals, the significance of their freedom to choose among policies and strategies to win support goes unheeded.

The obsession with leaders is even less satisfactory for the study of extra-legislative parties, and yet local activists and local supporters are as much a part of a broadly defined political party as are the legislative leaders and notables: indeed, as will be discussed below, the centre of gravity of the post-Confederation parties was located in the constituencies. It is to this subject that attention must turn if the imbalance in the study of political parties is to be redressed and if the territorial dimension of Canadian political parties, which up to now has been absent from the discussion, is to be introduced.

The study of extra-legislative parties traditionally takes place within narrow confines, with the customary distinction being drawn between parties of mass participation, like the Co-operative Commonwealth Federation and the NDP, and those like the Liberal and Progressive Conservative parties who place a low priority on rank-and-file participation. With regard to policy formulation and leadership selection, this comparison may have less meaning today in light of the organizational changes that have occurred in the two "old parties" in the last quarter-century. Nonetheless, the distinction lingers.

What is missing from these discussions and what the focus on parliamentary leaders in modern political parties ignores is the subject of candidate selection. In a system of party government, one way of balancing the bias in favour of parliamentary leadership is for local supporters to seek control of the constituency nominating process. This after all was one of the objectives of the Progressives, although they went further in ambition than most advocates of localism, experimenting tentatively in 1921 with primary elections for delegates to constituency nominating conventions. However, the concern to balance central power, to delimit it and thus guarantee a broadly based distribution of influence, has been evident within all Canadian political parties. It is a desire not easily met.

Centralization is the organizing principle of legislative parties, but legislative parties cannot become the party in government unless they make national, extra-legislative appeals; then the organizing principle becomes decentralization. Thus, for political parties in a parliamentary system, there is a contradiction between how they must organize to exercise power and how they must organize to win power. The tension between the two requirements is permanent. In a geographically small, culturally homogeneous country with a unitary government, like Britain, reconciliation in favour of the centralizing principle is at least practicable. However, in a continental country, with a culturally divided society and a federal government, like Canada, reconciliation itself seems uncertain, and the tendency may be at one time to favour centralization and at another decentralization.

In Canada, candidate selection is generally agreed to rest on local decisions, except in rare instances. Candidates are normally local residents who are conscripted or co-opted by local party leaders to run for nomination; parachuting of candidates by central headquarters is almost non-existent. Exceptions are made for party leaders who have led a peripatetic existence. The most recent of these is Brian Mulroney, who joins Mackenzie King (the most travelled local candidate of all) and a legion of others with the willing, even enthusiastic, acceptance of constituency leaders. With this exception, involvement of central officials is a delicate matter. It would be misleading to claim that it never happens; it happens, for instance, through the appointment of a sitting candidate to an office of federal patronage, thus opening a seat in the larger interests of the national and not just, presumably, the constituency party. There is, however, little reason to quarrel with the observation of Robert Williams (1981), one of the few students of selection procedures in Canada, when he says: "This most important responsibility provides a reason for local organizations to flourish and to remain relevant in a political age dominated by leadership" (p. 119).

The effect of local autonomy in this matter is not confined to elections alone. Recruitment is "an organizational task for parties": it attracts interest and support, it educates, and it provides aspirants with an introduction to the skills of leadership and elections. It can have detrimental effects as well: high turnover of candidates can hurt the riding organization, for in its wake can follow frustration, disarray and even faction. This is the experience of such local parties long excluded from power as the Liberals in Alberta.[8]

Local autonomy in candidate selection, then, is a fact of Canadian political life and a crucial element to understanding the structure of political parties. Its influence may be demonstrated by reference to a subject where the factor of localism has been underestimated: women and politics. The literature on the very low percentage of women members of Parliament recognizes the importance of party as a mediating "structure, serving as a critical bridge between the political aspirant and elective office" (Brodie and Vickers 1981, 326; Kornberg et al. 1979, chap. 8). It analyzes the degree of receptivity to female candidates evident among major and minor parties and in different regions of the country. What it does not do adequately, however, is to weigh the importance of decentralization in the performance of this function in the 282 federal constituencies. Nor, relatedly, does it take into account the exclusionary effect of the single-member-district/simple-plurality-vote system. One advantage of a list system would be to give those who compile the list (the central party apparatus or its agents) the latitude to place women, native people or other politically excluded persons at the top of the list. Thus, an enterprising party might well decide that this is a way to underline its commitment to gender equality in this country.[9] Admitting the crucial role of the constituency in candidate selection in no way disputes the findings on women parliamentarians, but it does suggest that the explanation for the findings is to be found more at the local level than in the parties' central offices.

Localism in candidate selection is a corrective to the leadership orientation that infects the study of political parties in Canada. It may in fact be one of the few countervailing forces — perhaps even the principal one — to the national organization. Localism may actually increase in response to legislation that limits campaign expenditures but subsidizes candidates' expenses. Its survival is a reminder of the importance of territory in the organization of Canadian political life. This discussion of leadership and candidate selection (of centralization and decentralization, if you will) underlines the geographic linkage which political parties are traditionally supposed to provide. This is as important a theme in the study of Canadian political parties as that of party government. Parties perform a multitude of functions; among the most generally agreed upon are that they structure the vote, integrate and mobilize the electorate, recruit leaders, organize governments, formulate policy and aggregate interests (see King, 1969). These may be boiled down to two general functions: parties govern and parties represent. Candidate selection falls within this second general function but so, too, does territorial integration. As institutions that predated Confederation, the role of political parties in linking centre and periphery was special.

Political Parties and Territorial Expansion

The Canadian centre is a political one or, more precisely put, there is a political centre and then there are economic and cultural centres. A.R.M. Lower (1939) once noted that while Toronto shared with Montreal the domination of the West's trade and finance, "it was much more successful than Montreal in building up a human connection," a connection which has continued in the media to the present day. The same might be said for all of English Canada. For French Canada, Montreal's cultural hegemony, especially in the electronic age, is unrivalled. The national capital, on the other hand, is not a metropolis that attracts artistic or business talent, nor does it influence events beyond the political realm and even there it must guard against provincial incursions on all sides. The unity which comes with the concentration of national activity in one centre is denied to Canada. The linkage between the governing centre and its constituents must necessarily be political and either partisan or administrative in character.

Ottawa is political in several senses. Possessing no natural or historical claim to be the seat of national government, it was selected using political (and military) criteria. Its influence in directing the destiny of the Dominion has lain, in the first instance, with its parliamentary authority, supplemented always by its spending power. It was here that representatives of the former colonial elites assembled as the new federal Parliament, and it was from here that the political parties, hesitantly and often inexpertly, extended their hold over the new reaches of the Dominion. The incorporation of the provinces admitted to the union after 1867 and securing the allegiance of the original but unhappy Maritime provinces, particularly Nova Scotia, was the task of political parties. It was they who traded in sentiment and loyalties, though the question of fidelity to the new federation was usually backed up with convincing patronage ranging from postmasterships to railroads. For those areas of the country distant from the centre and in an era when the state performed only the minimal functions of law and order (reduced still further in Canada by dependence upon the British military for defence), the Canadian federal government created bureaucratic departments (agriculture, fisheries and especially the interior) whose powers and patronage, when placed at the disposal of the governing party of the day, aided in this task of incorporation.

If the contribution of political parties was crucial in the "rounding out" of Confederation, its effect did not rest there. Britain and the United States have been described by some European observers (Badie and Birnbaum, 1983, chap. 8) as "weak state models," by which is meant that they did not seek "to dominate the periphery via the stewardship of an outside administration (*intendants* or *Landräte*)." The same could be said of Canada, for here as there it was "the civil society" that organized itself, especially through representative institutions, to control its own development. (The first half-century of active nation-building occurred in the absence of a professional civil service; by contrast, the era of province-building since 1950 has been coincident with the growth in size and competence of provincial bureaucracies.) The implications for the federal policy were momentous, especially in the realm of administration. A professional civil service was slow to develop, and its influence is still less than in countries like West Germany and France. In its place was favoured a small, patronage-based service which could be supplemented, when expertise was required, by royal commissions or, if the expertise was needed on a permanent basis, by the creation of Crown corporations. Much the same happened on the provincial level: Saskatchewan, which for the first four decades of this century possessed a model "party machine," achieved a record in the frequency and versatility of its royal commissions (Fowke, 1948). Administrative courts were unnecessary in practice and unpopular in theory; the latter attitude still prevails and has, indeed, strengthened in response to the activities of a range of federal regulatory agencies which, while not administrative courts, would nonetheless incur the wrath of A.V. Dicey.[10]

Canadian practice, responding to Canadian conditions (a federal, bilingual and continental society), departed occasionally from the "weak state model," but it was a matter of degree and then only of slight degree. Deviations were usually limited to federal policies affecting the West: the creation of the Department of the Interior, whose territorially specific mandate was unlike that of any other department of government in Canadian history; the formation of the North West Mounted Police to assure peaceful western development; and the retention of the Prairie provinces' natural resources until 1930. For a time, these policies established a special relationship between Ottawa and the Prairie provinces. Critics labelled it "colonial" because of the opportunity offered for federal involvement in the affairs of the territories, beginning with the events leading to provincial autonomy in 1905 and continuing for more than a generation afterward. Thus, the weak state model was compromised temporarily, to allow for federal direction of the unique settlement period, but in principle and generally in practice, Canada remained a country committed to voluntary action for its growth, with political parties among the most prominent and visible agglomerates of volunteers.

As a consequence, political parties can be looked on historically as agents of territorial and social inclusion. C.B. Macpherson (1962, pp. 20–27) dismissed the introduction of competitive parties into Alberta as an irrelevant manifestation of quasi-colonialism on the part of the federal government. Even he, however, did not rule out the contribution of party as an organizing device, responding to the perceived inequities of national economic policies and, more particularly, expressing provincial agrarian discontent. The social implications of parties, especially the Liberal Party, in mobilizing the waves of immigrants who arrived in Canada after 1896, are matched in importance in Canadian history only by the territorial inclusion of new provinces under the Conservatives before them. Both enterprises were imbued, said the cynics, by overweening partisan self-interest: the guarantee of more votes either, as in Sir John A. Macdonald's case, by violating the "rep. by pop." principle when negotiating the entry of new provinces into Confederation, or, as in Sir Wilfred Laurier's case, by sedulously courting the immigrants who settled by the tens of thousands on the Prairies (Cartwright, 1912, pp. 94–95).[11] The motives of both men may be open to question but not the result of their actions: the nationwide expansion of political parties that had originated in the St. Lawrence heartland. Both parties sought votes, but to win them each adopted a new and broader view of Canada. For the Conservatives this was reflected in the enunciation of the National Policy and for the Liberals in the reception of immigrants whose needs liberated that party from its Roman

Catholic and, more particularly, its Quebec confines. In each instance, strong incentives to establish provincial and ethnic linkages made possible new structures of national integration.

The growth of national political parties was expected and accepted, as the evolution of the franchise and voting laws bore witness. Liberal and Conservative perceptions of the nature of federalism might differ, as was made abundantly clear in the franchise debates of the last quarter of the nineteenth century when the right relationship of central to provincial governments was at issue. What was never in question was that the party was the proper instrument to achieve the objective of national integration (Morton, 1943). All this changed after the First World War, Union Government, civil service reform, and the appearance of a strong agrarian third party. Old loyalties were questioned, partisan administration deplored, and the political consensus of a half-century dissipated. The war, as well, put an end to other certainties that had conditioned politics: imperial security gave way to Dominion autonomy in external affairs, which led in time to a close alliance with the United States; the economic optimism of the Laurier years evaporated to be replaced by a two-decade-long (1916–35) search for security in grain, Canada's principal industry. The effect of both changes was to push government, at first hesitantly and then resolutely, into broad but previously little explored policy areas. The implications for parties were at that time only dimly perceived.

All of this is history and appears of slight relevance to modern party concerns, but it is history that underlines the centrality of party to Canadian development. The ambit of party is more extensive and more intrusive than modern commentaries often admit. Perhaps parties in Canada never penetrated society's institutions as they did in some European countries. They are not communitarian, and neither Liberal nor Progressive Conservative youth and women's associations are any match for the economic, welfare and recreational enterprises of continental parties. Nonetheless, the pervasiveness of party in the expansion of Canada, their virtually coterminous existence, and the determining influence of a handful of party leaders in shaping the federation are beyond question. Sir John Willison's (1919) observation about politics almost a century ago, "To be out of office was to be out of the world" (p. 122) is as accurate a measure of the strength of party spirit on all sides now as then.[12]

Models of Party Government

Post-Confederation Political Parties

Before 1914, political parties dominated the federal system; the governing parties, Conservatives under Sir John A. Macdonald and Liberals under Sir Wilfrid Laurier, were creating the Canadian nation. After 1918, this paramountcy disappeared in the face of regional revolt and sectional change. In its place, William Lyon Mackenzie King established a form of party and governmental leadership which, in this paper, is labelled as accommodative. That approach directed Canadian politics through the interwar years and then, with declining vigour, until the end of the Louis St. Laurent era. With John Diefenbaker as prime minister, the primary goal of intergroup consensus began to give way to a pan-Canadian approach to leadership, an approach that was sympathetic to group interests but even more favourable to a conception of Canada as a nation of individuals. This break with the accommodative model became clearer under Lester Pearson and then guided the leadership of Pierre Trudeau. The details of the evolution follow but before embarking on that discussion it is necessary first to summarize the character of political party leadership in the period between Confederation and the First World War and then to comment on the changes in economic, political and social conditions which preceded and accompanied the disruption of the war and to which the old political parties had to adjust when that conflict had ended.

It is argued earlier in this paper that political parties played a central role in the territorial expansion of Canada, that they made national integration possible because they provided the ligament for a society whose economic and cultural ties were slow to grow. One student of the period has said of the federal government that it was "the single most important energizing agency" in post-Confederation Canada (Stewart, 1980, p. 16). This assertion would seem to conflict with the earlier description of Canada as a weak state model of national consolidation, but there is no inconsistency, for two reasons. First, the growth of the nation in these years was in the West, and it has already been admitted that in that region there was a deviation from the model in the form of such regionally specific features as a federal department of the interior, federal retention of the Prairies' natural resources and the creation of the North West Mounted Police. A more important reconciling factor lies in the vehicle of that active federal government; it was the Conservative and Liberal parties, the alter egos of their respective federal governments, which were the organizing forces in Canadian society and politics. As Gordon Stewart (1980) noted:

> There was no aristocratic or traditional landed class that still had an influence in public affairs; there was no lingering peasant presence upon which a political movement could be based; there was no rapidly expanding capitalist class deriving wealth and power from industrialization; there was no mass labor movement seeking to form its own party. In these conditions the federal political parties, representing the dominant middle class and particularly the professionals were extraordinarily influential in Canadian society. (p. 15)

Donald Creighton (1953) has noted that the original provinces of Confederation constituted only a fragment of British North America and that, as Sir John A. Macdonald liked to phrase it, "even in the existing union, it would be a long time . . . before the gristle hardened into bone" (p. 3).

As Stewart has brilliantly shown, Macdonald was the first to see that political parties could be the agents of nourishment.[13] And it was he, personally and throughout his career, who used "patronage to build up not merely party loyalty but party structures outside the assembly." The features of the system he created are described in illuminating detail by Stewart, but for the purposes of this discussion, the principal points to note are the following: patronage pervaded the political system; it was systematically followed; and Macdonald played a central role in its conduct. The chief result of this development, which Stewart emphasized was "taken over, as with so much else, by Laurier," was a party system both intensely local in its interests and profoundly personal in its management by the party leader. For Canadian politics, the effect of this approach to party management was to ignore and even resist change that could not be accommodated within the framework of constituency politics. There was "a structural problem in the federal parties" which made it difficult for them to respond to the new forces of urbanization, industrialization and provincialism that became manifest toward the turn of the century. It was an "effective party structure" but not, says Stewart, a "modern" one.

This depiction of Macdonald and Laurier runs counter to their popular image as nation builders. Their achievements in securing and rounding out Confederation would seem to place them alongside the pan-Canadian leaders who, it was suggested earlier, view Canada as a collection of individuals to whom national appeals are made that override divisions of class or religion. There is an ambiguity, then, between the popular perception of these singular leaders as nation-builders and the reality of Macdonald's and Laurier's intense localism in managing politics; party structures should imitate, not conflict with, governmental objectives. The explanation for the poor fit between party practice and governmental performance lies in the unique era of expansion following the post-Confederation years.

For Macdonald, "the primacy of the Dominion" was the measure of all things. Therefore, repeal of the Union, in the case of Nova Scotia's discontents, was "not even a matter for discussion"; negotiating "collectively rather than individually" with the unruly provinces in 1887 was out of the question (Creighton, 1955, pp. 3, 473). The role of the Dominion in national affairs was paramount, as demonstrated in settlement of the West, development of eastern industry and construction of a transcontinental railway. The continuing thread of Macdonald's era and of Laurier's, over four decades together, was expansion of territory, of economy, of population. More than anything else, the experience of expansion set Macdonald and Laurier apart from their successors. Great enterprises successfully achieved marked their administrations. It was argued earlier that the goal of expansion more than any other motivated the Fathers of Confederation, for from expansion would come not only economic well-being, but also political breathing space and military security. This was purposive federalism, and while its outward sign might be great enterprises, its inward logic demanded the creation of a party system based on minute attention to local constituencies. Only if the party were built in each constituency, in each new territory added to the Dominion, would the majority be there in Parliament available to the leader to advance his nation-building ambition. Macdonald and Laurier were the creators not only of modern Canada but of modern political parties in Canada. They learned to command the party in Parliament by dominating the party outside Parliament.

The appeals of post-Confederation politics were national, the practices local. Nevertheless, the combination worked and by the opening of the twentieth century, national political parties and national integration through the political parties was achieved. Party competition right across the country was secured for the first time by 1896 (Reid, 1932). However, as already intimated, the party system was based on a society whose foundations were beginning to crumble. The success of the national economic policy and the First World War guaranteed that Canada would not remain the fixed society of local, agricultural communities that the creators of the post-Confederation party system had known. In the West, the arrival of the immigrants created another agricultural society of ethnic communities and gave the original party system a second life, which lasted until the disruption of the grain trade during and after the war. In the Maritimes, where emigration and the tariff undermined the region's industrial base, the society grew more entrenched and more dependent on staples than before, so that the old party system could continue unchallenged by new economic and social forces (Acheson, 1977). At the centre, however, and then in the West, the strains became evident as the premises of post-Confederation politics confronted, but did not yield to, the changes of twentieth-century society.

To the reasons usually cited for this transition (the growing partisanship among provincial farmers coupled with new demands on their governments to act in areas of legislative responsibility allocated to the provinces) should be added one other of long-term import for governing the federation. The homogeneous political elite of 1867 (homogeneous in the sense of having brought Confederation into being and of having nurtured the new national institutions of Parliament, cabinet, the civil service and parties) was no longer ascendant.[14] New provincial elites had been formed and, in some instances, separated from the federal: Saskatchewan's early political leaders were graduates of federal politics. Even in Quebec and Ontario, it had taken at least two decades for provincial elites to secure a hold against Macdonald's centralized federalism.

The First World War accentuated this phenomenon of changing elites by accelerating trends in urbanization and industrialization which were already evident before the conflict and had their most direct and immediate impact in Ontario and, to a lesser extent, in Quebec. Rural and agrarian interests no longer held the unchallenged attention of the federal government, and it was this change in the relative importance of agrarian and non-agrarian interest which W. L. Morton (1950) suggested was an important contributing factor to the rise of the Progressives. Neither the tariff nor freight rates explained the farmers' electoral combustion; rather, they saw a future in which agriculture served but did not rule Canada, and they resisted. They also failed.

Agriculture might be declining relative to industry, although a decade and a half later, responding to western farm pressure and in opposition to private traders, the federal government "nationalized" the collection and marketing of wheat. The economic transition, however, did not mean that government was in the pocket of Canadian commerce. In fact, the experience of agriculture following the war was a harbinger of the federal government's later response to demands of other economic and social groups. Ottawa, as already stated, is the political, not the economic or cultural, centre of Canada. While there have been notable exceptions, the most obvious being C.D. Howe's long tenure in the business-related portfolios of the governments of William Lyon Mackenzie King and Louis St. Laurent, the federal government has also experienced difficulties in working with the business community. Unlike the societies of traditional European capitals (or even those of most Canadian provincial capitals), businessmen and politicians do not rub shoulders in Ottawa. A similar separation might have happened but did not in the United States; there an easy movement between public and private sectors occurs. Part of the reason lies in the separation of governmental institutions, the "multiple crack" phenomenon, to use Morton Grodzins' (1967) picturesque phrase, which offers a variety of access to those who approach government.[15] Despite the need for contact, Canada has fewer arrangements for continuing consultation among these groups than exist in most other industrial countries, where the isolation is less acute.[16] It is now clear that the isolation is not limited to agriculture or traditional business matters but extends in other directions as well, including labour questions and science policy (Fish, 1983).[17]

With the end of the wartime emergency, the conflict of demands on government, generated in part by this economic transition, had become a permanent feature of national politics. Demands on government were not new of course, nor was conflict, but they mounted in the 1920s and government set its modern course by responding with regulatory action and shared-cost programs. The Liberals, who after 1921 formed the government most of the time and who for this reason will receive disproportionate attention because of their influence on federal and governmental development, greeted with reluctance this changing attitude toward the role of government. Philosophically, the party and its leader, Mackenzie King, opposed activism and warned repeatedly of the dangers of intervention. This is one reason why it is impossible to find the Liberal

Party, as opposed to the Liberal government, reforming its organization to accommodate change. There were other reasons as well. The party first and last was an electoral organization; policy discussion during the long King era was strange, even forbidden, territory for the rank and file. It continued this way until the late 1950s. As well, and this was to become a significant factor once policy did rise to the surface of party consciousness, Anglo-American-style parties congenitally resist manifestations of professionalism. Proponents of professionalism might argue that it strengthens party by providing intellectual resources to debate and helps formulate policy; nonetheless it is invariably held suspect as being a limit on participation and a restraint on political activity (see Blondel, 1963, pp. 128–30; and Fairlie, 1968, chaps. 1 and 2). This was to be the experience of the Liberal Party: during the King and St. Laurent years, professionalism was shunned; during the Pearson and Trudeau years, non-elected managers gained unprecedented influence in Ottawa only to encounter strong opposition from Liberal supporters distant from the capital (Smith, 1981, pp. 62–71, 84–89, 148–149).

To these old and new examples of restriction on Ottawa's contact with the country's geographic hinterland and economic base must be added the cultural isolation of the capital for the French-Canadian member of Parliament. McMenemy and Winn (1976, pp. 75) treat this form of isolation as "a proxy for distance." Nothing has been said so far in this paper about French-English relations and parties, but any discussion of the party tradition in Canada would be remiss and misleading in not stressing its central place and the fundamental role of party from the outset. Territorial incorporation and social inclusion, argued here as primary functions of political parties, have special significance in the context of maintaining Quebec's commitments to Canada.

The Accommodative Approach: The King and St. Laurent Years

From 1920 on, Ottawa began to lose control of organized forces in Canadian life: farmers first, then business and labour, and still later, the provinces. It took the Second World War with the vast powers it conferred to order events (powers and a confidence thus engendered which continued for another dozen years) to restore the federal government to its former dominance. It was in the years between the wars, however, that a revised form of political rule took shape under Mackenzie King, one which checked the disintegration implicit in the events surrounding the conclusion to the First World War. Inheriting a divided party and faced with what still remains the largest electoral revolt in federal political history, King began a record of leadership whose most outstanding characteristic was his success at accommodating the factions and divisions in Canadian society. The test of his political dexterity continued through depression, drought, war and reconstruction: an unprecedented series of challenges to occur in the space of one man's tenure in office as prime minister and of such magnitude as to give cause for the expressions of self-pity in his diary. The legion of critics notwithstanding, it was a remarkable achievement and not only for political longevity.

The foregoing is not an apologia for King or his party but a reminder of two facts: the importance of dominant though not necessarily commanding leadership (the electorate is right to grant it so much weight) and the kaleidoscopic demands made on leadership in the second half-century since Confederation. One of King's remarkable skills was his ability to recognize and give rein to the political talent around him, although his biographer (Neatby, 1976) notes that the independence and power his colleagues were given as reward could also limit their influence: "their success as the advocates of the interests of their region made them less acceptable in other parts of the country" (p. 15). Opportunities to hone this skill recurred throughout his leadership as he sought to deflect the depredations of bumptious third parties and pugnacious provincial governments. It is not necessary to describe King's organizational and political triumphs; this has been done with admirable care by Reginald Whitaker (1977). From the perspective of a study of national political parties, the importance of the King years is that the key to party organization, the basic tenet of political life, was federalization. The provincial base of party organization had always been significant, for Liberals and Conservatives alike. During the tenure of Mackenzie King, however, the "decidedly federal nature" of the party became an article of faith and practice, one which profoundly affected political rule in the country and one which equally distinguished King's leadership from that of Macdonald and Laurier in the post-Confederation period.

The linkage was provided by ministers who dominated their regions, such as James G. Gardiner, C.D. Howe, Ernest Lapointe, and Angus Mac-Donald in the King cabinet; the names alone conjure up associations with strong administration and partisanship. However, "ministerialism" (the term is Whitaker's) did not convert the cabinet into a holding company of provincial chiefs. Always, there was King's insistence on the need for consensus, regardless of time, before decisions were implemented. King's deftness in defusing the Progressive threat in Parliament and in the general elections from 1921 through 1926 took time and patience. Gardiner, then still in Saskatchewan, wanted to meet the farmers' challenge head-on, but King's will prevailed, as it always did on political strategy. The farmers could be accommodated and, later, the interests of labour met, if the party acted judiciously and reasonably. The latter injunction made sense if it were realized that the Liberals should represent, that it was their natural obligation to represent, the interests of farm and labour. King did not see such economic groups, even when organized politically, as the enemy but only as the misguided. His pompous and turgid rhetoric, his platitudes, made him an easy target for ridicule, and his parliamentary opponents often fell into the trap of resorting to that and doing nothing else.

The earlier era of national expansion had passed, but King's sense that the Liberals had a mission to guarantee national unity and social justice provided an integrating force for his government and party which held in check strong and potentially divisive tendencies. Any number of illustrations of this shrewdness could be cited, but King's decision not to contest the Hamilton East by-election in 1931 reveals his skill from several perspectives. Here was a rare instance of central authorities intervening locally to prevent a Liberal nomination. It was King's opinion that if the Liberals stood to one side and allowed the Labour and Conservative candidates to do battle, Labour would win, which it did, and that the Labour candidate, Humphrey Mitchell, could be co-opted into Liberal ranks, which he was, eventually becoming Minister of Labour between 1941 and 1950. As Whitaker (1977) noted:

> The riding lost its traditional Tory cast and has since been a Liberal stronghold, where the party has drawn considerable support from the unionized working class electorate. . . . The Liberal party thus gained a labour base in a working class constituency which might otherwise have turned to the CCF, and drew in a representative of organized labour to the federal labour ministry. (p. 46)

As Macdonald and Laurier had before him, King excelled as a party leader, but his methods were different. If the earlier prime ministers had perfected the uses of patronage to create and hold constituency loyalties, King favoured a position at one remove from such direct involvement. He supported party organization and organizers in their work because it protected him from innumerable local squabbles, but distance had an added advantage. Unlike his predecessors, King throughout his years in office had to calculate in his political strategies the potential of third-party activity. Intimate involvement with constituency matters could only complicate the negotiations and compromises he always sought in order to include rather than exclude interests within the Liberal Party. On the other hand, King maintained a strong belief in his judgment of what was best for the party and would, if need be, interfere in organizational matters. This meant overriding, on occasion, the advice of ministers whose responsibility for Liberal welfare in their respective provinces or regions King normally respected. One example is his disagreements with James G. Gardiner over how to combat the Progressive challenge in the 1920s.

King's concern for the party, however, was paramount, and this awareness, perhaps more than any other factor, accounts for the Liberal Party's multiple successes before and after the Second World War. Ward (1977b) has described how the party established acceptable relationships between (among others) the parliamentary and extra-parliamentary wings of the party, between the leader and his supporters, between federal and provincial organizations, and between contributors of campaign funds and those who let government contracts. (p. 43)

King's accommodative tactics, however, did not vanquish all opponents, and it was indicative for future Canadian politics that his chief failures lay in dealing with provincial governments of disparate partisan complexion: in Alberta where the Liberals were a lost cause provincially and federally after 1921, in Quebec where they monopolized federal politics but, by the mid-1930s, faced implacable provincial opposition in the Union Nationale, and in Ontario where the fiercest opponents to the national Liberal Party in elections at either level were the provincial Hepburn Liberals.

Neatby (1976) has written that King "did not realize that regional frustrations were too profound to be resolved by political tactics" (p. 247). It was a curious weakness in a party of such talent and strength, with a leader so attuned to changes in public opinion, although it is true that a regional lieutenant like Gardiner, with roots in the West, remained equally impervious to the tremors of ferment there. Federal government emergency power and its use during the Second World War to deal with defence, external relations and economic production matters, blunted national sensibility to provincial concerns remote from these great questions of state. The imperatives of wartime government also coincided with the recommendations of the Rowell-Sirois Report (Royal Commission on Dominion-Provincial Relations), thus placing a "burden" on the federal civil service which Harold Innis (1940, p. 568) described as "disquieting." Growth of the federal bureaucracy, even when intended to help the provinces, restricted their internal development: money and knowledge might move out from the centre, but it did so at the cost of provincial initiative and responsibility. Innis' reservations about treating the provinces as "static institutions" concerned economic adjustment, but the same could be said of political adjustment, the first major failures of which were evident even under so successful a party leader as Mackenzie King.

The accommodative party of King continued nine more years in power under Louis St. Laurent, but appearance disguised reality in several important respects. Unlike King, who always maintained an interest in party matters (but kept his distance from its conduct in his own mind as well as in public), St. Laurent "never had any genius for organization."[18] At the very time when bureaucracy was growing fastest and party needed tending, interest in it waned. The extra-parliamentary party, which had been Mackenzie King's sounding board, petrified. The cabinet ministers now indeed became the provincial chiefs they had always threatened to become. The centralism of Canadian federalism, let loose during the war years, was given free rein by the detachment of the leader from the affairs of the party. If localism had made the parties of Macdonald and Laurier unresponsive to social change of national proportions, the isolation of the Liberal leadership from constituency opinion in the early 1950s brought about an equivalent rigidity only now as a result of loss of touch with the people. The party leaders turned inward to instruments of government. As Ward (1977b) remarked:

> In that right turn the party virtually merged with the state, so that top civil servants, all appointed, and ministers, all members of Parliament, became almost indistinguishable from one another. (p. 43)

The interpenetration of party and bureaucracy, which before the First World War had taken place only at the lowest level of the civil service and which had been prohibited by the introduction of the merit principle through the Civil Service Act of 1918 and its regulations, returned after the Second World War in the guise of shared attitudes, if not common membership, at the highest level. Partisan sclerosis ensued though the symptoms of the disease, let alone the fatal prognosis, remained veiled to "the government party" almost to the end.

A second distinction between the King and St. Laurent eras, scarcely developed yet important for the evolution of Canadian political parties, was the articulation during the 1950s of attitudes and policies that might be called pan-Canadian. King had been a nationalist in that he sought to define dominion status and promote Canadian autonomy in peace and war. However, he avoided actions which would disturb relations between groups of Canadians and, particularly on the national question, between English and French Canadians. Only at the end of his period in office was there a suggestion of a new, pan-Canadian approach, in the form of the Canadian Citizenship Act of 1946. Although it was the first legislation of its kind, it was a harbinger of an attitude the St. Laurent government was to reveal on several occasions. Generically, the policies flowing from this approach might be seen as defining or promoting "national status." This, in fact, is how they are grouped in the guide to the St. Laurent papers in the Public Archives of Canada, the bulk of which, relating to this subject, were opened to the public in January 1984. They include, among other matters, discussion of a national anthem, a distinctive flag, the 1949 amendment to the BNA Act included in a new section 91(1), and dropping such customary usages as "dominion" and "royal."

In these circumstances, the government's objective had to be inferred from its actions, since nowhere is there an explicit statement of pan-Canadian attitudes. In other areas, especially the relatively unexplored domain of cultural policy, more concrete evidence of a change in direction from the King years is available. The 1951 Report of the Royal Commission on National Development in the Arts, Letters and Sciences (the Massey Commission) made a strong claim for federal government activity "in the general education of Canadian citizens" and argued that, if Ottawa does not act, "it denies its intellectual and moral purpose, the complete conception of the common good is lost, and Canada, as such, becomes a materialistic society" (p. 8). The St. Laurent government never spoke so boldly on behalf of the federal power, but its actions following the report's recommendations (establishment of university grants, creation of the Canada Council, introduction of a national television system, heightened support for existing cultural agencies) testified to its acceptance of a responsibility to act, at least in the nebulous realm of culture, for all Canadians.

The impact of cultural policy on the self-definition of citizens has yet to be evaluated in Canada. It seems indisputable, however, that the St. Laurent government's decisions in this area of public policy were of immense importance. On the one hand, they promoted on many fronts a Canadian cultural community which before 1950 had one public base, the Canadian Broadcasting Corporation; on the other hand, they stopped the drain to the metropolis of artists who in earlier years had had to abandon their region or culture if they were to find commercial work. Much could be said of the long-term influence of this set of policies on Canadians as individuals and as a people, but for the purpose of this discussion it is enough to end this section of the paper by making two points. First, such national policies would never have been considered by Mackenzie King, partly because it would have been foreign to him to think of federal government playing this kind of educative role and partly because he would have been concerned about their impact on his accommodative approach to politics. Second, these policies were not welcomed in Quebec for the very reasons King would have cited; they interfered with provincial jurisdiction and they demonstrated a federal system which had lost its balance and in which the central government knew no self-restraint.[19]

The Pan-Canadian Approach: Diefenbaker, Pearson and Trudeau

The defeat of the Liberals in 1957 marked the end of the accommodative party identified with Mackenzie King and modified by Louis St. Laurent. John Diefenbaker and the Progressive Conservatives did not bring this skill with them nor did they acquire it in office. Diefenbaker was chosen leader in 1956. In the 20 years before that, the party had had five leaders (R.B. Bennett, R.J. Manion, Arthur Meighen, John Bracken and George Drew), as well as an 18-month period in 1940 and 1941 when there was no leader. Conservative disorganization reflected the instability that follows rapid changes in leadership and precluded the integration of national, provincial and constituency associations: "Much of the organization," a student of the party wrote on the eve of Diefenbaker's coming to power, "exists almost entirely as 'window dressing' to impress the public"

(Williams, 1956, p. 110). Further, abrupt reversals in policy designed to attract or to repel in turn advocates of social welfare and private enterprise aggravated the problem and prevented the creation of a dependable support base among the electorate.

The Diefenbaker administration, especially after the 1958 sweep, appeared set to give stability to a party unfamiliar with that condition. But the forces of regionalism which had percolated and boiled over, even under King, now grew much stronger. It was Diefenbaker's misfortune to preside over the federal government as the Quiet Revolution burst on the scene in Quebec. Whether the federal Liberals, given their old dominance in the province, could have done better at meeting the challenge of Jean Lesage's Quebec Liberals is problematic. What is certain is that under Mr. Diefenbaker, the horde of western MPs in the Progressive Conservative caucus and the handful of Quebec ministers in cabinet proved unsympathetic and unequal to the task. Not for the first time were the costs of the Tory exclusion from Quebec to be paid by a Progressive Conservative government in Ottawa (and perhaps by Canadians across the country). William Hamilton, Postmaster General in that cabinet, later said that "none of [the French-Canadian ministers] approached a few of the outstanding ministers from other provinces" (Stursberg, 1975, p. 198). The front bench was not the only problem in Parliament. On the back benches sat nearly 50 MPs from Quebec whose Tory credentials were their good standing with Maurice Duplessis' Union Nationale, a warranty that expired when both Duplessis and Paul Sauvé, his highly regarded successor, died in 1959. Although there were an unprecedented number of Quebec MPs, there were now, proportionately, even more who were not from Quebec, for the sweep of 1958 had given Diefenbaker the largest majority in Canadian history. He had taken all but five seats in the four western provinces. These, plus the Ontario seats, created an imbalance between government and opposition members in the House and between Quebec and non-Quebec members in caucus that was to plague the new prime minister and exacerbate the problems he faced.

One of Mr. Diefenbaker's major difficulties was political abundance; its effect, paradoxically, was to immobilize the executive. Decisions in cabinet occurred infrequently and then after excruciatingly inconclusive debate. The "Chief's" electoral dominance in the West, the uncertain base of the PCs in Quebec and the divisions evident between Toronto and non-Toronto Ontario Tories meant that this cabinet was a far cry from St. Laurent's "corporation" of provincial chieftains. Personal style, too, influences political leadership, and Mr. Diefenbaker's style was to be that of extreme caution in delegating authority; at the same time, he experienced great (and inevitable) difficulties in coordinating decisions himself.

In the end, it was style, style determined by a personality one colleague (Jacques Flynn in Stursberg, 1975, p. 218) described as "flamboyant," which "started something new in many areas." The "something new" was policies and actions in the period between 1957 and 1963 which deliberately and directly appealed to Canadians as Canadians regardless of where they lived or what language they spoke. Mr. Diefenbaker's concept of his country was not a community of communities but, as he repeatedly avowed, "One Canada." The Bill of Rights, the national development policy (with its vision of the North, its Roads to Resources and National Energy Board), the extension of hospital insurance and the creation of the Royal Commission on Health Services under Mr. Justice Emmett Hall, these and other national policies revealed a pan-Canadian approach to political leadership which, in its explicitness, went far beyond the actions of the St. Laurent government before him.

The explicitness resulted in part from Mr. Diefenbaker's own personal interpretation of his policies. Unlike Mackenzie King's consensual style which avoided direct displays of leadership or St. Laurent's collegial cabinet, Mr. Diefenbaker repeatedly demonstrated that he saw himself as the leader of the people. There were specific party reasons for this: he was leading a party only recently long out of power and riven by division, in particular between progressive Prairie Conservatives and non-radical central-Canadian Conservatives. This was not a new division; it had plagued John Bracken, but Mr. Diefenbaker devised, through his appeals to the people, a new approach to overcoming it. This explanation, by itself, would make his seeking of direct access to the people only a partisan strategy, but it was more than this.

Mr. Diefenbaker was a product of the Prairies and, for whatever combination of personal and societal factors, acutely conscious of ethnicity. He was indeed the first national party leader to give evidence of this consciousness: one which struck a responsive chord not only in the "old ethnic" West but also in the "new ethnic" East — especially southern Ontario.[20] As a result, he took pride in his appointment of the first Ukrainian to the cabinet (Michael Starr of Oshawa) and the first Indian to the Senate. His sensibility to perceived discrimination and to the need to recognize previously unrecognized groups, thereby including them (for he thought they had not been included before) in the political system, derived from a common conviction that all Canadians were equal and none privileged.

Multiculturalism married to liberal individualism in the leadership of a Progressive Conservative was bound to create intra-party tension and thereby press the leader to look to the electorate to vindicate his interpretation of Canada. The same priorities were also to bring friction with French Canada, especially as the flowering of the Quiet Revolution became manifest. Mr. Diefenbaker's response was of a piece with his response to all groups in Canada. He would recognize them by some distinctive act; among others, in this instance, by introducing simultaneous translation of debates in the House of Commons and appointing the first French Canadian since Confederation to the office of governor general. He vehemently rejected, however, any policy that implied special status in Canada for the province of Quebec or for French Canadians (as he did for any other Canadians). It was over a proposal that the Progressive Conservative Party recognize Canada as composed of *deux nations* that he fought his last battle as leader, right up to the 1967 Progressive Conservative leadership convention (see Churchill, 1983).

Mr. Diefenbaker unequivocally introduced a pan-Canadian approach to leadership in the politics of the country but, as will be argued below, this approach did not disappear with the end of his prime ministership. In fact, the significance of this interregnum in the long period of Liberal rule was that it established an approach to leadership that Lester Pearson and Pierre Trudeau were to develop further and with distinctive adjustments, especially to accommodate French Canada. As well, they were to experiment, as Diefenbaker did not, with party reorganization to try to make the Liberal Party fit more closely their governments' national, pan-Canadian policies. Mr. Diefenbaker had neither the time nor the inclination to do this. On political matters, as opposed to administrative ones where his ministers acknowledge that he respected their departmental prerogatives, his leadership was markedly personal. "He really believed," said Alister Grosart, national director of the Progressive Conservative Party from 1957 on, "that he was elected, to put it in the corniest terms, the prime minister of all the people. He really felt that he had to be very very careful . . . to make his decisions in the interests of all the people and not for political reasons" (Stursberg, 1975, p. 151).

Quite separate from the electoral or personality dimensions of Mr. Diefenbaker's leadership, but of long-term significance for the development of Canadian political parties, was his relationship to the bureaucracy. The first transition of government between parties in 22 years presented a test for the British-Canadian model of a non-partisan civil service at the ready to serve any parliamentary master. The decision as to how adequately it performed its task is open to interpretation; Mr. Diefenbaker and some of his ministers remained forever suspicious of the bureaucracy's alleged Liberal proclivities, springing less perhaps from outright partisan attachment than from a symbiotic relationship engendered by decades of proximity. The non-elected side of "the government party" continued in office, according to Walter Dinsdale (Stursberg, 1975, p. 47), Diefenbaker's Minister of Northern Affairs and Natural Resources, and it proceeded to harass its new political masters: "I was constantly being pursued by certain departmental officials confronting me with crises that I must deal with immediately."[21]

This was only one side of the bureaucracy question. The other was the concern Innis had expressed two decades before, about the bureaucracy's effect on federalism. Diefenbaker had charged the Liberals and their civil servants with being insensitive to regional concerns; his own administration went some way to reverse this trend with policies of regional economic development (for example, the Agricultural and Rural Development Act, northern development, and Atlantic Provinces Adjustment Grants) that harkened back to activities identified with J.G. Gardiner and the PFRA (Prairie Farm Rehabilitation Act). When Mr. Diefenbaker spoke of his close relationship to the people, he had in mind not only pan-Canadian policies like the Bill of Rights, but also these and other countervailing policies which were attempts to reverse the centralism he identified with the Liberals.

The Diefenbaker government collapsed as a result of an issue of high bureaucratic content but traditionally of low concern in domestic politics and of slight structural effect on Canadian political parties. The area was defence and foreign policy. The question which proved to be incendiary was whether Canada should acquire or had agreed to acquire nuclear warheads for missiles placed on Canadian territory. It brought the government into conflict not only with U.S. politicians and their military advisors but with its own advisors, especially in the Department of External Affairs, a department uniquely identified with earlier Liberal policies to foster Dominion autonomy (and therefore in conflict with Mr. Diefenbaker's personal attachment to Anglo-Canadian ties) and more directly the modern creation of the former secretary of state for external affairs and now Liberal leader, Lester Pearson.

The triangle of government, party and bureaucracy which had brought down the Liberal Party after two decades of rule, proved the nemesis of the Progressive Conservative Party in a quarter of that time. The difference between the two events was that with the Liberals the parts had become so interrelated, if not fused, that "the Government party had lost touch with opinion not sponsored by the elites with which it was in daily and intimate contact" (Whitaker, 1977, p. 210); with the Progressive Conservatives, the relationship was never close enough to provide a workable partnership. On the particular question of the nuclear warheads for missiles, Mr. Diefenbaker chose the route dictated by public opinion as he discerned it. Thus, in opposition to the advice of his Minister of Defence, Douglas Harkness, who subsequently resigned from the cabinet, he refused to accept the warheads (Stursberg, 1976, p. 25).

Whether a decision to accept the warheads would have saved the minority government of Mr. Diefenbaker from the disintegration that soon followed the decision to reject them is a matter for conjecture. The party and government were so divided over policies, military and otherwise, and over personalities, principally Mr. Diefenbaker and his leadership, that it seems improbable it would have lasted for long. From the perspective of this paper, the most significant factor in the debate of 1962–63 was Mr. Diefenbaker's dependence in this tumultuous period on his appeal to the people. The pan-Canadian approach to leadership which, it has been argued, characterized Mr. Diefenbaker's years as prime minister, guided him up to his defeat and indeed afterward in his struggle to retain leadership of the Progressive Conservative Party.

The return of the Liberals in 1963 signalled neither a return to accommodative policies as practised by Mackenzie King nor the incorporation of provincial political communities through a minister at the centre, as seen in the St. Laurent cabinet. Instead, what has been described as pan-Canadianism, an attempt to create a Canadian community, became firmly established, first as the policy of the Pearson government and then of the Trudeau government. However, the policies that now appeared challenged the unhyphenated Canadianism of Mr. Diefenbaker. In its place and from the outset of his administration, Mr. Pearson sought to construct a country-wide nationalism based on bilingualism and biculturalism. In a speech in the House of Commons which he later described in his Memoirs as the speech of which he was the "most proud," he depicted Confederation as "a settlement between the two founding races of Canada made on the basis of an acceptable and equal partnership" (Munro and Inglis, 1975, pp. 239, 67–69). Here was the mustard seed of a policy which was to germinate and blossom through royal commission, statute and administrative order over the next two decades and transform Canada's perception of itself.

The old mold of triumphant unilingualism outside of Quebec was to be broken and a new era of cooperative federalism was prophesied. The error of the past, said Mr. Pearson, was the centralist assumptions the federal government had taken from the Rowell-Sirois Commission's report (Munro and Inglis, 1975, p. 238). There was a contradiction here between, on the one hand, advocating a policy which would transcend provincial boundaries and on the other, promising a retreat from interventionist central government. The success of the one undertaking would appear to challenge the other, for stronger, more active provinces would be less amenable to the assertion of federal language policy. This would be particularly the case where the assumptions of that policy had the least validity — in the West. Not only were there few Francophones in the Prairie provinces, there were also proportionately fewer Anglophones than elsewhere. Here bilingualism and biculturalism ran up against Mr. Diefenbaker's ethnic world.

This paper is not concerned with the history of this policy or with its worth. What is pertinent, however, is that there was such a policy, that it was based on assumptions having little regard for either the West or the East, and that in the West, there was a tradition (embodied in Mr. Diefenbaker) of objecting to perceived special status. Mr. Pearson might say that the days of centralism had ended, but to westerners long sensitive about the question of their economic and political status in Canada, bilingualism and biculturalism betrayed the claim and added a new dimension to an old set of grievances.

Pan-Canadianism was not limited to language, however. Under Mr. Pearson, medicare and the Canada Pension Plan were policies with national content too, for they dealt with social matters and individual concerns that did not coincide with provincial boundaries. The same was true during Mr. Trudeau's years in office; to bilingualism in the early period and medicare restored as an issue of national debate most recently must be added energy, constitutional reform and the Charter of Rights. These have affected all parts of the country because of their individual, regional and national importance and will be discussed further toward the end of this paper.

At this point, it is necessary to turn to the subject of party organization during the Pearson and Trudeau years. Unlike their predecessors in office, both Liberal leaders experimented with party reorganization and in particular, both experimented with party reforms in the 1960s. Participatory democracy, the sophisticated use of polling and public relations agencies, the use of the mass media, and the emphasis on the leader (to the detriment of regional chieftains) all reflected the same motivation as their major government policies, which was to speak to Canadians directly, in a national language, and without intermediaries.

The lesson the Liberals drew from their defeats in 1957 and 1958 was that "ministerialism" as practised in the St. Laurent period was at fault and that the party must be "rejuvenated." To this end, two unprecedented experiments in reform ensued: one, to create "pan-Canadian" structures free from provincial entanglements and the other, to promote a "mass membership party" that encouraged individual participation.[22] Each reform was associated with a dominant extra-parliamentary figure, the first with Keith Davey, the national organizer for the period in question (1961–66), the second with Richard Stanbury, party president between 1968 and 1973, and each had a detrimental effect upon relations between Liberals at the centre and those in the regions.

The urbanizing and industrializing trends which the Progressives had resisted a half-century before and whose centralizing efforts Mackenzie King sought always to ameliorate by political means now reached full force in the Liberal Party's reforming zeal. The voice of reform spoke a vocabulary that rang strange in the ears of hinterland Liberals. The primacy granted to rank-and-file participation in policy formulation, the belief that policy should be the product of exchange of opinion and not a balancing of interests, the rejection of patronage as a perversion of principle and a vestige of old-style politics, the commitment to "nationalized" standards (be it in health, welfare or the dairy industry, among others) were all new ideas to the party of King and St. Laurent.[23] The vanguard of change was the Toronto-and-district riding associations; here tradition fell first because demographic and economic change was strongest and here the stakes were greatest once redistribution showed more concern for reflecting population growth than for protecting political fiefdoms. With the Liberals ever dominant in Quebec and the Diefenbaker Conservatives entrenched in the West, the focus of attention shifted.

Electoral strategy alone did not account for the shift either. Technology and increased sophistication in political knowledge also played a part. To overcome the gap in communication with which the end of "ministerialism" presented them, the Liberals resorted to myriad structures and techniques borrowed from abroad (especially from the presidential campaign of John F. Kennedy in the United States), showing particular enthusiasm for public relations agencies and opinion polls whose Canadian offices were in Ontario.[24] Television, too, played an important role. Transmission from Toronto and Montreal had begun in 1952, and a microwave network for instantaneous national programming was in place by 1958. More than radio, television's influence was to centralize: considerations of cost and scarce expertise discouraged multiple production facilities, with a consequent sacrifice of regional perspective. The impact of these changes has only now begun to be evaluated (Siegel, 1983; Fletcher, 1981).[25]

The first set of reforms (between 1961 and 1966), which transferred organizational and electoral matters into the hands of committees whose members were appointed by the federal party leader, were in place for the election of 1963. But neither then nor in 1965 did Mr. Pearson secure the majority he and the federal campaign committee desired. The depressing news came always from the West; in 1963 three seats in the Prairies, in 1965 only one. The second set of reforms, devised to promote participatory democracy, were scarcely in place at the time of the Trudeaumania election (1968), when the Liberals won their first majority in a decade (with 11 out of 45 Prairie seats). By the time of the next election (1972), when the Stanbury reforms were fully operational, the Liberals lost their majority and were back to three Prairie seats.

The centrepiece of the Stanbury reforms was the politicization of government through opening decision making to rank-and-file participation. By so doing, it was believed, the scope of government would expand, for in the language of the period, the political agenda would be defined by the mass and not by the elite. Along with a policy organization of gargantuan proportions, there were a host of innovations in the form of "the political cabinet," a national as well as a provincial advisory council (composed of representatives of caucus, the Prime Minister's Office, Liberal headquarters and regional caucuses) and regional desks in the PMO to inject party considerations into government decision making. The impact of the parts and the whole of this reform enterprise proved disappointing when measured by observable policy emanating from government. That, perhaps, should not have been surprising, for parties are not, in Finer's word, "republics" whose members dictate to their leader (Finer, 1980, p. 180). If not surprising, however, it was nonetheless a premise that underlay Liberal action in these years. It is not necessary to detail its successes and failures; it is enough to note that it was tried. The contrast between the earlier accommodative party of King and St. Laurent and its opposite, a pan-Canadian party under Pearson and Trudeau, illuminates the circuitous journey that Canada's dominant political party had made during five decades of policy and organizational change. By 1980, the Liberal quandary of being in power but out of favour in the West appeared insurmountable, certainly by organizational means. It was this situation more than any other that contributed to the new urgency in finding an answer to the problem of regional representation.

Representation and Political Parties

In the foregoing sections of this paper it has been argued that party-in-government is the central fact of Canadian politics. The concentrated power which is its hallmark affects everything else and not least the evolution of the political parties themselves. Because of the resources they confer on their leaders, political parties have functioned as crucial institutions in the expansion and development of Canada. At different times, party leaders have adopted different approaches to the exercise of power, designing or redesigning policies and party organizations to enhance localism, to promote accommodation and to foster nationalism. While with each development it is possible to see the influence of changing economic and social factors, so too is it possible to see even more clearly the influence of individual leaders and their personal perception of how national politics should be conducted. However, the analysis of political parties so far has been primarily theistic in character, that is, power and direction have been seen to emanate from the centre. There is, however, another perspective, recognized earlier but left until now for elaboration, and that is the view from the constituencies, from the regions. Party government is also representative government and the question of representation, which in Canada almost always means the representation of interests which are territorially based, must be addressed.

The performance of political parties as representative institutions is a complex subject which may be approached from several directions. In the discussion that follows, the forum, the manner and the mechanics of regional representation will receive attention under three subheadings: political parties and the House of Commons; protest parties; and political parties and the electoral system.

Political Parties and the House of Commons

Although the Fathers of Confederation looked to the Senate to represent the regions, that institution never played the role envisaged by its framers. It was the cabinet and the popularly elected House of Commons, from which nearly all the ministers were drawn, which became and remain the principal foci of the representation question, and the House of Commons was not designed to give weight to regionalism. The three formulas used since Confederation in the redistribution of seats have secured at best rough justice for a federal state which from its beginning has experienced substantial movements of population but always massive disproportion between its concentration in two provinces and its dispersal in the rest.[26] The result is not surprising in light of the conflicting goals each formula was intended to meet and of which "rep. by pop." was always a negotiable item. With each redistribution, the major concern of Members of Parliament has been the effect of boundary changes on their present or future relationship to constituents.

A broader focus than this is rare though not unknown, as for example, in the debate at the end of the nineteenth century and in the early years of this one over the franchise (not its extension so much as which level of government would define it and for what purpose). The Liberals charged the Conservatives, who wanted a federally defined franchise separate from provincial franchises, with mistakenly treating "the country as a single community," when political reality for the Liberals was quite different: "Only in the provincial legislature are individuals represented as such. In the federal parliament it is the provinces which are represented by provincial delegations" (Morton, 1943, p. 78).[27] Nearly a century later, in the constitutional debate of 1981–82, these party positions were reversed, with the national stance struck by the Liberals and the Progressive Conservatives talking of a "community of communities." Stands taken on great issues of constitutional interpretation once in a century do not constitute a party platform; they occur so rarely as to be almost outside parliamentary life. More typical and more in conformity with the practice of redistribution is the journeyman view of Parliament, that "the prime relationship for every MP is the constituency that elects him."[28]

There are several reasons for the narrow, constituency focus, of which the single-member-district/simple-plurality-vote is only one: "Nothing . . . sharpens the mind of the MP so much as the thought of winning or losing some votes" and, excluding that band of huge constituencies between the northern territories and the settled areas of Canada, these votes are concentrated in geographically limited territory. Another reason for the constituency focus is the electoral insecurity of members. Unlike their British counterparts, they have no party organization at the municipal level to call on, so that the burden of electioneering falls on them alone.[29] Similarly, individual candidate responsibility is enhanced here, in contrast to the United States, because of the infrequent campaigns and the small number of elected offices. The cumulative effect of these factors is that "never in the past 50-odd years had more than one-third of the House of Commons been made up of safe seats" (Lovink, 1973, pp. 362–63).[30] A third reason for the strength of the constituency focus among MPs is the occupational and educational background of the candidates who are elected. It is well documented that there is a large proportion of lawyers and a small proportion of businessmen in Parliament. However, the increase in the range of occupations represented today compared to a century ago does not parallel that found in society. The effect of resistance to change, according to Paul Pross (1982, pp. 109, 110), has been to make Parliament "anachronistic"; Parliament's principle of localism, in the form of the individual member, renders it "ineffectual" for modern policy making (Pross, 1982, p. 31).[31] Members of Parliament today may be ineffectual, but they are able enough to defend their own interests, and it is often repeated that they must be "given" a larger role to play in Parliament if they are to acquire the expertise they lack: "The member of Parliament is a eunuch in this area. He needs resources and he needs investigative skills that he just does not have with the research structure behind his investigative functions right now."[32]

The question as to whether elaborate and costly research facilities will make for more informed and presumably more competent MPs is beyond the scope of this paper. In any case, the traditionally high turnover, which accentuates the constituency focus already encouraged by other factors, makes any proposal to educate MPs an expensive and short-term solution to the localism from which Parliament now allegedly suffers. The effect of all this is twofold. On the one hand, it promotes a close relationship between constituent and member, one facilitated by ease of communication and greater mobility. The MP from the West or Atlantic Canada today visits the riding more frequently during the session than ever in the past, even though he spends longer periods in Ottawa than used to be the case. On the other hand, today groups proliferate at accelerated speed and the liabilities under which MPs work make contact with groups unsatisfactory: "The individual MP can press individual remedies for individual cases," says Finer (1980, p. 178), "but only a party system is capable of generating the collective policy necessary to redress the grievances of a category." Put differently, in order to turn the discussion to regional representation, only parties can, as Irwin says (1960, p. 240), "reduce gross and inarticulate populations to practicable proportions for purposes of representation." They alone are suited to make the correctness of representation convincing.

The impracticability of looking to the individual member as regional spokesman requires elaboration, for there is always the contrast of the U.S. Congress.[33] Long ago the Canadian Progressives thought that the key to understanding lay in the structures of party in parliamentary democracy: caucus, discipline and nomination. Party constituted a thraldom from which there was no institutionalized escape. Without primaries to open up nominations and with patronage and the whips to enforce discipline, dissent died or was expelled. These arguments have been repeated at intervals ever since 1921, not only by third-party critics but also by disgruntled old-line party members. At one level, the frustration is fed by a sense of impotence; constituency views do not receive parliamentary expression because they are not approved of by party leaders. In other words, it is the suppression of Edelman's (1964, 1971) symbolic use of politics that chafes. This, rather than the difficulty of achieving practical change in party policy, accounts for the sense of stasis in the body politic. "There is no fluidity to a majority," noted one observer.[34] At another level, the frustration is fed by the public perception and media attention that is given to intra-party dissent: "Every time there is a division of opinion within the caucus, it is perceived . . . to be a crisis of leadership."[35] The negative publicity that accompanies such differences is as much of a restraint on the expression of diverse views as is the activity of the whip.

Party discipline is one manifestation of the centrality of partisanship in Canadian politics and one found as frequently in opposition as in governing parties. The Progressives were right to see it as the structuring principle of Parliament. It remains so, and attempts at parliamentary reform must seek to curb its excesses while harnessing the energy it injects into democratic government. The contrast between Canada and a federation like West Germany is striking for the strong partisanship found in the one but not in the other; not only is coalition government perennially shunned but also the daily life of the House of Commons is molded by the partisan rivalry that infects virtually all debates and procedures. It is frequently said that Parliament is held in low repute by the public (an attitude that televised debate has not changed) and that, as a result, there has been a loss of public confidence in the operation of political institutions (Canadian Bar Association, 1982, chap. 2). Such hand-wringing must be treated with suspicion if only because it has happened too many times before and has proven to be unwarranted. Even if the low esteem is proven, the explanation may lie elsewhere. It could spring from misunderstanding or impatience with the way the institutions work. That, however, is another matter.

Canadian MPs envy their colleagues at Westminster for the greater independence of members and for the greater efficiency of government which they perceive there. Their British colleagues and the British electorate, however, do not share this admiration. At Westminster, as in Ottawa, members want to participate more, but there is less now than previously that they can affect or effect. Frustration follows, for there, as here, the executive dominates. A.H. Birch (1964, p. 166) said there are two languages of Parliament: "the Liberal language" which says that Parliament "possesses sovereignty" to hold ministers to account and to control the executive, and "the Whitehall language" which says that Parliament is "an arena or forum to air grievances."[36] In Canada and in Britain, the Whitehall version rules. The importance of Parliament as a national forum is not thereby disparaged. It still calls government to account, and in debating and arriving at valid, sustainable decisions, it generates public acceptance of its policies. What makes Canada distinct is the matter of regional representation, more particularly its inadequate expression. That problem, however, has less to do with the operation of parliamentary government as practised in Ottawa and a great deal to do with the fact that regions have slight power to influence party officials before the whip is laid on.

Protest Parties

Ever since 1921 and the explosive appearance of the Progressives, regional protest parties with representation in provincial and federal legislatures have been a standard component of Canadian politics. In fact, their variability and durability have distinguished the Canadian party system when it is compared with that of other countries. Their share of the national vote garnered in general elections in the last 50 years has never fallen below 12 percent (1958) and has reached a high of 32 percent (1945). Since 1962 it has hovered around the 25 percent level, and protest parties have formed governments in more than half of the provinces (Ontario, British Columbia, Alberta, Saskatchewan, Manitoba and Quebec).[37] However, although still in power in three provinces and with 24 percent of the vote in the 1980 general election, the regional protest party, with one notable exception, is a shell of its former self. Time and the exercise of power have stilled its anger, and the non-partisan world of federal-provincial relations has robbed it of its effectiveness. On this last point, Richard Simeon (1972) in his major study of Canadian federalism, has shown that "party differences have very little to do with federal-provincial conflicts. Party, in fact, seems to be almost the least important line of cleavage in the system." In other words, the more that federal-provincial conflict becomes a matter for executive negotiations, the less relevant are party differences to its settlement.

The notable exception to the decline of the regional protest party is, of course, to be found in Quebec. Any study of political parties written after 1976 must distinguish between regional protest parties like Social Credit and the NDP in the West and the Parti Québécois in Quebec. Clearly, to equate protest movements simply because they take the form of third parties and to take no account of their different objectives is to confuse the analysis. The PQ's advocacy of sovereignty association, more passionate perhaps before the 1979 referendum than after, but still vigorous into the 1980s, sets it apart from other protest parties. Unlike any of them, it proposes a new relationship between one province and the rest of the country. The protests of T.C. Douglas, as premier of Saskatchewan, William Aberhart, premier of Alberta, and W.A.C. Bennett, premier of British Columbia, contained no nationalist ambitions, except perhaps for Canada itself through a reformed party system. However, as Léon Dion (1976) has demonstrated, Quebec's history is structured by nationalism or, better still, nationalisms: conservative, liberal, social-democrat and socialist. Each, he argues, has had a different meaning for the self-definition of Québécois and for their relationship to the rest of Canada.[38]

Regional protest parties occupy a special place in Canadian political literature. These parties, in particular the phenomenon of Social Credit, gave impetus to the study of political parties. As noted earlier, the ten-volume study of Social Credit in Alberta written between 1950 and 1959 was the first and is still the most ambitious research project on Canadian political parties. That this series should have had a protest party as its subject (one which within three years of completion of the project was to experience fission and, in another decade, exhaustion in its home province) was the result of a perspective on Canadian politics shared by national politicians and academics alike. The Progressives, Social Credit, and the Co-operative Commonwealth Federation were viewed as aberrations from the Canadian norm, to be accommodated if Mackenzie King had his way, destroyed if western Liberals like James G. Gardiner or W.R. Motherwell, ministers in the King cabinet, had theirs. Because Canadian parties are low in ideological content, any dissent or faction is subject to misinterpretation by politicians; they are seen as the plots of spoilers or the misguided.

For the academics, the interpretations have been more sophisticated, but they too share what might be called the "eccentric" view of third party proliferation. Protest parties were understood as the product of frontier-metropolitan tension, or the response to a "quasi-colonial" relationship, or another variant of North American agrarian radicalism. Each saw the protest as a reaction to forces generated elsewhere; each was centralist in its interpretation. (None of the scholars in the Social Credit series was provincialist in his research interest; only one of the ten in this series on Alberta actually resided there, and he wrote about the Liberal Party.) Politicians and academics embraced what Frank Underhill called a "literary theory of the constitution."[39] Canada had inherited a British-styled constitution and deviations from what happened in Britain were just that — deviations, to be curbed by the governors and studied by the scholars. Both saw the political system as sound but subject to idiosyncratic attack. Neither appreciated that the Constitution embraced several governments, each the fulcrum of its own political system. Of the ten volumes on Alberta, none examined Social Credit in power or Alberta's governmental institutions. (This is still the case; there are seven provincial studies in the Canadian government series published by the University of Toronto Press, but Alberta, along with British Columbia and Quebec, does not figure among them.)[40]

Since scholarship illuminates understanding and helps determine the range of political debate and experiment, another reason for this strong centralist perspective on parties is worth considering, even if at first it appears tangential to the study of the national party system.

It is hard to credit how little had been published 30 years ago about provincial institutions and processes.[41] Political science was identified "predominantly [with] constitutional law and constitutional history," which, in essence, meant a fondness for studying one of two subjects: judicial interpretation of the British North America Act or the evolution of Dominion status (Macpherson, 1938, p. 160). Provincial literature hewed to the same line but with a different purpose: to stop any province marching along the new road to autonomy. Articles appeared asserting that "The Provincial Legislatures Are Not Parliaments"[42] and that "Lieutenant Governors Are Not Ambassadors."[43] Claims by provincial premiers like Maurice Duplessis of Quebec, Mitch Hepburn of Ontario, and William Aberhart of Alberta to a revised status for their provinces in Confederation were met by scholarly rebuttal in articles with titles like "Canada: One Country or Nine Provinces?"(MacFarlane, 1938).[44]

The centralist perspective of the journals ran counter to the trend of the courts but represented the dominant view of the era's fledgling social scientists, then concentrated in a few universities, for whom provincial meant parochial and the study of either was a matter of little consequence. Devaluation of provincial government and politics was confirmed, paradoxically, by that grand inquest into the state of Canadian federalism, the Royal Commission on Dominion-Provincial Relations (1937–40). Four decades after completing its work, the Rowell-Sirois Commission remains unrivalled in the scope of its inquiry: the volume and expertise of research delineate the inherent complexity of provincial, regional and national questions, while the provincial government briefs (from all but Quebec) even now constitute an unexcelled depiction of provincial economies at one stage of their development, as well as a rare sample of political sentiment for a single period.[44] Despite this, the commission's immediate influence contrasted unexpectedly with its overall consequences.

The Rowell-Sirois Commission brought together, for the first time, Canada's nascent and scattered social science community and then linked it for two decades in near perfect union with the federal government. Thus, although it recommended a restored balance to Confederation by redistributing functions and fiscal resources for the benefit of the provinces as well as the federal government, its impact on scholarship was to give precedence to central government questions at the expense of provincial. By stimulating the social sciences in Canada, the Rowell-Sirois Commission may be seen to have had a long-run influence on the study of provincial government and politics, but in the short run its effect was negative, reinforcing the bias already evident against "parochial" research.

With respect to the study of protest parties, that bias was less pronounced in the attitudes of succeeding academics and politicians, and even some of the original interpreters revised their theories. S.M. Lipset, who in *Agrarian Socialism* (1950) had written the pioneer study of the Cooperative Commonwealth Federation in Saskatchewan, qualified the emphasis he originally placed on sociological factors and gave more attention to electoral and constitutional differences between Canada and the

United States. The more productive question to ask, he now suggested, was why there was such a range of third parties in Canada. The focus thus moved from province to nation. En route, Macpherson's class analysis of Alberta was criticized for its limited perspective, and in its place Lipset (1954) hypothesized that Social Credit had emerged out of the tension inherent between the centripetal demands of cabinet government and the centrifugal requirements of a federal society.

In the intervening years, institutional explanations received support from the work of Maurice Pinard (1971) and Denis Smith (1972). Pinard argued that third parties arise in situations of prolonged one-party dominance where the major opposition party so atrophies that the electorate must seek change elsewhere when it finally becomes dissatisfied with the governing party. The theory originated in Pinard's work on Social Credit in Quebec in the early 1960s, but it applied as well to what happened in Alberta in 1921 and Saskatchewan in 1944. The Liberals held sway after 1905, in both provinces, with the Conservatives becoming a spent force by the time of the crucial elections. Disaffected government supporters consequently turned from old parties to new.

Denis Smith's corrective to Macpherson's class analysis stressed the relevance of political leadership and, of equal importance, the forum in which it is exercised. According to parliamentary theory of the last century, the classic location was the floor of the popularly elected chamber, although the experience of the Prairie provinces raised questions as to the accuracy of this judgment. In those provinces, legislative opposition was often numerically weak and where more than one party was in opposition, federal party loyalties frequently discouraged combinations against the provincial government. Legislative traditions were weak as well, and politicians discovered that in order to gain and keep power they had to appeal to the public outside the legislature.

The study of protest parties in the West has waned as the parties themselves have faded or become part of the Prairie political landscape.[46] Only in Quebec does this original branch of political inquiry survive and even there it has experienced transformation, becoming as already noted, less a study of party activity and rather more an investigation of nationalism (Stein, 1973; Saywell, 1977). The focus has shifted to governments, as the large body of literature on intergovernmental relations testifies.[47] The reasons for this are well known: the growth in the past quarter-century in provincial responsibility, revenue and resources (human as well as natural) and the decline in nation-building and nation-maintaining (that is, wartime government) activities. How this happened is an involved story of jurisdictional interpretation, greater relevance of provincial powers to modern society, and a revolution in the nature of intergovernmental fiscal relations; all of these, thankfully, are beyond the scope of this paper to explain. What is necessary is to note the impact of these changes on party.

The change in intergovernmental relations undercuts the old parties but so too does it undermine protest parties. The federal-provincial party linkages which characterized the King–St. Laurent period of accommodative politics have atrophied. This has come about more in some parts of the country than others but to an extent which makes intra-party harmony unlikely and unnecessary to achieve.[48] The fractious relations between federal Liberals and the few provincial Liberals in power (for example, Ross Thatcher in Saskatchewan) or even with provincial Liberals not in power (for example, in British Columbia) and the fruitless union between the short-lived Conservative government of Mr. Clark and the dominant Lougheed government in Alberta make the point.[49] Conversely, and depending on the issue, the federal Liberals have found a sympathetic ear sometimes with New Democrats in Saskatchewan and Manitoba and sometimes with Progressive Conservatives in Ontario or New Brunswick. When the Liberals are in power federally, provincial Liberals anywhere can expect to have a rough time of it as they are scorned by other provincial parties for their nominal allegiance to federal policies. That has long been standard electoral strategy. More recently and more remarkably, the same weapon has been used against incumbent governments (for example, the Saskatchewan NDP in 1982). The big controversies of that campaign (higher gas prices and high interest rates), despite their obvious federal content, became matters for which the provincial government was held responsible, as a result of either acts of commission or acts of omission. The onus for unpopular federal policies was placed on provincial shoulders even when the political parties in each instance were different. The party connection is no longer relevant; it is enough for an indictment that federal and provincial governments of whatever stripe cooperate, as in this instance they did in the energy pricing board.

Political Parties and the Electoral System

The western protest parties attacked the rigidity of Canada's political institutions. The Co-operative Commonwealth Federation went further and attacked the economic system, proposing instead to build a class-based party system. In this respect the CCF was centralist, pan-Canadian and ahead of its time, for the 1930s and 1940s were decades when the accommodative approach dominated political leadership. Quebec's protest parties sought to defend and to assert the Québécois' distinctive interest against the English-Canadian majority. Western protest parties challenged the operation of the national political system in terms of its fairness in sharing power; Quebec's parties eventually questioned its legitimacy.

Political change in the last two decades demonstrates that complaints about the system's rigidity have been exaggerated. On the one hand, Mr. Diefenbaker's triumph on the Prairies in 1958 (when he captured 47 of 48 seats, after taking only 14 in 1957) dealt a severe blow to the claims of the CCF and Social Credit to be the voice of regional protest, a blow that signalled a realignment in party support which continues to the present. On the other hand, his conquest of Quebec in 1958 proved transitory, as the Liberals under Lester Pearson and then Pierre Trudeau recaptured and held fast that traditional Grit bastion. Pan-Canadian policies pursued by these Liberal leaders, and discussed at length earlier in this study, help to explain both developments. Language policy split the Progressive Conservatives under Mr. Diefenbaker and bequeathed to his successor an intractable faction of opponents, mainly from the Prairies, who deprived the party of the unity necessary to win the support needed to form a government in 1972. Liberal social policies in the 1960s, just as patriation of the Constitution in the early 1980s, created sufficient identity of interest between the Liberal and New Democratic parties to compromise NDP distinctiveness in the first area and to alienate Prairie support in the second. Evidence of the latter is clear in disagreements with the Saskatchewan NDP government and the defection of four Prairie MPs over the resource clause in the constitutional resolution. The Progressive Conservative Party waxed, and the protest parties waned in response to the new nationalist model of party government followed by the Liberals in Ottawa.[50]

Pan-Canadian policies, however, did not generate pan-Canadian legislative support, a truth to which the NDP and the CCF before it could testify. The CCF-NDP had long been aware of the problem of transforming electoral support into comparable parliamentary strength. That knowledge gained wider circulation in the 1960s, as a sequence of minority governments (1962, 1963, 1965) ensued whose common characteristic was a marked regional imbalance in legislative support. It was this development that made the electoral system a subject for discussion, for until the 1960s, the influence of plurality elections on federal politics had received scant academic attention. That changed with the publication in 1968 of "The Electoral System and the Party System in Canada, 1921–1965," by Alan C. Cairns.

Cairns dispelled the haze that surrounded the subject of the electoral system, one so opaque that it obscured both its origin and its operation. More than anything else, this might be considered the principal achievement of his article; it raised the electoral system to academic consciousness. Like so much else inherited from Britain, the conduct of elections had been accepted with remarkably little comment. Those questions that had traditionally exercised opinion had to do with the ballot, its form and secrecy, and the administration of the count, but never with the principle of what constituted victory at the polls.[51] The electoral system was another manifestation (like candidate selection) of the strength of localism in political life. Moreover, until there were more than two parties in a contest, such a question seldom arose, and even when third parties appeared it still might go unheard if the electoral base of the protest party was concentrated (as it often was) in solidly agrarian or nationalistic territory. In this latter situation, the two old parties might have been expected to ponder the implications of the plurality electoral system, but there is scant evidence that they did.

Even later when, in a province like Saskatchewan, the CCF competed with the Conservatives and the Liberals for election, the question of the fairness of the method of counting votes proved temporary. After the CCF formed a government in 1944, the controversy lapsed; the Conservatives had been annihilated; the Liberals valued a system that had kept them in power for 40 years and now gave them a monopoly of the opposition; and the CCF looked upon it as a rite of passage which proved their maturity. In the other western provinces the question was never posed even this clearly. In British Columbia, Liberals and Conservatives had manipulated the electoral system in 1952 to keep the CCF out of office and had got a Social Credit government as reward. Alberta had experimented with alternative methods of counting the vote and then gone back to a plurality system province-wide with no one paying much attention to either result, since the United Farmers and then Social Credit seemed invincible. Finally, in Manitoba, a fluid but always moderate coalition of partisans maintained proportional representation for decades "to help break the hold which the Eastern-dominated Liberal and Conservative parties had on the province" (Donnelly, 1963, p. 75; Scarrow, 1962, p. 4).

What the Cairns article did was to elaborate on the matter of "fairness" in the context of national elections and, even more importantly, to demonstrate what had never been an issue in the provinces but was an issue nationally — the regional implications of the system's operation. Its territorial dimension was now made plain. The exclusion of the Tories from Quebec extended back more than a half-century; the retreat of the Liberals from the West was more recent. So much was obvious in the reports of the chief electoral officer. What had not been and what was now graphically depicted was that there were two worlds to elections — that of the popular vote and that of parliamentary representation. While the fit may never have been perfect (the Byzantine formulas for redistribution saw to that), in the last quarter-century it had become even less so. The consequences were not only of numerical interest but of direct relevance to the concerns of the opposition, caucus and leaders. The electoral system molded the party system which, in turn, set constraints on the government and opposition. Its cumulative effect was to distort while it converted votes into seats, assigning, as it did, whole provinces and regions to individual parties.

The conclusion drawn by some critics of the electoral system was that proportional representation was to be preferred to plurality elections. It would, so the argument went, bring regional voices now excluded into the ranks of the national parties and, presumably, make the discussions of those parties of broader concern. That was one conclusion. Another was that proportional representation would promote a national political debate sensitive to regional particulars but at the same time transcending localism. For this to occur, attitudes about party discipline and the prerogatives of party leadership would have to change. It is indicative of the hold which the concept of party government has on Canadians that such modifications in party practices were never discussed. Instead, proportional representation was viewed as a reform to strengthen political parties by making them more representative.

That was the argument, although whether in fact proportional representation would affect parties so beneficially is not at all certain. The ambiguity surrounding the subject is intense. What effect would proportional representation (modified or total) have on the existing parties, on relations between federal and provincial wings of parties, and on leadership? Would it, as sometimes charged, put too much power into the hands of party bureaucrats, the very people in the Liberal Party under attack as "non-accountable, non-legitimate, non-elected members of the party"?[52] If only a modified system were introduced, would there not be two classes of MPs: list representatives and "real" representatives? Would not the list representatives be the unsuccessful candidates who are now appointed to the Senate?

Sample testimony given before the Special Joint Committee on Senate Reform[53] suggests the range of existing opinion. Robert Stanfield proposed that "a political party should have to earn its representation in all regions," thereby opposing a system that rewards parties that secure small fractions of the vote. John Meisel, on the other hand, dissented from this view, and thus favoured a system to elect more and diverse interests and encourage greater party responsiveness. On this subject, where party interest is as vested as might ever be expected, Canada's parties offer meagre enlightenment. In 1979, after he had announced his retirement, Mr. Trudeau mused about the advantages of proportional representation. In 1979 as well, NDP leader Ed Broadbent went further and proposed expanding the House by 100 seats and dividing them equally among the five regions, with the parties being allocated shares of each region's 20 seats equal to their share of the regional vote. But this was the leader's proposal, not the party's. The New Democrats at their convention in 1981, expressing partisan sentiment as strong as any heard from a Canadian party, roundly condemned proportional representation as a means of keeping the Liberals in and the NDP out of power indefinitely.[54] In the brief period of the Clark government, among the number of proposals to reform Parliament and make government more sensitive to regional interests electoral reform was mooted, but that is as far as it went.

The year Cairns' article appeared was also the year Mr. Trudeau led the Liberals to form the first majority government since the Diefenbaker sweep of 1958. As well as the majority, he won 11 of 45 seats in the Prairie provinces, the largest Grit contingent since 1953, giving him a broader regional base to build on than Mr. Pearson had. Whatever the promise of those returns, it was lost in 1972 along with the Liberals' majority and eight of the Prairie seats. Liberal standings in the three Prairie provinces improved marginally in 1974, only to fall again in 1979 when the government was defeated; Liberal fortunes collapsed the following year in British Columbia as well. At the same time, the Liberals were given a convincing majority federally. (Tables in the Appendix give this information in more detail.) The returns after 1968, however, did nothing to assuage the concern earlier expressed about the detrimental effect of the electoral system: majority government too often was elusive. When it occurred, the winning party's success was not distributed across all regions and even when inroads were made in difficult electoral terrain they might be washed away in the next contest. Liberal fortunes in the West matched Progressive Conservative rejection in Quebec. A victory for either party meant that at least one part of the country was excluded from government. This balkanization of Canadian politics, so frequently assailed, extended beyond Parliament and elections and into the ever-growing realm of intergovernmental relations. Federal governments, destitute of regional support to the West or to the East, nonetheless had to deal with provincial governments (in the same regions) who, thanks to the operation of the electoral system, might claim with emphatic assurance to represent all interests within their boundaries.

Representation and the Appointment Power

The first thing to be said about regional representation is that since Confederation written constitutional provisions to ensure it have failed. The Senate enshrined the principle, but perennial aspersions on that body's work and episodic bouts at reform testify to resounding failure in its realization. The Senate, it should be admitted, is not alone in eliciting public apathy and even hostility: "The overwhelming litany of complaint on virtually every political issue . . . gives evidence of considerable public dissatisfaction [and] little indication that Canadians have confidence that the political system will solve any of their problems."[55] It is in light of such criticism that then Justice Minister Mark MacGuigan (1983) proposed territorial and minority representation as two of four suggested functions of a reformed second chamber; the others would confer responsibility in areas of intergovernmental relations and legislative review. The MacGuigan discussion paper admits that function cannot be separated from the method of senatorial selection, distribution of seats or allocation of powers. Although these are considerations that vitally affect political parties, they must be disentangled from the question of one institution's reform, if only because regional representation is not confined to that particular body.

Expanding "constitution" to include convention as well as statute broadens the ambit of representation, as the following illustrations suggest. Commentators on all sides agree that "every province must have, if at all possible, at least one representative in the cabinet" (Dawson, 1970, p. 92). Regional representation here has been a guiding star of federal and provincial politicians alike. Sir John A. Macdonald wanted Joseph Howe in 1869 because, as "a representative man," his admission to cabinet would symbolize the "pacification" of Nova Scotia (Saunders, 1916, I:191). Over a century later, in August 1983, following the resignation of Newfoundland's only cabinet minister, Pierre Elliott Trudeau was pressed both by colleagues and by Newfoundland's premier to find a replacement because the province could not go "unrepresented."[56] Regional representation on the Supreme Court of Canada results from a combination of statute and convention: since 1875, the act has provided for judges (two, now three) from Quebec, and long-standing custom requires sectional representation from the other regions. The appearance of the first woman member of the Court complicates convention, for territory may have to give way to other considerations, like gender, although to date this has rarely happened. Again, regulatory agencies are invariably composed with regional considerations in mind, although often not to the satisfaction of particular provinces, some of whom now demand a hand in selecting a portion of the agency's personnel.

Places in the Senate, Supreme Court, cabinet and regulatory agencies are commonly filled by appointment. Of similar provenance are royal commissions and ministerial advisory committees. Traditionally, they too are representative with respect to the country's regions but occasionally (and more recently) with respect to special constituencies. The appointment principle, which animated nascent political parties in the 1830s and whose excesses the advocates of responsible government sought to curb, did not by any means disappear in the new federation. During the Confederation debates in the legislature of the united Canadas, A.A. Dorion described its pervasive continuation in the form of appointed lieutenant governors and an appointed Senate, including even the Speaker of that chamber, as "most illiberal," but he was in the minority in objecting (Waite, 1963, p. 92). Whatever the intent of the Fathers of Confederation, the practice since 1867 has been to use the appointment power to reflect Canada's federal composition. Indeed, because it might be counted a chief instrument to that end, it would be a useful contribution to understanding Canadian political development if prime ministerial exercise of this power were studied in relation to realizing the federal principle.

It would be of special benefit to compare the use of the appointment power under each of the three models of party government discussed earlier in this paper. As already noted, Professor Gordon Stewart has argued that patronage was the motive power of the Macdonald and Laurier years, its use giving the leader personal contact with every constituency. Mackenzie King's caution not to be involved too directly in day-to-day party operations and his astute sense of the need to accommodate diverse interests reduced the leader's overt participation in appointments but not the effectiveness of the process itself. Detailed examination of the appointment power may await study, but both King's papers and those of a lieutenant like James G. Gardiner, for example, show that the process was not politically inflammatory nor those chosen by it deemed less legitimate than elected officials. This has not been the case in recent years when the pan-Canadian approach to leadership has dominated federal politics. It is tempting to see a relationship between the growth of a national, participatory ethic on the one hand and increased condemnation of political appointments on the other. If there is merit in this supposition, then the implications of the continued use of the appointment power (either to assuage regional sensitivity or to acknowledge regional demands) are indeed serious.

Whether Mr. Pearson or Mr. Trudeau used the appointment power differently from their predecessors in office remains open to investigation, but that perceptions of its use and of its utility have become more critical is beyond dispute. Increasingly, it is asserted that the legitimacy of an appointee is diminished because, regardless of experience or qualifications, he is not directly accountable to the people on a regular basis.[57] A change in public attitudes rather than a change in governmental practice may therefore explain the increased attention which the appointment power seems to attract. Disregarding frequent newspaper criticism, consider as a barometer the comment of an academic observer of Canadian politics in the late 1970s: "Patronage for retiring or defeated Liberal candidates and various other hangers-on was dispensed on a scale unprecedented in recent memory" (Meisel, 1981, p. 48). These included "at least 200 of the order-in-council appointments" and "no fewer than fifty-nine judges," all of whom were former Liberal candidates or spouses of the same. Meisel notes as well the "blatant" electoral purpose for which appointments were used: the appointment and therefore, "neutralization" of non-Liberals to the Senate and the Canadian Grain Commission. As well, "electoral opportunities were enhanced through wholesale appointments to the International Joint Commission, the National Parole Board, the National Energy Board, the Immigration Appeal Board and the Canadian Pension Commission, and similar bodies."[58]

Criticism of the use of the appointment power is not limited to those outside the ranks of government. In fact, within the Liberal Party during the 1970s, there was an acrimonious debate on this subject. The sides in the debate were drawn generally between those Liberals who believed that participatory democracy required the party to reform its patronage ways and those Liberals (mainly to the east and west of central Canada) who looked to patronage as a traditional lubricant of politics and (especially in the West) as an essential instrument for keeping the party alive in a hostile environment.[59] Patronage, however, was a two-edged sword in places where the party was weak. The effect of "good" appointments was to lose leaders or potential leaders the local party could ill afford to see go; the effect of "bad" appointments was to lose supporters, often local notables, who grew frustrated at national party insensitivity or indifference to local opinion. Progressive Conservative experience is limited because the party has been out of power so long. Nevertheless, during the brief period of the Clark government, appointments did become a fractious issue: here the criticism stemmed from Mr. Clark's failure to fill up positions before the 1980 election. The combination of inexperience and changing public attitudes made that government hesitate to act, despite intraparty pressure from the constituencies (Simpson, 1980, p. 108-13).

The place where the appointment power is in most visible disrepute among democratic reformers is the Senate. The Senate is an obvious arena for constitutional change, especially since it does a spectacular job of not representing the units of the federal system. It therefore fails, the critics claim, in the primary role of an upper chamber in a federation.[60] Instead, the Senate is perceived as a refuge for tired politicians of the two old parties, for those who are electoral liabilities, or for those who never get so far as to be liabilities but who cannot get elected and yet merit some reward. Constant repetition of this practice hurts the reputation of Senate and party. It does a disservice to those senators who are active legislators, and it complicates proposals for reform, since any other selection process raises the spectre of injecting party even further into the Senate's operations.

The practice of placing key party officials in the Senate can affect the nature of party organization in ways quite distinct from the benefits of security and freedom from onerous obligations conferred by a senatorial appointment. Those provinces which by themselves are regions are favoured with a large number of senators, and these contingents become the base of national party organizations. Senatorial regions made up of several provinces do not assume similar prominence, because of smaller numbers of senators and because disagreements among multiple sets of provincial and federal partisans encourage factionalism. Where a governing party is weak, as the Liberals are in the West, and where it appoints senators to cabinet as provincial spokesmen, the differences are further aggravated. In those provinces whose senatorial representation is small (four, six or ten), the choice of a senator to fill a vacancy to "represent" such provinces easily stirs rancour among the remaining three, five or nine (the numbers are often smaller because of perennial vacancies). To the public, this may seem eccentric. To party loyalists who scrutinize the bona fides of each appointee, the result may even seem perverse: two of the three Prairie senators from Saskatchewan, Alberta and British Columbia appointed to the cabinet in 1980 did not start their political careers as Liberals, while the third was rumoured to have lost his cabinet position in 1983 as a result of pressure from fair-weather Liberals.[61] From a broader perspective, the appointment of senators to cabinet worsens the partisanship in the upper chamber, whose best work, all commentators agree, is done in an atmosphere generally free of such divisiveness.

The "ministerialist" organization in the days of Mackenzie King acted as a counter-attraction to the senatorial lodestone; whether it was any less centrifugal in its effect might be debated. If it is debated, James G. Gardiner's long sway over Alberta as well as Saskatchewan needs to be remembered (Ward, 1977a). In any case, today there is no ministerialist organization, although until September 1984 there were senators who were cabinet ministers. That might explain the reminiscence of Senator George McIlraith when he appeared before the Special Joint Committee on Senate Reform: "The Senate [once] was independent . . . there was less of the party concept in it."[62]

Conclusion: Potential Parties and National Integration

This study has taken as its fundamental premise the centrality of party government (more specifically, party-in-government) in the evolution of Canadian political parties and even in the growth of Canada itself. The claims made here for parties are great: they are agents of territorial and social inclusion, of economic expansion, and of national identification. They are, in fact, "political systems in themselves" with a multitude of functions and a multidimensional life, but most crucially they are, in the hands of their leaders, autonomous institutions (DeVree, 1980, p. 211). Although they may respond to change, they do not only respond; they initiate and determine events as well, and by this power they affect the lives of all Canadians.

The most recent model of party and governmental leadership is the pan-Canadian, and its structuring influence on the self-perception of Canadians cannot be exaggerated. Consider, for example, the finding that "Liberal voters in the West in 1979 were very likely the people who felt national unity and Quebec relations are major issues" (Pammett, 1981, p. 217). The 25 percent of the electorate in the West who supported the Liberals then and in 1980 was the subject of anguish among party strategists, who ponder how to increase the number and who attribute its current size to unpopular Liberal policies. However, it is at least worth asking whether in the absence of Liberal language and national unity policies western support would not have gone even lower. Could it not be that this vote represents "restructured" support in response to pan-Canadian policies (rather than a vestigial Liberalism from the days of Mackenzie King) and to a different kind of party leadership?

This paper argues that the brokerage theory of politics offers a poor explanation of Canadian party development. It does not allow for the direct, national approach to leadership which has characterized Canadian politics at least from the time of Lester Pearson and which, as demonstrated above, was evident even during Mr. Diefenbaker's prime ministership. A very different attack on the brokerage theory has recently been made by John Wilson (1983, p. 181), who questions whether Canada is a nation at all, in the conventional sense of one whose symbols and perspectives are more national than regional. Instead, he argues that political behaviour federally is a continuation of political behaviour in the provinces. Wilson's argument and that of this paper agree that brokerage theory is in error when it brands Canadian political parties as failures. Wilson rejects the charge because he rejects the assumption that there must be some kind of underlying uniformity in the national party system. This paper accepts that there is an underlying uniformity; indeed, it makes models of party and governmental leadership its centrepiece. However, with Wilson, it seriously questions the validity of the failure charge.

Moreover, it argues that the pan-Canadian approach to leadership, with its reduced sensitivity to provincial communities (the reverse side of its commitment to policies that touch Canadians directly: medicare, the Charter of Rights, the Constitution, energy, language), is a far more useful explanation of the current Canadian political scene than is brokerage theory. In particular, it explains the heightened conflict in federal-provincial relations already mentioned, and which is a cardinal feature of the country's modern politics. Pan-Canadian policies push the provinces into an exaggerated defence of provincial concerns because, unlike the era of Mackenzie King or St. Laurent, whose cabinets were composed of provincial spokesman, or the period of Macdonald or Laurier, when localism controlled by the leader triumphed, the provinces today see no defenders of their interests at the centre.

That is the source of the demand for institutional change: the belief that the central government does not understand the regions, that it does not hear them. On this, however, the regions are wrong. They do not see the real issue. The governing party can court the regions at any time, just as governing parties did in the past. The truth is that the Liberals under Mr. Trudeau chose not to do so, and the reason was that the governing party held a different view of Canada. Canada, as Mr. Trudeau repeatedly said during the constitutional discussions, was composed of more than its parts.

If this interpretation is accurate, then the question must be asked: how useful will institutional reforms be in changing political behaviour? The question is more easily posed than answered. It is nonetheless worth commenting that in the past parties have shown themselves neither easily subject to control nor predictable in their response to change.

Traditionally, political parties have rested outside the scope of statute law, although this immunity has been breached in the last decade by election expenses legislation. Because parties touch multiple levels of public and private life, the impact of specific reforms is not easily isolated. Certainly, for instance, there is no way of predicting at one election, let alone at several over the space of a decade or a generation, the effect of giving millions of voters preferential choice. Reforms possess the potential to surprise, as the experience with leadership conventions suggests.[63] On the one hand, a convention of delegates, representative perhaps of the party but not society, drawn from across the land and assembled to perform a common act, is an integrating and nationalizing event in the country's politics. On the other hand (which has taken longer to show itself), the contest among the candidates and the search for delegate support can have a disintegrating impact on existing structures. There is reason to believe that contradictory impulses are latent in electoral reform as well.

Although it began with the Liberals in 1919 as a strategy to unite a divided party, the leadership convention before 1968 was more what Bagehot called "dignified," rather than efficient. The 1948 and 1958 conventions approximated a laying-on-of-hands ceremony, with the old leader playing a key part in the convention's choice. Mr. Pearson favoured Mr. Trudeau, but the presence of eight serious candidates and the availability of national television with its multiplier effect on rank-and-file participation immensely changed the character of the undertaking. In this, the Liberals were imitating the Progressive Conservatives, who had chosen Robert Stanfield in 1967 at a convention in which nine serious candidates were present and which followed several years of spectacular intra-party fighting aimed at removing Mr. Diefenbaker. Although the Conservatives had had frequent recourse to conventions to find leaders in the 1930s, '40s and '50s, it was the 1967 meeting and the Liberal convention following close in 1968, that whetted public appetite for leadership debate.

But it did not end there. Biennial party meetings where leadership review might become an issue fed political excitement more regularly than general elections could. Because of extensive television coverage, leadership is no longer a matter of caucus or even intra-party discussion: partisan opponents as well as party members become engaged. With candidates appearing in constituencies across the country, something analogous to James MacGregor Burns's (1982) useful concept of a "followership" for each candidate is formed. Significantly, in a country where territory has been so dominant an organizing principle in political life (Bakvis, 1981), it is not territory but ideology, doctrine or policy that is stressed in the quest for delegates who, when assembled, stand as virtual representatives of nationwide bodies of opinion. At its base the convention's weakness is the same as that of the parliamentary parties criticized by the Progressives long ago: the selection process. Rather than using an American-style primary contest to fit an American-modelled institution, delegates, like party candidates, are the choice of limited numbers of local activists whose practices occasionally call for turning a blind eye. The convention's chief weakness and its chief characteristic is the independence of the delegates in casting their votes. An individual secret ballot gives advantage to the new and the fresh; experience in the forum where the leader must work has never determined the convention's choice.

If experience is any guide, the introduction of leadership conventions has increased the power of the leader of the governing party, for it gives him a basis of authority separate from that of the parliamentary caucus. For the major opposition party, the effect has been quite different — institutionalizing intra-party criticism of the leader who has failed to bring the party to power. This effect further protects the governing party's security. The impact of an altered electoral system on party behaviour can only be surmised, but it is not improbable that proportional representation, through the compilation of the lists, could similarly enhance the leader's power. Institutional reforms can have unexpected results, but the Canadian experience is that they reinforce existing models of leadership.

Henry Fairlie has said, with Macaulay, that North American parties are "all sail and no anchor."[64] However, federal Liberal problems in the West or federal Progressive Conservative problems in Quebec have been problems of sail: theories and policies of organization, theories and policies of the economy, theories and policies of nationalism. It is no wonder that leadership preoccupies Canadian politics: appointments rest with it; party organization serves it; and policy reflects it.

The challenge to Canadian parties has been to assert and make firm their claim to be national. At different times and under different leaders, national integration has proceeded by various means: the incorporation of people and territory through local patronage supervised personally by leaders like Macdonald and Laurier; the accommodation at the centre of multiple interests and communities by Mackenzie King and St. Laurent; and the nationalization of individual Canadians into a single community (though of two languages and many cultures) through policies enunciated first by John Diefenbaker and later by Pierre Trudeau. Only in this last model of leadership has there been an attempt to incorporate all the people and all the territory. In the past, Quebec, to a greater extent than elsewhere, had been treated differently and allowed its separate development.

However, the integrative capacity of political leadership committed to a pan-Canadian ideology, but one deprived of a territorial base other than the nation as a whole, is flawed. In the absence of provincial chieftains whose responsibilities once extended from cabinet through province to constituency, and in the absence of leaders who used to superintend constituency party-politics through control of local notables, national parties now find themselves isolated from an electorate which is still distributed among 282 districts. Pan-Canadian appeals are horizontal, the electorate's view of politics vertical. The significant questions are whether pan-Canadianism can be combined with localism and, if that proves possible, whether the combination will produce national parties with greater integrative capacities.

The combination is possible if the structuring effect of the pan-Canadian appeal is extended into the constituency. That, of course, would require a level of debate and a mechanism to regulate it which have never before been present in local politics. As noted earlier in this paper, constituency energies have traditionally been devoted to electoral campaigning and candidate selection. The experience of each of the old parties in recent years is that leadership contests and elections reveal, to a degree, the strata of opinion in each constitutency and that the conflict of values represented by the strata create problems of legitimacy when a choice must be made between potential delegates or candidates. The introduction of primaries would be one method of resolving such conflicts, to the benefit of constituency harmony and national party unity. The advantage of pre-election contests within the constituencies would be to bring national appeals, made by electoral aspirants or by contestants for delegate selection to leadership convention, directly before individual party supporters. As it is now, the selection of candidates or convention delegates is made through procedures in constituencies that ignore the choice of values being presented to local supporters and that highlight once again the contestants' personal qualities.

Modern Canadian politics is characterized more by patronage at the top of the party hierarchy than at the bottom. The parties of the post-Confederation and the accommodation periods derived much of their structural consistency from the distribution of local patronage. This is hardly feasible any longer. Local activists are more probably animated by their attachment to a party's pan-Canadian policies — for example, bilingualism. In itself such activist attachment is not sufficient for the party locally or nationally. What is required is the unifying and broadening effect of constituency debate, which would de-emphasize personality while promoting the opportunity to dissent within party ranks and not outside them. Currently, without a local base where local advocates can espouse, debate or oppose pan-Canadian policies, constituency dissent as well as support is muted, and policies appear to be imposed upon the electorate rather than emanating from it.

The Liberals' pan-Canadian policies were designed to incorporate Quebec, but they estranged the West. The Progressive Conservatives' "One Canada" and their "community of communities" succeeded in the latter but failed in the former. In power and with access to appointments and instruments of policy, the Liberals in a quarter-century made no gains in the West. Out of office and without access to the levers that power brings, the Progressive Conservatives were excluded from Quebec for much longer. The two situations, though comparable, are different: given the choice, the Liberals did not trim to win regional support. Instead, through policies of national breadth, they sought to effect fundamental change in constitutional condition and citizen perceptions. Party-in-government has succeeded in aggregating a large and growing number of voters irrespective of place. The political contest has been redefined to set nation ahead of region. Language, energy, and medicare are national issues, although their origins can be traced back to the provinces — namely, Quebec, Alberta and Saskatchewan. Through them, region is drawn into nation even when rejecting pan-Canadian policies, and national integration through debate is achieved.

Appendix A
Selected Tables

TABLE 1-A1   Federal Election Results, 1878–1984

Election Year	Party Forming Federal Government	Total Seats	Conservative Seats	Conservative Votes (%)	Liberal Seats	Liberal Votes (%)	Progressive Seats	Progressive Votes (%)
1878	Con.	206	140	53	65	45		
1882	Con.	211	138	53	73	47		
1887	Con.	215	128	51	87	49		
1891	Con.	215	122	52	91	46		
1896	Lib.	213	88	46	118	45		
1900	Lib.	213	81	47	132	52		
1904	Lib.	214	75	47	139	52		
1908	Lib.	221	85	47	135	51		
1911	Con.	221	134	51	87	48		
1917	Con.[a]	235	153[b]	57	82[c]	40		
1921	Lib.	235	50	30	116	41	65	23
1925	Lib.	245	116	46	99	40	24	9
1926	Lib.	245	91	45	128	46	20	5
1930	Con.	245	137	49	91	45	12	3
1935	Lib.	245	40	30	173	45		
1940	Lib.	245	40	31	181	51		
1945	Lib.	245	67	27	125	41		
1949	Lib.	262	41	30	193	49		
1953	Lib.	265	51	31	171	49		
1957	P.C.	265	112	39	105	41		
1958	P.C.	265	208	54	49	34		
1962	P.C.	265	116	37	100	37		
1963	Lib.	265	95	33	129	42		
1965	Lib.	265	97	32	131	40		
1968	Lib.	264	72	31	155	45		
1972	Lib.	264	107	35	109	38		
1974	Lib.	264	95	35	141	43		
1979	P.C.	282	136	36	114	40		
1980	Lib.	282	103	32	147	44		
1984	P.C.	282	211	50	40	28		

TABLE 1-A1 (CONT'D)

Election Year	CCF-NDP Seats	CCF-NDP Votes (%)	Social Credit Seats	Social Credit Votes (%)	Recon-struction Seats	Recon-struction Votes (%)	Other Seats	Other Votes
1878							1	2
1882								
1887								
1891							2	2
1896							7	9
1900								1
1904								1
1908							1	2
1911								1
1917								3
1921							4	6
1925							6	5
1926							6	4
1930							5	3
1935	7	9	17	4	1	9	7	3
1940	8	8	10	3			6	7
1945	28	16	13	4			12	12
1949	13	13	10	4			5	4
1953	23	11	15	5			5	4
1957	25	11	19	7			4	2
1958	8	9		2				1
1962	19	14	30	12				
1963	17	13	24	12				
1965	21	18	5	4	9[d]	5[e]	2	1
1968	21	17	0	1	14[d]	5[e]	0	1
1972	31	18	15	8				
1974	16	15	11	5			1	1
1979	26	18	6	5			0	2
1980	32	20	0	2			0	2
1984	30	19	0	0			1	

Source: Adapted from Hugh G. Thorburn, *Party Politics in Canada,* 5th ed. (Scarborough: Prentice-Hall, 1985), p. 349.

Notes: a. Wartime Coalition.
 b. Government.
 c. Opposition.
 d. Créditiste seats.
 e. Créditiste votes (%).

TABLE 1-A2 Percentage of Seats in Each Region Won by Governing Party in Canadian General Elections, 1867–1984

| Election | Governing Party | % Seats Won by Governing Party in each Region | | | | |
		Canada	West	Ontario	Quebec	Atlantic
1867	CONS[a]	55.8	—	56.1	69.2	29.4
1872	CONS	51.5	90.0	43.2	58.5	48.6
1874	LIB	64.6	20.0	72.7	50.8	79.1
1878	CONS	66.5	90.0	67.0	69.2	55.8
1882	CONS	66.2	72.7	59.3	73.8	67.4
1887	CONS	57.2	93.3	56.6	50.8	55.8
1891	CONS	57.2	93.3	52.2	46.2	72.1
1896	LIB	54.9	47.1	46.7	75.4	43.6
1900	LIB	62.0	70.6	39.1	87.7	69.2
1904	LIB	65.0	75.0	44.2	83.1	74.3
1908	LIB	60.2	51.4	41.9	81.5	74.3
1911	CONS	60.2	51.4	83.7	41.5	45.7
1917	UNIONIST (CONS)	65.1	96.5	90.2	4.6	67.7
1921	Lib[b]	49.4	8.8	25.6	100.0	80.6
1925	Lib	40.4	33.3	13.4	90.8	20.7
1926	Lib	47.3	34.8	28.0	92.3	31.0
1930	CONS	55.9	44.9	72.0	36.9	79.3
1935	LIB	69.8	48.6	68.3	84.6	96.2
1940	LIB	72.7	59.7	67.1	93.8	73.1
1945	LIB	51.0	26.4	41.5	83.1	69.2
1949	LIB	72.5	59.7	67.5	90.4	73.5
1953	LIB	64.2	37.5	58.8	88.0	81.8
1957	Prog. Cons	42.3	29.2	71.8	12.0	63.6
1958	PROG. CONS	78.5	91.7	78.8	66.7	75.8
1962	Prog. Cons	43.8	68.1	41.1	18.7	54.5
1963	Lib	48.7	13.9	61.2	62.7	60.6
1965	Lib	49.4	12.5	60.0	74.7	45.5
1968	LIB	58.7	40.0	72.7	75.7	21.9
1972	Lib	41.3	10.0	40.9	75.7	31.2
1974	LIB	53.4	18.6	62.5	81.1	40.6
1979	Prog. Cons	48.2	73.8	60.0	2.7	56.3
1980	LIB	52.1	2.5	54.7	98.7	59.4
1984	PROG. CONS	74.8	76.2	70.5	77.3	78.1

Sources: Adapted from Robert J. Jackson, Doreen Jackson and Nick Baxter-Moore, *Politics in Canada: Culture, Institutions, Behaviour and Public Policy* (Scarborough: Prentice-Hall, forthcoming); Chapter X, 6 in Special Joint Committee on Senate Reform, 28 June 1983, 10A:2.

Notes: a. LIB/PROG. CONS = Majority Government
b. Lib/Prog. Cons = Minority Government

TABLE 1-A3 Regional Composition of Government Caucus and House of Commons, Canadian General Elections, 1867–1984

Election	Governing Party	Regional Composition of Government Caucus				Regional Composition of House of Commons			
		West	Ontario	Quebec	Atlantic	West	Ontario	Quebec	Atlantic
1867	CONS[a]	—	45.5	44.6	9.9	—	45.3	35.9	18.8
1872	CONS	8.7	36.9	36.9	17.5	5.0	44.0	32.5	18.5
1874	LIB	1.5	48.1	24.8	25.6	4.9	42.7	31.6	20.9
1878	CONS	6.6	43.1	32.8	17.5	4.9	42.7	31.6	20.9
1882	CONS	5.8	38.8	34.5	20.9	5.2	43.3	31.0	20.5
1887	CONS	11.4	42.3	26.8	19.5	7.0	42.8	30.2	20.0
1891	CONS	11.4	39.0	24.4	25.2	7.0	42.8	30.2	20.0
1896	LIB	6.8	36.8	41.9	14.5	8.0	43.2	30.5	18.3
1900	LIB	9.1	27.3	43.2	20.5	8.0	43.2	30.5	18.3
1904	LIB	15.1	27.3	38.8	18.7	13.1	40.2	30.4	16.4
1908	LIB	13.5	27.1	39.8	19.5	15.8	38.9	29.4	15.8
1911	CONS	13.5	54.1	20.3	12.0	15.8	38.9	29.4	15.8
1917	UNIONIST (CONS)	35.9	48.4	2.0	13.7	24.3	34.9	27.7	13.2
1921	Lib[b]	4.3	18.1	56.0	21.6	24.3	34.9	27.7	13.2
1925	Lib	23.2	11.1	59.6	6.1	28.2	33.5	26.5	11.8
1926	Lib	20.7	19.8	51.7	7.8	28.2	33.5	26.5	11.8
1930	CONS	22.6	43.1	17.5	16.8	28.2	33.5	26.5	11.8
1935	LIB	20.5	32.7	32.2	14.6	29.4	33.5	26.5	10.6
1940	LIB	24.2	30.9	34.2	10.7	29.4	33.5	26.5	10.6
1945	LIB	15.2	27.2	43.2	14.4	29.4	33.5	26.5	10.6
1949	LIB	22.6	29.5	34.7	13.1	27.5	31.7	27.9	13.0
1953	LIB	15.9	29.4	38.8	15.9	27.2	32.1	28.3	12.5
1957	Prog. Cons	18.8	54.5	8.0	18.8	27.2	32.1	28.3	12.5

TABLE 1-A3 (CONT'D)

Election	Governing Party	Regional Composition of Government Caucus				Regional Composition of House of Commons			
		West	Ontario	Quebec	Atlantic	West	Ontario	Quebec	Atlantic
1958	PROG. CONS	31.7	32.2	24.0	12.0	27.2	32.1	28.3	12.5
1962	Prog. Cons	42.2	30.2	12.1	15.5	27.2	32.1	28.3	12.5
1963	Lib	7.8	40.3	36.4	15.5	27.2	32.1	28.3	12.5
1965	Lib	6.9	38.9	42.7	11.5	27.2	32.1	28.3	12.5
1968	LIB	18.1	41.3	36.1	4.5	26.5	33.3	28.0	12.1
1972	Lib	6.4	33.0	51.4	9.2	26.5	33.3	28.0	12.1
1974	LIB	9.2	39.0	42.6	9.2	26.5	33.3	28.0	12.1
1979	Prog. Cons	43.4	41.9	1.5	13.2	28.4	33.7	26.6	11.3
1980	LIB	1.4	35.4	50.3	12.9	28.4	33.7	26.6	11.3
1984	PROG. CONS	28.9	31.7	27.5	11.8	28.4	33.7	26.6	11.3

Sources: Adapted from Robert J. Jackson, Doreen Jackson and Nick Baxter-Moore, *Politics in Canada: Culture, Institutions, Behaviour and Public Policy* (Scarborough: Prentice-Hall, forthcoming); Chapter X, 7 in Special Joint Committee on Senate Reform, 28 June 1983, 10A:3.

Notes: a. LIB/PROG CONS = Majority Government
   b. Lib/Prog Cons = Minority Government
   Rows may not add up to 100.0 percent due to rounding.

Notes

This paper was completed in March 1984, before the sweeping victory of the Progressive Conservative Party in the general election of September 1984. In the autumn of 1984 it is still too soon to say anything about what effect the change in government will have on the subjects discussed in this paper.

1. See testimony before the Special Joint Committee of the Senate and House of Commons on Senate Reform, *Minutes of Proceedings and Evidence*, June 2, 1983, p. 6 (witness: Peter Russell), June 14, 1983, p. 34 (witness: Richard Simeon), June 21, 1983, p. 14 (witness: R.M. Burns) and June 28, 1983, pp. 9–10 (witness: John Meisel).

2. The difference between the two North American federations must not be overstated, however. The Americans, too, had a continent to subdue, just as British North America's two founding peoples could not be oblivious to the representation question. Witness the debate over the composition of the Senate. However, in the one, "the federal division of powers served a representative function by creating a structure of mutual balance and influence between the two main levels of government" (Beer, 1978, p. 15), while in the other, imbalance was the cardinal feature. For as Jean Baptiste Eric Dorion said of the proposed federal government, "All is strength and power" (Waite, 1963, p. 147).

3. The ten volumes are written by Morton (1950), Masters (1950), Burnet (1951), Macpherson (1953), Mallory (1954), Mann (1955), Fowke (1957), Thomas (1959), S. D. Clark (1959) and Irving (1959). Some works of distinction on Liberals and Conservatives are written by Granatstein (1967), Whitaker (1977), English (1977) and Wearing (1981). The author of this paper has also written two studies of the Liberal Party: see Smith (1975, 1981).

4. Among the most insightful are books by Dawson (1958), Neatby (1963, 1976), Pickersgill (1975) and Munro and Inglis (1975). See also Thomson (1967), Diefenbaker (1977) and Graham (1960).

5. Given his long tenure as leader, Mackenzie King's views on party organization are obviously of considerable importance to this study. However, as Whitaker (1977, p. 30) comments: "The man with the reputation as the master of ambiguity in his public statements was, on this particular issue at least, fundamentally ambiguous in his own mind as well as in his public expression."

6. They include in that figure all mentions of local candidates as well as other prominent politicians.

7. Selective interest in political parties is a permanent feature of the media: "The vast amount of information now available [on party finance] has been very little used [by the media]. No one has seriously examined in detail the sources of donations to parties and how these may have changed since [the passage of the Election Expenses Act in] 1974" (Seidle and Paltiel, 1981, p. 277).

8. See "Recruiting Candidates for Elected Office: How Parties Make Them Run," *Parliamentary Government* 2 (2) (1981), pp. 12–14; see also Smith (1981, pp. 64–65).

9. See testimony of William Irvine before the Special Joint Committee of the Senate and House of Commons on Senate Reform, *Minutes of Proceedings and Evidence*, June 22, 1983, p. 13.

10. Regulatory activity by government has increased since the Second World War. In Atlantic Canada and in western Canada, the Canadian Transport Commission has been added to the list of "devils" once dominated by the banks and the railroads. The CTC is only one agency; others include the NEB and CRTC, for example. The relationship between the growth of regulation and regionalism needs study. A lucid summary of the conflict of principle inherent in "regulatory agencies and the federal system" is found in Schultz (1981). In testimony before the Special Joint Committee of the Senate and House of Commons on Senate Reform, *Minutes of Proceedings and Evidence*, June 16, 1983, pp. 12–13, McWhinney alludes to the comparative advantages of royal commissions, administrative tribunals and legislative bodies as watch-dogs of government but favours parliamentary bodies because of their combined advantages of "constitutional legitimacy" and speed.

11. Criticisms that Laurier was "mollycoddling" the "foreigner" not as a "disciple of British institutions and citizenship — but because of his almighty power at the ballot box" was stock Tory fare up to and during the First World War (Smith, 1975, chap. 4).

12. In this respect, Canada differs, one is tempted to say radically, from a country like West Germany, whose political structures and processes have in recent years been drawn warmly to the attention of Canadians. Even aside from features that markedly distinguish each federation — the one a small, populous, historic, but now divided country, the other a transcontinental, multicultural state settled through mass immigration — Germany's integration is, and always was, intensely administrative. This has had profound effects on attitudes towards such subjects as leadership, legislative opposition, intergovernmental cooperation and the limits of partisanship. For helpful examinations of these questions in the Bonn Republic, see Dyson (1975) and Pridham (1973).

13. The remainder of this paragraph is based on Stewart (1980, 1982).

14. There is a great need in the study of Canada's development to look more closely at generations and political change. Societal adaptation is a crucial factor in peaceful territorial expansion. See, for example, Prang (1983).

15. For Canadian contrasts, see Gillies (1981). The mobility in question is particularly important to new governments who seek informed but non-bureaucratic advisors: see Canadian Study of Parliament Group, *Seminar on New Parliament, New Government, Old Public Service: The Changing of the Guard* (Ottawa, October 25, 1979). The ignorance of businessmen about the ways of government has long been a subject for comment by politicians; see Cartwright (1912, p. 340) and the papers of Sen. R.J. Stanbury, vol. 5, in the Public Archives of Canada, especially his 1969 paper on "The Attitudes of Businessmen."

16. See "The MP as Broker: Business/Labour/Government Relations," *Parliamentary Government* 2 (1) (1980), pp. 13–15.

17. In discussing caucus research offices, "one director noted that staff hiring has a strong political requirement. It is difficult to get the best combination of skills when party affiliation is the primary consideration" (Fish, 1983, p. 33).

18. This is the assessment of Brooke Claxton, who first was Minister of National Health and Welfare and then Minister of National Defence in the King cabinet and who kept the latter portfolio in the St. Laurent cabinet; see volume 79 of the Claxton papers in the Public Archives of Canada, especially his memorandum on "What should the Liberals do" (undated typescript post-1957).

19. This was the central criticism of the Tremblay report, which appeared in Quebec in 1957; see Kwavnick (1973). For an example of specific criticism of a single program, see "Federal Grants to Universities" in Trudeau (1968).

20. The scope of this paper does not permit consideration of regional contrasts in ethnic demography. Its importance for the development of Canadian political parties after 1950, however, demands investigation. The National Liberal Federation papers in the Public Archives of Canada contain many files related to ethnic organizational matters, for southern Ontario especially. To this writer's knowledge, they have not been used for academic research.

21. Almost 20 years later, another minister in the next Progressive Conservative government had the same complaint about "corridor decisions." See F. MacDonald (1980, p. 30). The now classic statement on bureaucratic cunning is in Crossman (1979, pp. 92, 148).

22. The details of each set of reforms can be found in Smith (1981) and Wearing (1981).

23. At least the reformers believed they were new. Mackenzie King had entered national politics advocating social reform, and party stalwarts like C.G. Power had long argued the need for electoral reform. See Ward (1966).

24. Already there was a prescient remark on this trend, as usual by Innis (1946, p. 85): "The Gallup Poll has possibly made politics more absorbing. But statistics has been particularly dangerous to modern society by strengthening the cult of economics and weakening other social sciences and the humanities."

25. According to Siegel (1983), "The 'modern media' have become agents of denationalization by serving as roadways for foreign, largely American, cultural values."

26. With rare exceptions, commentators tend to neglect migration in their discussions of Canada's political development and in comparisons they draw with countries of less recent settlement. For example, between 1931 and 1976 Saskatchewan experienced consistently negative values in net migration, while Ontario and British Columbia always enjoyed growth through migration. For the other provinces the net totals have been mixed. See Leacy (1983, A339–49).

27. See also speech of Edward Blake, MP and former premier of Ontario, to the House of Commons, *Debates*, 1885, pp. 1180–92.

28. See David MacDonald, "Is Lobbying MPs Worth the Effort?" *Parliamentary Government* 2 (1) (1980), p. 11.

29. See David Collenette and Ian Deans, "Westminister on the Rideau?" *Parliamentary Government* 3 (3) (1982), p. 5.

30. The percentage was higher still in the first half of Confederation (Ward, 1963, pp. 115–18). Courtney (1973, p. 154) reports that there is some evidence to suggest that the turnover may, in fact, be higher in the Liberal Party than in either the Progressive Conservative or New Democratic parties.

31. See "From Private Life to Public Life: Making the Transition," *Parliamentary Government* (1) (1979), pp. 3–5.

32. Quotation is by A.R. Huntington, Progressive Conservative MP, testifying before the House of Commons Special Committee on Standing Orders and Procedures, *Minutes of Proceedings and Evidence*, (November 30, 1982), p. 40. See also David MacDonald, "Is Lobbying MPs Worth the Effort?" *Parliamentary Government* 2 (1) (1980), p. 12.

33. See Gibbins (1982, chap. 3). Canadians, however, should not be selective in the characteristics of American government they stress. See also the sections dealing with the United States in Aberback et al. (1981). There and in Grodzins (1967), the interpenetration of bureaucratic and political roles is stressed.

34. See Darcy McKeough, "Parliamentary Perceptions," *Parliamentary Government* 3 (3) (1982), p. 7.

35. See testimony of Bill Blackie before the House of Commons Special Committee on Standing Orders and Procedures, *Minutes of Proceedings and Evidence*, (July 6, 1982), p. 35.

36. Here and in a chapter on "The Liberal View of the Constitution," Birch (1964) uses the word "liberal" to refer to such nineteenth-century English ideas as "one man, one vote, one value," Parliamentary sovereignty and the "rule of law."

37. See Appendix for federal election results.

38. There is an extensive literature on Quebec nationalism; a good place to begin reading in English is Cook (1966). A study which specifically links nationalism to political parties is Quinn (1963).

39. In an article in *Canadian Forum*, January 1930, reprinted in *Constitutional Issues in Canada, 1900–1931*, edited by R. MacGregor Dawson (London: Oxford University Press, 1933), p. 135.

40. The seven studies are written by MacKinnon (1951), Beck (1957), Thorburn (1961), Donnelly (1963), Schindeler (1969), Noel (1971) and David E. Smith (1975).

41. By this writer's count, there are seven pieces written by Spender (1938), Wrong (1924), Clark (1924), Reid (1936), Kraft (1944), Harvey (1944) and Forsey (1942).

42. Article by Arthur Beauchesne in the *Canadian Bar Review* (1944): 137–46.

43. Article by Eugene Forsey in *Saturday Night*, March 20, 1948, pp. 12–13.

44. Article by R.O. MacFarlane in *The Dalhousie Review*, vol. 18, (1938–39): pp. 9–16. Two other topics of cyclical interest were the redrawing of provincial boundaries and provincial secession; see Arthur Lower, "Nonsense — Our Big Provinces Behave Like Imperial Provinces and Should Be Carved Up," *Maclean's*, October 15, 1948. Discussion of the possible secession of Quebec has produced a voluminous bibliography, but that subject is neither new nor limited to Quebec; see for example Thompson Hardy, "Secession in Canada II: The Prairies," *Canadian Forum*, June 1924, pp. 266–68; F.C.

Pickwell, "Prairie Chartists Drop Secession," *Saturday Night*, March 28, 1931, p. 2; and S. Leonard Tilley, "Will the Maritimes Secede?" *Maclean's*, August 15, 1936, pp. 17, 22–24.

45. The Prairie provinces' statements run to several hundred pages. The case for Alberta was directed not to the Rowell-Sirois Commission but to "the SOVEREIGN PEOPLE of Canada and their Governments." Ontario's statement includes a jaundiced view of the claims of the other provinces or, in Mr. Hepburn's words, "working over accounts presented by sister provinces." *Statements by the Government of Ontario to the Royal Commission on Dominion-Provincial Relations*, I (Prime Minister's Statement, Toronto, 1983) p. 29.

46. There are always exceptions to such generalizations, the most recent and most informative being Morley et al. (1983).

47. The literature is vast; among the most useful introductions are those by Simeon (1972), Smiley (1980) and the Institute of Public Administration of Canada (1979). See, too, the extensive and apposite publications of the Institute of Intergovernmental Relations, Queen's University, Kingston, Ontario.

48. The data provided by Clarke et al. (1977, chap. 6) underscore the separation that has taken place. Electoral choice and party image duplicate the bifurcation found in party organization.

49. For a recent example, see the comment by the B.C. Liberal leader on the removal of Senator Ray Perrault from cabinet: "A backroom clique of Liberals with Social Credit connections. . . have had their knives out for Senator Perrault. [They] are highly connected with Liberals not only by convenience, but by conviction." *Globe and Mail*, August 17, 1983, p. 9.

50. The transmutation in 1961 of the CCF, along with the Canadian Labour Congress, farm groups and other "liberally minded Canadians," into the NDP, the Canadian counterpart of the British Labour Party, was another important factor in undermining its traditional regional protest role. In fact, it created a Janus-like organization of provincial-agrarian and federal-labour interests that, to the sorrow of its leaders, infrequently meld in national politics. McMenemy and Winn (1976, p. 81) compare France and Canada: "The leadership of the left in both countries . . . may come from the core, but the electoral strength resides in the periphery."

51. It needs to be emphasized that modern ideas on the subject are just that — modern. See Sir Goronway Edwards (1964, 1965). I would like to thank my colleague, Duff Spafford, for bringing these two articles to my attention. In her "political" novel, *Felix Holt*, George Eliot notes the persistence of favourable attitudes towards "uncontested" elections into the period following the First Reform Act, 1832; see George Eliot, *Felix Holt* (London: Penguin Books, 1972), pp. 409–10.

52. *Globe and Mail*, November 9, 1982, p. 7.

53. See testimony before the Special Joint Committee of the Senate and House of Commons on Senate Reform, *Minutes of Proceedings and Evidence*, June 21, 1983, p. 75 (witness: Robert Stanfield), and June 28, 1983, p. 28 (witness: John Meisel).

54. *Globe and Mail*, July 2, 1981, p. 7.

55. Clarke et al. (1977, p. 31). The same authors also note that "symbolic" attitudes towards community, regime and authorities are distressingly low. In interviews with 2,445 respondents, not one referred to national events or persons; all those who mentioned government in general did so in neutral terms (the capital, the Parliament buildings), and of those who referred to the political actors of the day, 40 percent of the responses were neutral; 37 percent negative and only 23 percent positive (p. 28). "In general, the parties and politicians who run the political system are regarded with distaste by most of the public" (p. 31).

56. See, too, *Globe and Mail*, August 17, 1983, p. 9. The need for balance extended early and far: even to the Sudan expedition. The plan for a composite Guards Camel Corps, taken from regiments in each province, won approval, in part, because the "several provinces would feel they were represented"; Marquis of Lorne to Tupper, February 27, 1885 (Saunders 1916, 2:50).

57. See testimony of David Elton before the Special Joint Committee of the Senate and House of Commons on Senate Reform, *Minutes of Proceedings and Evidence*, June 14, 1983, p. 29.

58. Public displeasure at patronage appointments, dispensed at the time of Mr. Trudeau's retirement in June 1984, plagued his successor, John Turner, throughout the election campaign that followed. The use of the appointment power to neutralize opponents was not original with Mr. Trudeau. At a time when it was an offence to refuse an appointment as an electoral official, Macdonald made repeated use of Liberals in these offices (Ward 1963, p. 175).

59. Alive, perhaps, but with low expectations. When Senator R.J. Stanbury, Liberal Party president from 1969 to 1973, criticized graft and patronage in Nova Scotia politics, he was put right by one Liberal supporter. "Of course things are corrupt down here. As long as you have the feudal system in operation, as it is in Nova Scotia, you'll have privilege, graft, favoritism and the buying of sins and errors." Governments were changed in Nova Scotia, he was told, not "to improve the fabric of life but to find out if the next fellow will share the graft a little more liberally. . . . Decisions here are still largely made by the 'opinion-makers' [who will] pass the word down and the word they pass down will stick. . . . God has decreed that there shall be those who master and those who serve. The masters, therefore, are not exploiting — they are . . . in a position to solve problems with a minimum of charity, to grant jobs, to punish by firing, and to reward meanly, for long and faithfull service — a watch, a story in the newspaper, a dinner, a twenty-five dollar cheque etc." His correspondent concluded that what was needed was another Diefenbaker (presumably this time in the Liberal Party) who could "show . . . these humble people . . . what was in them"; Public Archives of Canada, *Stanbury Papers*, vol. I, *W.A. Lindsay to Stanbury*, October 6, 1969.

60. A new, theoretical work on federalism (King 1982, pp. 88–89) supports this contention.

61. *Globe and Mail*, August 17, 1983, p. 9.

62. See testimony before the Special Joint Committee of the Senate and House of Commons on Senate Reform, *Minutes of Proceedings and Evidence*, June 21, 1983, p. 41 (witness: Sen. George McIlraith), June 2, 1983, p. 25 (witness: Sen. Hartland de Montarville Molson).

63. On the subject of conventions, see Courtney (1973).

64. Henry Fairlie, "Letter from Washington," *Encounter*, January 1973.

Bibliography

Aberback, Joel D., Robert D. Putnam, and Bert A. Rockman. 1981. *Bureaucrats and Politicians in Western Democracies*. Cambridge, Mass.: Harvard University Press.

Acheson, T.W. 1977. "The Maritimes and Empire Canada." In *Canada and the Burden of Unity*, edited by David Jay Bercuson, pp. 87–114. Toronto: Macmillan.

Badie, Bertrand, and Pierre Birnbaum. 1983. *The Sociology of the State*. Translated by Arthur Goldhammer. Chicago: University of Chicago Press.

Bakvis, Herman. 1981. *Federalism and the Organization of Political Life: Canada in Comparative Perspective*. Kingston: Queen's University. Institute for Intergovernmental Relations.

Beck, J. Murray. 1957. *The Government of Nova Scotia*. Toronto: University of Toronto Press.

Beer, Samuel. 1978. "Federalism, Nationalism and Democracy in America." *American Political Science Review* 72 (March): 9–21.

Bercuson, David Jay. 1977. *Canada and the Burden of Unity*. Toronto: Macmillan.

Bernard, André. 1977. *La politique au Canada et au Québec*. 2d ed. Montreal: Les Presses de l'Université du Québec.

Birch, A.H. 1964. *Representative and Responsible Government: An Essay on the British Constitution*. Toronto: University of Toronto Press.

Blondel, J. 1963. *Voters, Parties, and Leaders: The Social Fabric of British Politics*. London: Penguin Books.

Brodie, M. Janine, and Jane Jenson. 1980. *Crisis, Challenge and Change: Party and Class in Canada*. Toronto: Methuen.

Brodie, M. Janine, and Jill Vickers. 1981. "The More Things Change: Women in the 1979 Federal Election." In *Canada at the Polls, 1979 and 1980: A Study of the General Elections*, edited by Howard R. Penniman, pp. 322–36. Washington, D.C.: American Enterprise Institute.

Burnet, Jean. 1951. *Next Year Country*. Toronto: University of Toronto Press.

Burnham, Walter Dean. 1983. *The Current Crisis in American Politics*. New York: Oxford University Press.

Burns, James MacGregor. 1982. *The Vineyard of Liberty*. New York: Knopf.

Cairns, Alan C. 1968. "The Electoral System and the Party System in Canada, 1921–1965." *Canadian Journal of Political Science* 1 (March): 55–80.

Canadian Bar Association. 1982. *Report of the Canadian Bar Association Committee on the Reform of Parliament: Parliament as a Lawmaker*. Ottawa: Canadian Bar Association.

Cartwright, Sir Richard. 1912. *Reminiscences*. Toronto: William Briggs.

Churchill, Hon. Gordon. 1983. Conservative convention, Toronto, September 6–9, 1967. In " 'Deux Nations' or One Canada: John Diefenbaker at the 1967 Conservative Convention." *Canadian Historical Review* 64 (4): 597–604.

Clark, A.B. 1924. "The Single-Chamber Legislature of Manitoba." *National Municipal Review* 13 (April): 225–33.

Clark, S.D. 1959. *Movements of Political Protest in Canada, 1640–1840*. Toronto: University of Toronto Press.

Clarke, Harold D., Colin Campbell, F.Q. Quo, and Arthur Goddard, eds. 1980. *Parliament, Policy and Representation*. Toronto: Methuen.

Clarke, Harold D., Lawrence Le Duc, Jane Jenson, and Jon H. Pammett. 1977. *Political Choice in Canada*. Toronto: McGraw-Hill Ryerson.

Clotfelter, James. 1975. "The Future of Political Parties as Organizations and Symbols." *Public Administration Review* 35 (September-October): 554–66.

Cook, Ramsay. 1966. *Canada and the French-Canadian Question*. Toronto: Macmillan.

Courtney, John. 1973. *Selection of National Party Leaders*. Toronto: Macmillan.

Creighton, Donald. 1955. *John A. Macdonald: The Old Chieftain*. Toronto: Macmillan.

Crossman, Richard. 1979. *The Crossman Diaries: Selections from the Diaries of a Cabinet Minister, 1964–1970*. Edited and with an introduction by Anthony Howard. London: Methuen Paperbacks.

Dawson, R. MacGregor. 1933. *Constitutional Issues in Canada, 1900–1931*. London: Oxford University Press.

———. 1958. *William Lyon Mackenzie King: A Political Biography, 1874–1923*. Toronto: University of Toronto Press.

———. 1970. *The Government of Canada*. 5th ed., revised by Norman Ward. Toronto: University of Toronto Press.

DeVrees, Johan K. 1980. "In Pursuit of the Common Weal: A Theory of Emergence and Growth of the Political Party." *Acta Politica* 15: 191–218.

Diefenbaker, Rt. Hon. John G. 1977. *One Canada: The Tumultuous Years, 1962–1967*. Toronto: Macmillan.

Dion, Léon. 1976. *The Unfinished Revolution*. Montreal: McGill-Queen's University Press.

Donnelly, M.S. 1963. *The Government of Manitoba*. Toronto: University of Toronto Press.

Dwivedi, O.P., ed. 1982. *The Administrative State in Canada: Essays in Honour of J. E. Hodgetts*. Toronto: University of Toronto Press.

Dyson, Kenneth H.F. 1977. *Party, State, and Bureaucracy in Western Germany*. Beverly Hills: Sage Publications.

Edelman, Murray. 1964. *The Symbolic Uses of Politics*. Urbana: University of Illinois Press.

————. 1971. *Politics as Symbolic Action: Mass Arousal and Quiescence*. Chicago: Markham Publishing Company.

Edwards, Sir Goronway. 1964. "The Emergence of Majority Rule in English Parliamentary Elections." In *Transactions of the Royal Historical Society*. Fifth Series 14: 175-96.

————. 1965. "The Emergence of Majority Rule in the Procedure of the House of Commons." In *Transactions of the Royal Historical Society*. Fifth Series 15: 165-87.

English, John. 1977. *The Decline of Politics: The Conservatives and the Party System, 1901-1920*. Toronto: University of Toronto Press.

Fairlie, Henry. 1968. *The Life of Politics*. London: Methuen.

Finer, S.E. 1980. *The Changing British Party System, 1945-1979*. Washington, D.C.: American Enterprise Institute.

Fish, Karen. 1983. *Parliamentarians and Science: A Discussion Paper*. Ottawa: Science Council of Canada.

Fletcher, Frederick J. 1981. *The Newspaper and Public Affairs*. Vol. 7: Royal Commission on Newpapers. Ottawa: Minister of Supply and Services Canada.

Forsey, Eugene. 1942. "Sectional Representation in Maritime Provincial Cabinets since 1867." *Public Affairs* 6 (Autumn): 23-24, 30.

Fowke, V.C. 1948. "Royal Commissions and Canadian Agricultural Policy." *Canadian Journal of Economics and Political Science* 14 (May): 163-75.

————. 1957. *The National Policy and the Wheat Economy*. Toronto: University of Toronto Press.

Gibbins, Roger. 1982. *Regionalism: Territorial Politics in Canada and the United States*. Toronto: Butterworth.

Gillies, James. 1981. *Where Business Fails*. Montreal: Institute for Research on Public Policy.

Graham, Roger. 1960. *Arthur Meighen: A Biography*. 3 vols. Toronto: Clarke, Irwin.

Granatstein, J. L. 1967. *The Politics of Survival: The Conservative Party in Canada, 1939-1945*. Toronto: University of Toronto Press.

Grodzins, Morton. 1967. "American Political Parties and the American System." In *American Federalism in Perspective*, edited by Aaron Wildavsky, pp. 133-35. Boston: Little, Brown.

Harvey, D.C. 1944. "Representation in the Assembly of Nova Scotia." *Public Affairs* 7 (Summer): 217-23.

Innis, H.A., ed. 1938. *Essays in Political Economy in Honour of E. J. Urwick*. Toronto: University of Toronto Press.

————. 1940. "The Rowell-Sirois Report." *Canadian Journal of Economics and Political Science* 6 (November): 562-71.

————. 1946. "On the Economic Significance of Cultural Factors." In *Political Economy in the Modern State*. Chap. 6. Toronto: Ryerson Press.

Institute of Public Administration of Canada. 1979. *Intergovernment Relations in Canada Today*. Toronto: Institute of Public Administration of Canada.

Irving, John A. 1959. *The Social Credit Movement in Alberta*. Toronto: University of Toronto Press.

Irwin, William P. 1968. "Representation and Apportionment." *Parliamentary Affairs* 21 (Summer): 226-45.

King, Anthony. 1969. "Political Parties in Western Democracies: Some Sceptical Reflections." *Polity* 11 (2): 111-41.

King, Preston. 1982. *Federalism and Federation*. Baltimore: Johns Hopkins Press.

Kornberg, Allan, and Harold D. Clarke, eds. 1983. *Political Support in Canada: The Crisis Years*. Durham: Duke University Press.

Kornberg, Allan, Joel Smith, and Harold D. Clarke. 1979. *Citizen Politicians — Canada: Party Officials in a Democratic Society*. Durham: Carolina Academic Press.

Kornberg, Allan and Judith D. Wolfe. 1980. "Parliament, the Media and Polls." In *Parliament, Policy and Representation*, edited by Harold D. Clarke et al., pp. 35-58. Toronto: Methuen.

Kraft, Theodore. 1944. "The Civil Services in the Canadian Provinces." *Public Affairs* 7 (Summer): 217–23.

Kwavnick, David, ed. 1973. *The Tremblay Report: Report of the Royal Commission of Inquiry on Constitutional Problems.* Toronto: McClelland and Stewart.

Leacy, F.H., ed. 1983. *Historical Statistics of Canada.* 2d ed. Ottawa: Statistics Canada.

Lipset, S.M. [1950] 1968. *Agrarian Socialism: The Co-operative Commonwealth Federation in Saskatchewan.* Reprint. Garden City, N.Y.: Anchor Books, Doubleday.

———. 1954. "Democracy in Alberta." *Canadian Forum* 34: 175–77, 196–98.

———. 1976. "Radicalism in North America: A Comparative View of the Party Systems of Canada and the United States." *Transactions of the Royal Society of Canada.* Fourth Series, 14: 19–55.

Lovink, J.A.A. 1973. "Is Canadian Politics Too Competitive?" *Canadian Journal of Political Science* 6 (3): 341–79.

Lower, Arthur R.M. 1939. "Geographical Determinants in Canadian History." In *Essays in Canadian History Presented to G. M. Wrong,* edited by R. Flenley, pp. 229–52. Toronto: Macmillan.

MacDonald, Hon. Flora. 1980. "The Minister and the Mandarins." *Policy Options* 1 (3): 29–31.

MacGuigan, Hon. Mark. 1983. "Reform of the Senate." Discussion paper presented to the Special Joint Committee of the Senate and House of Commons on Senate Reform, June 16, 1983, Ottawa.

MacKinnon, Frank. 1951. *The Government of Prince Edward Island.* Toronto: University of Toronto Press.

Macpherson, C.B. 1938. "On the Study of Politics in Canada." In *Essays in Political Economy in Honour of E.J. Urwick,* edited by H.A. Innis, pp. 147–65. Toronto: University of Toronto Press.

———. 1953. *Democracy in Alberta: Social Credit and the Party System.* Toronto: University of Toronto Press.

———. 1962. *Democracy in Alberta: Social Credit and the Party System.* 2d ed. Toronto: University of Toronto Press.

Mallory, J.R. 1954. *Social Credit and the Federal Power in Canada.* Toronto: University of Toronto Press.

———. 1984. *The Structure of Canadian Government.* Rev. ed. Toronto: Gage Publishing.

Mann, W.E. 1955. *Sect, Cult and Church in Alberta.* Toronto: University of Toronto Press.

Masters, D.C. 1950. *The Winnipeg General Strike.* Toronto: University of Toronto Press.

McMenemy, John, and Conrad Winn. 1976. *Political Parties in Canada.* Toronto: McGraw-Hill Ryerson.

Meisel, John. 1962. *The Canadian General Election of 1957.* Toronto: University of Toronto Press.

———. ed. 1964. *Papers on the 1962 Election.* Toronto: University of Toronto Press.

———. 1981. "The Larger Context: The Period Preceding the 1979 Election." In *Canada at the Polls, 1979 and 1980: A Study of the General Elections,* edited by Howard R. Penniman, pp. 24–54. Washington, D.C.: American Enterprise Institute.

Morley, J. Terrence, Norman Ruff, Neil A. Swainson, R. Jeremy Wilson, and Walter Young. 1983. *The Reins of Power: Governing British Columbia.* Vancouver: Douglas and McIntyre.

Morton, W.L. 1943. "The Extension of the Franchise in Canada: A Study in Democratic Nationalism." *Canadian Historical Association Annual Report*: 72–81.

———. 1950. *The Progressive Party in Canada.* Toronto: University of Toronto Press.

Munro, John A., and Alex I. Inglis, eds. 1975. *Mike: The Memoirs of the Right Honourable Lester B. Pearson.* Vol. 3. Toronto: University of Toronto Press.

Neatby, H. Blair. 1963. *William Lyon Mackenzie King: The Lonely Heights, 1924–1932.* Toronto: University of Toronto Press.

———. 1976. *William Lyon Mackenzie King: The Prism of Unity, 1932–1939.* Toronto: University of Toronto Press.

Noel, S.J.R. 1971. *Politics in Newfoundland*. Toronto: University of Toronto Press.

Pammett, Jon H. 1981. "Elections." In *Canadian Politics in the 1980s*, edited by Michael S. Whittington and Glen Williams. Toronto: Methuen. pp. 206–20.

Penniman, Howard R., ed. 1975. *Canada at the Polls: The General Election of 1974*. Washington, D.C.: American Enterprise Institute.

———. 1981. *Canada at the Polls, 1979 and 1980: A Study of the General Elections*. Washington, D.C.: American Enterprise Institute.

Pickersgill, Hon. J.W. 1975. *My Years with Louis St. Laurent*. Toronto: University of Toronto Press.

Pinard, Maurice. 1971. *The Rise of a Third Party: A Study in Crisis Politics*. Englewood Cliffs, N. J.: Prentice-Hall.

Prang, Margaret. 1983. "The Family and Canadian Federalism." Paper presented to Joint CHA-CPSA Session, Learned Societies Meeting, June 1983, Vancouver.

Pridham, Geoffrey. 1973. "The CDU/CSU Opposition in West Germany, 1969–1972: A Party in Search of an Organization." *Parliamentary Affairs* 25 (Spring): 201–17.

Pross, Paul. 1982. "Space, Function, and Interest: The Problem of Legitimacy in the Canadian State." In *The Administrative State in Canada: Essays in Honour of J. E. Hodgetts*, edited by O. P. Dwivedi, pp. 107–29. Toronto: University of Toronto Press.

Quinn, Herbert F. 1963. *The Union-Nationale: A Study in Quebec Nationalism*. Toronto: University of Toronto Press.

Reid, Escott M. 1932. "The Rise of National Parties in Canada." *Papers and Proceedings of the Canadian Political Science Association* 4. Reprinted in *Party Politics in Canada*, 4th ed., edited by Hugh G. Thorburn, pp. 12–20. Scarborough: Prentice-Hall. 1979.

———. 1936. "The Saskatchewan Liberal Machine Before 1929." *Canadian Journal of Economics and Political Science* 2 (February): 27–40.

Saunders, E.M. 1916. *The Life and Letters of the Right Honourable Sir Charles Tupper, Bart. K.C.M.G.* 2 vols. Toronto: Cassell.

Saywell, John. 1977. *The Rise of the Parti-Québécois, 1967–1976*. Toronto: University of Toronto Press.

Scarrow, Howard A. 1962. *Canada Votes: A Handbook of Federal and Provincial Elections Data*. New Orleans: Hauser Press.

Schindeler, F.F. 1969. *Responsible Government in Ontario*. Toronto: University of Toronto Press.

Schultz, Richard. 1981. "Regulatory Agencies." In *Canadian Politics in the 1980s*, edited by Michael S. Whittington and Glen Williams, pp. 320–22. Toronto: Methuen.

Seidle, F. Leslie and Khayyam Zev Paltiel. 1981. "Party Finance, the Election Expenses Act, and Campaign Spending in 1979 and 1980." In *Canada at the Polls, 1979 and 1980: A Study of the General Elections*, edited by Howard R. Penniman, pp. 226–79. Washington, D.C.: American Enterprise Institute.

Siegel, Arthur. 1983. *Politics and the Media in Canada*. Toronto: McGraw-Hill Ryerson.

Simeon, Richard. 1972. *Federal-Provincial Diplomacy: The Making of Recent Policy in Canada*. Toronto: University of Toronto Press.

Simpson, Jeffrey. 1980. *The Discipline of Power*. Toronto: Personal Library.

Smiley, D.V. 1980. *Canada in Question: Federalism in the Eighties*. 3d ed. Toronto: McGraw-Hill Ryerson.

Smith, David E. 1975. *Prairie Liberalism: The Liberal Party in Saskatchewan, 1905–1971*. Toronto: University of Toronto Press.

———. 1981. *The Regional Decline of a National Party: Liberals on the Prairies*. Toronto: University of Toronto Press.

Smith, Denis. 1972. "Prairie Revolt, Federalism and the Party System." In *Party Politics in Canada*, 3d ed., edited by Hugh G. Thorburn, pp. 204–15. Toronto: University of Toronto Press.

Social Science Research Council. 1982. "The Political Economy of National Statistics." *Items* 36 (3): 29–35.

Spender, Richard C. 1938. "The Unicameral Legislature of Ontario." *American Political Science Review* 32 (February): 67–80.

Stein, Michael. 1973. *The Dynamics of Right-Wing Protest: Social Credit in Quebec*. Toronto: University of Toronto Press.

Stewart, Gordon. 1980. "Political Patronage under Macdonald and Laurier, 1878–1911." *American Review of Canadian Studies* 10: 3–12.

———. 1982. "John A. Macdonald's Greatest Triumph." *Canadian Historical Review* 63 (1): 3–33.

Stursberg, Peter. 1975. *Diefenbaker: Leadership Gained, 1956–1962*. Toronto: University of Toronto Press.

———. 1976. *Diefenbaker: Leadership Lost, 1962–1967*. Toronto: University of Toronto Press.

Thomas, L.G. 1959. *The Liberal Party in Alberta: A History of Politics in the Province of Alberta, 1905–1921*. Toronto: University of Toronto Press.

Thomson, Dale. 1967. *Louis St. Laurent, Canadian*. Toronto: Macmillan.

Thorburn, Hugh G. 1961. *Politics in New Brunswick*. Toronto: University of Toronto Press.

———. ed. 1979. *Party Politics in Canada*. 4th ed. Scarborough, Ont.: Prentice-Hall.

Trudeau, Pierre Elliott. 1968. *Federalism and the French Canadians*. Toronto: Macmillan.

Van Loon, Richard J., and Michael S. Whittington. 1981. *The Canadian Political System: Environment, Structure and Process*. 3d ed. Toronto: McGraw-Hill Ryerson.

Waite, P. B., ed. 1963. *Confederation Debates in the Province of Canada, 1865*. Toronto: McClelland and Stewart.

Ward, Norman. 1963. *The Canadian House of Commons: Representation*. 2d ed. Toronto: University of Toronto Press.

———. 1966. *A Party Politician: The Memoirs of Chubby Powers*. Toronto: Macmillan.

———. 1977a. "The Politics of Patronage: James G. Gardiner and Federal Appointments in the West, 1935–57." *Canadian Historical Review* 58 (3): pp. 294–310.

———. 1977b. Review of *The Government Party*. *Globe and Mail*, October 22, 1977.

Wearing, Joseph. 1981. *The L-Shaped Party: The Liberal Party of Canada, 1958–1980*. Toronto: McGraw-Hill Ryerson.

Whitaker, Reginald. 1977. *The Government Party: Organizing and Financing the Liberal Party of Canada, 1930–1958*. Toronto: University of Toronto Press.

Whittington, Michael S., and Glen Williams, eds. 1983. *Canadian Politics in the 1980s*. Toronto: Methuen.

Wildavsky, Aaron, ed. 1967. *American Federalism in Perspective*. Boston: Little, Brown.

Williams, John R. 1956. *The Conservative Party of Canada, 1920–1949*. Durham: Duke University Press.

Williams, Robert J. 1981. "Candidate Selection." In *Canada at the Polls, 1979 and 1980: A Study of the General Elections*, edited by Howard R. Penniman, pp. 86–120. Washington, D.C.: American Enterprise Institute.

Willison, Sir John. 1919. *Reminiscences: Political and Personal*. Toronto: McClelland and Stewart.

Wilson, John. 1983. "On the Dangers of Bickering in a Federal State: Some Reflections on the Failure of the National Party System." In *Political Support in Canada: The Crisis Years*, edited by Allan Kornberg and Harold D. Clarke, pp. 171–222. Durham: Duke University Press.

Wrong, G.M. 1924. "A Contrast: The Single-House Legislature of Ontario." *National Municipal Review* 13 (March): 169–72.

2

The Role of National Party Caucuses

PAUL G. THOMAS

Introduction

A country like Canada, with significant regional, economic and social diversities, needs institutions that both permit the expression of disagreements and facilitate the development of a national consensus. It is something of a cliché but nonetheless true that Canada is a difficult country to govern. Dissatisfaction with the policies of the national government and tensions among regions have been a recurrent feature of political life. The inability of national political institutions to reflect and satisfy the concerns of Canadians, especially those who live outside central Canada, has led to strong regional discontent. The two main political parties have not been flexible enough to accommodate fully the political expression of the range of diversities found within the country. Political protest movements and new political parties have often based their appeal on the promotion of regional causes.

The clash of regional interests has seemed greater during the last decade because of the regional nature of party support within the House of Commons. In terms of electing members to the Commons, none of the parties was truly national in appeal. Each was locked into a regional stronghold. The Liberals dominated Quebec. The Conservatives dominated the West, with some competition from the New Democratic Party. Atlantic Canada was shared by the two older parties. Thus Ontario became the focus of the real political struggle and was seen as the arbiter of what policies would be adopted. Inevitable disagreements over national policies were heightened by the additional dimension of a partisanship that was expressed along regional lines. For example, the Crow's Nest Pass freight rates for grain and the National Energy Program pitted not only Liberals against Conservatives but also East against West. The skewed nature of party representation in the House of Commons diminished the capacity of national institutions to accommodate regional grievances. Party caucuses more closely resembled contending regional blocs than truly national bodies that could accommodate regional divergences.

Denied what they regarded as effective representation in national institutions, Canadians looked increasingly to their provincial governments, acting within the forum of intergovernmental relations, to promote and defend their regional interests. Surveys revealed that Ottawa was seen as more remote and less responsive than provincial governments. Sensing public support for their role, provincial governments became more aggressive in their insistence on prior consultation over national policies and in their right to criticize. Heightened federal-provincial conflict resulted. The apparent weakening of national-level political representation for certain regions and the on-going intergovernmental struggles led to proposals for reforms to central institutions that would make them more sensitive to regional attitudes, concerns and demands.

Changes to the method of selection, the regional composition and the powers of the Senate have been the most popular avenues of proposed reform.[1] Much less attention has been paid to changing the House of Commons to enable it to serve as a more effective instrument for regional representation. Modifications to the electoral system designed to produce more geographically balanced parliamentary support among all three political parties have been proposed and debated in recent years (Elton and Gibbins, 1980; Courtney, 1980; Irvine, 1979). Adoption of free votes on all matters except those involving a clear question of confidence in the government has also been suggested as a way to liberate MPs from the alleged thralldom of party discipline (Special Committee on Standing Orders and Procedures, 1983, p. 5; Special Joint Committee of the Senate and the House of Commons on the Constitution of Canada, 1972, p. 22; Forsey, 1974). Enhancement of the input of Commons committees to legislation, review of government spending, and on-going evaluation of programs have been discussed primarily as a means of holding the executive more accountable, but also as a way of increasing the influence of the public's elected representatives. Various changes to the rules of the House of Commons have been suggested as a way to enable individual MPs to present their ideas to Parliament (and beyond) and, on occasion, to have those ideas serve as the basis for government action.

Although such proposals seek, in whole or in part, to increase the responsiveness of the executive and of Parliament to regional views, they all encounter the obstacle of partisanship and the capacity of key actors to resist changes that might upset the political equilibrium, to their disadvantage. The concentration of power in a cabinet-parliamentary system and the related rigidities of party discipline make it difficult for change to occur, yet often deny the political system the flexibility necessary to accommodate mounting regionalism.

Political parties are central to the operation of modern cabinet-parliamentary government. Parliament is operated on the basis of competitive political parties, and the influence of parties on the cabinet-parliamentary system is pervasive. In theory, parties facilitate the organized aggregation and expression of society's multitudinous opinions by mobilizing support for ideas to be translated into legislation and spending. They also act as giant personnel agencies for the recruitment and election of individuals to public office.

The party able to command a majority of support within the House of Commons following an election provides leadership and direction to government, including the formulation of nearly all the business to be considered by Parliament. The other parties provide a visible and institutionalized opposition to the party in power, something considered valuable as a check on the possible abuse of executive power, as an outlet for minority opinions, and as a means of ensuring peaceful alternation in office. In addition to carrying on these broad functions, parties form the basis for the organization and performance of most aspects of the daily operations of Parliament. Of course, other institutions share certain of these functions. In order not to exalt unduly the role of parties, an assessment of their actual success or failure in performing these functions will be presented later.

Despite the fact that political parties are essential to the operation of cabinet-parliamentary government, their parliamentary roles and organization have received limited analysis to date. Important organizational arrangements and party offices within Parliament have not been described fully, much less analyzed in depth. This study examines the organization and operation of national parliamentary caucuses, an aspect of party organization about which little is known.[2] The term caucus refers to a regularly held private meeting of MPs and senators belonging to a particular political party. Historically, most senators have not played an active and influential role in the caucus deliberations of the two main parties. Because they are appointed rather than elected, the public does not view them as legitimate and effective regional representatives. There are, of course, examples of individual senators who have exerted influence in caucus because of their position in cabinet, their background knowledge of an issue, or their importance as regional spokespersons.

Caucus arrangements have evolved over the years to become more elaborate and more formal. The national caucuses of all three parties meet on Wednesday mornings when Parliament is in session. Smaller regional caucuses usually meet before the national caucuses, and the two main parties also hold periodic meetings of subregional groups of MPs and senators from particular localities. All three parties now establish subject-matter caucus committees covering broad policy fields. These meet periodically, whether or not Parliament is in session. In recent years, all three parties have held extended caucus meetings from time to time, usually lasting several days and often convened at a location away from Parliament Hill.

Each parliamentary caucus performs a variety of functions. This study, while examining all these functions, focusses on the opportunities provided by caucus for the expression, promotion and reconciliation of regional attitudes, concerns and demands. The convention of public party solidarity makes caucus an important forum for expressing regional viewpoints and achieving intraparty harmony. It is one of the political institutions that is supposed to permit conflict as well as facilitate agreement.

The discussion of the role of caucus begins in this section with a description of the essential and familiar features of cabinet-parliamentary government and the importance of political parties to our system of government. Contemporary challenges to the system of cabinet and party government are noted.

The second section of this paper reviews the origins and evolution of the caucus system in Canada. Caucuses have evolved from irregular and informal events to more complicated and formal structures with clearer roles. The influence of caucus within all parties has increased over the years, but progress has been slow and uneven. There are important party differences in the role of caucuses, reflecting the different histories and traditions of the three parties, the size of their parliamentary delegations, and the attitudes of their successive leaders toward caucus involvement in party decision making. The variable nature of caucus organization and activity makes it advisable to discuss each party separately.

Although all parties have a caucus, the one with the greatest potential influence on Canada's future is that of the governing party. Since the Liberal Party has been in office for most of this century, its experience serves as the basis for discussion of the role of the government caucus in the third section of this paper.

The fourth section examines the role of the caucus of Her Majesty's Loyal Opposition, a position occupied for most of this century by the Progressive Conservative Party. Since the opposition does not control government legislation and spending, its caucus meetings serve somewhat different purposes from those of the government. In particular, there is a greater emphasis on the tactics to be used in the permanent election campaign that is the essence of much Commons activity. Repeated failures to capture office and a related history of internal conflicts have adversely affected the organizational effectiveness of the Progressive Conservative caucus and the party's performance in Parliament.

Minor parties have been a well-established feature of the Canadian political landscape since at least the 1920s. The need for party solidarity imposed by the requirements of cabinet-parliamentary government has allegedly inhibited the expression of regional viewpoints within the two main parties and has contributed to the appearance of minor parties with a strong sectional appeal. Because of their origins, the ideologies they have espoused, and their smaller membership, the caucuses of the minor parties have been more informal and less structured than those of the two main parties. The fifth section of this paper examines the development and contemporary role of the Co-operative Commonwealth Federation and New Democratic Party caucuses.

The last section draws together the themes presented throughout the paper, states some conclusions, and offers some thoughts on how the role of party caucuses might be strengthened if this is considered desirable.[3]

Also relevant here is a brief introduction to the main concepts used in this study — the "representative" function and the "responsiveness" of party caucuses to "regional" needs and opinions. All three terms present problems of definition — all refer to complex, multidimensional phenomena that are interrelated and overlap in the real world. This is not the place to engage in an elaborate theoretical treatise, but some clarification of these concepts is appropriate.

What is representation and under what circumstances can it be said to occur? The term can refer to a situation where the membership of caucus generally reflects the distribution of significant social and political diversities throughout the country. The election of such a caucus would enhance the likelihood of effective representation.

Political representation takes place on several levels and in a multitude of ways. Regular elections are said to provide competitive political parties with a strong incentive to keep in touch with public opinion. To improve their chances for reelection, individual MPs petition government for developmental projects and other benefits for their riding, act as intermediaries with the bureaucracy on behalf of individual constituents, and take a variety of steps to maintain contact with interest groups and voters in their ridings. This broader, more encompassing concept of representation has been expressed in the rather general definition of representation as "acting in the interests of the represented, in a manner responsive to them" (Pitkin, 1967, p. 209; see also Eulau and Wahlke, 1978).

Of course this definition leaves much unsaid about how the representation process actually works. However, it is generally understood that for representation to occur, the interests of citizens must find expression in the actions of government. Until recently, however, the concept of responsiveness was not adequately defined. Eulau and Karps (1977) help to capture the complexity of responsiveness in the real world of politics by specifying four components.

"Policy responsiveness" refers to some meaningful connection between the policy preferences of a constituency and the positions taken by its representative in Parliament. If the constituency and the MP agree completely on policy, no matter how that agreement has come about, the representative is clearly responsive. When there is less affinity between constituency views and those of the member, it becomes debatable whether the MP is acting responsively in a policy sense. And of course there is the perennial question of whether MPs should act according to the desires of their constituents (if these can be determined) or according to what they think is in the constituents' best interest. This question is made more difficult by the fact that the system seems to require party loyalty.

"Service responsiveness" refers to the advantages and benefits that the MP is able to obtain for particular constituents. There are a number of services that MPs and their constituents may consider integral to the representation process. For several reasons, the provision of service to constituents has become more important during the last decade, and MPs have been provided with constituency offices and staffs paid for out of public funds to support this increased activity. Many MPs use their regular newsletters and columns in local newspapers to inform constituents of legislation that may be of interest and use to them. The newsletters also advertise the MPs' availability to help resolve problems encountered by constituents in dealing with the complex bureaucracy of modern government.

MPs and their staffs may spend a considerable proportion of their time on such casework activity. Whether the motivation for performing such errands on behalf of constituents is to enhance reelection prospects, to provide MPs with a sense of satisfaction when they intervene successfully on behalf of clients, or to act on the conviction that putting a human face on big government should be an important part of an MP's job is immaterial for our purposes. The important point is that the cumulative effort of individual MPs, who together probably handle hundreds of thousands of cases annually, must add something to citizens' perceptions of the responsiveness of the political system.

"Allocation responsiveness" refers to efforts by legislators to obtain more generalized benefits for their constituencies through intervention in the legislative and administrative process. MPs can stimulate requests for federal grants to create employment, attract industries, provide public works or take advantage of tax breaks. (Several job creation schemes in recent years have built in a role for the local MP in the processing of grant applications.) Once the application is submitted, the MP can lobby with ministers or officials for a favourable decision, then participate in the announcement of the grant or the sod turning of the project. To better appreciate the opportunities available through government programs, MPs normally seek assignments on House of Commons standing committees that match the economic and other interests of their constituencies. For example, MPs from slow-growth areas will serve on the regional development committee to be aware of changes to government legislation and programs and to be able to present the case for their areas.

"Symbolic responsiveness" is more psychological than material. It refers to the provision of intangible benefits to constituents. The representational relationship involves an element of trust, confidence and support for the elected member, who can generate this not only by securing material benefits on an individual or constituency-wide basis but also through symbolic actions. As Goodin (1984) notes, symbolic rewards seldom exist in isolation from more material benefits. When an MP announces a local employment grant, there are tangible as well as symbolic components to the action. Forcing the example into one category or the other ignores the fact that such actions carry symbolic significance. The extent to which a reward is symbolic depends greatly on the perceptions of the recipient. MPs seek to enhance their credibility and support by a variety of actions, such as advertising their services, making speeches in the House that extoll the advantages of their constituencies, or introducing private members' bills even though they have no prospect of being adopted. Such actions, even if futile, demonstrate an MP's responsiveness to local opinion. Obviously, even symbols can backfire; an MP must avoid straining credibility unduly.

Policy responsiveness, usually thought of as the heart of the representational relationship, is clearly just one component of successful representation. Especially in a cabinet-parliamentary system where the policy-making role of individual MPs is limited by structural arrangements that allow for dominance by the executive, the other dimensions of responsiveness must be recognized and studied.

Allocation and service responsiveness do not always accompany policy responsiveness. What matters in symbolic responsiveness is that constituents feel represented, whether or not the other components of responsiveness are fulfilled, since these components overlap in the real world. Pursuing the policy interests of their constituents merges with the MPs' search for allocation opportunities. The representation function can be pursued in both formal and informal, public and private ways. Within the House of Commons, MPs can employ official devices such as questions, debates, private members' bills and committee hearings, as well as unofficial party and all-party channels. MPs will act at times as individual representatives dealing with the executive arm of government and at times as party members dealing with party government.

One final term deserves some initial clarification. The concept of regionalism can have many meanings within political debate. As the Task Force on Canadian Unity (1979, pp. 10–11) notes, a basic distinction should be made between regionalism as a fact and regionalism as a value. Regionalism as a fact refers to the existence of various areas of the country with geographic, economic, social and political characteristics that distinguish them from other areas. Regionalism as a value refers to the perception that different regions exist within the country and often includes the notion that such regions represent a valuable feature of Canadian cultural and political life.

This paper adopts the following broad definition employed by McCormick et al. (1981, pp. 3–5): "Regionalism is a function of a territorially based diversity that achieves significant political articulation over a period of time." McCormick et al. go on to distinguish a regional voice from regional power, stating that it is not good enough for regional views to be merely heard but that the regions involved must have their needs and demands met at least some of the time. Regions will not and should not be bought off cheaply with symbolic and promissory rewards. While regions cannot expect to get everything they ask for, they should rightly expect to win sometimes and should have confidence that the policy-making process is not permanently rigged to their disadvantage. Otherwise, the problem of regional alienation will become even more difficult and pressing.

This study does not employ a strict definition of what constitutes a region. Most people have provincial units in mind when they talk of regions, but here the term also refers to groupings of provinces, such as the western and Atlantic provinces. Attention is also paid to the expression within caucus of subregional concerns, which refers to the political expression of territorial diversities within provincial boundaries.

Political Parties and Parliamentary Government

The essence of a political party is organization. As organizations, however, parties cannot be understood in isolation from the societal and institutional context in which they operate. Political parties have long been considered essential to representative and responsible government. Dahl (1980, p. 74) asserts that it "is not going too far to say that representative democracy in the state makes political parties possible, advantageous and inevitable." However, even if parties are inevitable and advantageous, it does not follow that they will always perform successfully or even adequately. Informed observers of Canadian politics over the last two decades argue that political parties have not performed all that well. There is talk of the "demise" of political parties and the failure of the party system to serve the needs of the country. There is clearly an element of exaggeration in such sweeping, negative assessments. Political parties are multifunctional institutions, and the failure of parties may relate more to certain functions than to others. King (1969) presents the following widely accepted list of party functions: structuring of the vote; integration and mobilization of the mass public; recruitment of political leaders; organization of government; formation of public policy; and aggregation of interests. Included within the function "organization of government" is the provision of a continuous and critical opposition within a cabinet-parliamentary system. In practice, these functions are not completely separate and emphasis on one may detract from another.

Knowledgeable observers of the Canadian party system appear to agree that it is with respect to the mobilization and integration of the public, the aggregation of interests and the formation of public policy that parties have recently encountered greater difficulties. The nature of the parties' shortcomings can only be briefly mentioned here. Party affiliations are weaker and less consistent in Canada than in many other democratic

systems. While the plurality electoral system exaggerates the regional composition of party support, the underlying reason why parties fail to win
seats in a region is the lack of sufficient popular support. Parties have
been weak generators of policy ideas, largely because policy development
has been subordinated to the perceived requirements of winning elections.
Parties have not been prepared to establish the necessary organizations
or to spend the money required for serious policy development.

With respect to the three other functions — the structuring of the vote,
the recruitment of political leaders, and the organization of government
— the parties are usually judged to have performed more successfully.
It should be reiterated that since party functions are interrelated, weak
performance in one function can have adverse consequences for the performance of other functions. This paper focusses on the relationship
between the functions of parties as promoters of national integration, as
aggregators of interests, as sources of public policy, and as the instruments
for providing government and opposition within the political system.

In the eyes of many critics, political parties have been almost too successful in helping to provide the structural framework for modern cabinet-
parliamentary government. By deciding which partisan groups become the
government and which the opposition, the parties organize government
in an important way. They also dominate the daily operation of cabinet-
parliamentary government. To paraphrase Bagehot, the party has become
the buckle that joins and controls cabinet and Parliament. The existence
of disciplined and cohesive political parties makes leadership and direction possible within government. At the same time, the pervasive influence
of parties and partisanship limit the contribution of both Parliament as
a body and its individual members to the process of governing.

In a modern cabinet-parliamentary system the initiative rests with the
leadership of the party in power — that is, in the cabinet. In theory, the
cabinet is collectively responsible to the House of Commons for the overall
direction of policy, while individual cabinet ministers are responsible for
the administration of their departments. All legislation involving the expenditure of funds must originate with the Crown, which now means the
cabinet, and only cabinet members can propose additional government
spending. A loss of confidence in the government by a majority of MPs
will bring about the resignation of the government and a fresh election
or, in a minority situation, perhaps its replacement by another party. In
practice, given a majority government, this is not a real threat, since MPs
invariably vote along party lines. The timing of an election within the normal five-year life of a Parliament rests with the prime minister. It has been
argued that a prime minister can use the threat of an election to stifle dissent within cabinet and caucus. However, the power to dissolve Parliament is a two-edged sword in the hands of the prime minister, who has
more to lose than party backbenchers, for going to the country with a
divided party will not enhance the government's chances for re-election.

Still, control over the timing of an election is an important advantage available only to the prime minister.

The major source of party cohesion in the Commons is considered to be the fact that the political fate of the government is theoretically on the line in most votes. Such an argument exaggerates the impact of constitutional rules on the daily behaviour of MPs. The threat of defeat in a majority government situation is seldom real; the sources of party solidarity appear to be more psychological than constitutional. Cohesion is based upon the acceptance of party voting as an essential feature of the parliamentary system, upon a sense of party loyalty, especially during difficult periods, and upon the satisfaction derived from seeing the party do well (Kornberg, 1967, pp. 129–36).

When disagreements within a party threaten to get out of hand, the leadership of the party in power has considerable powers of persuasion. In addition to the already-mentioned threat of election, these include the refusal to appoint a party member to the cabinet, a campaign to deny a member renomination by his constituency association, and the failure to reward a member with a parliamentary secretaryship or a committee chairmanship. Opposition parties have fewer similar rewards and punishments to distribute, and the prospect of division within their ranks is also regarded less seriously. It is difficult to discover how many members stifle their dissent for fear of ruining their career chances by antagonizing those in authority. In any case, sanctions are infrequently used, according to the party whips.

If MPs accept party discipline largely on a voluntary basis, they may be encouraged by trends in party politics. Canadian election campaigns have always emphasized party leadership, but the tendency has become more pronounced with the increase in the importance of the mass media, particularly television. Party backbenchers receive limited coverage in the mass media: they are elected as part of a team committed to supporting the existing leader and his policies, and are only occasionally able to build up an independent base of electoral support (Irvine, 1982). The leader's control of the party caucus has been further strengthened by the adoption of the practice of choosing leaders at national conventions.

The predictability and control made possible by the presence of disciplined political parties is often held to be a necessity, given the enormous scope and complexity of modern government. Although government has been growing in size since Confederation, the greatest expansion took place after the Second World War. A large and increasingly professional public service has developed. In addition, a larger, more differentiated society has led to the proliferation of pressure groups seeking programs and other support from governments. Elaborate networks of contact and communication have developed between administrative agencies and pressure groups within their functional areas of responsibility. To further ensure that they remain in touch with public opinion, departments and agencies have established advisory committees of non-governmental experts. Increased use of public opinion surveys has also helped governments keep in touch with public opinion in all its variety.

The rise of the "administrative" and "special interest" state has presented several problems for the parliamentary roles of political parties. First, the trends challenge the traditional assumption of the parliamentary system that the individual elected representative is the main communications link between citizens and their government. Industrial, agricultural, labour and other organizations have increasingly pressed for coherent national responses to problems that could not be dealt with locally because of the growing economic interdependence of the various sectors and regions of Canada (Pross, 1982). The interaction between interest groups and cabinet ministers or their departments involves the exchange of specialized information, knowledge and opinion. Such interaction is prior in time, and usually in importance, to the parliamentary stages of the policy cycle. These pre-parliamentary discussions and negotiations may eliminate the more contentious features of legislation, thus partly accounting for the lack of dissent within the governing party. It could be politically harmful for the government caucus to disown policies that are the product of protracted negotiations. Reliance upon the expertise found within large public and private information-gathering organizations threatens representative government. Possessing a transient membership and lacking the specialized knowledge available to the executive arm of government, Parliament finds it difficult to cope with the volume and complexity of contemporary public policy.

A corollary of more interventionist government and increased emphasis on competition among parties has been the tightening of government control over the procedures of the House of Commons. Throughout this century successive governments have used changes to the rules or standing orders to permit expeditious completion of an expanded legislative workload. The right of private members to sidetrack government business through adjournment motions was greatly restricted (1906); the power of government to curtail debate by closure was established (1913); time limits were applied to individual members' speeches (1927, 1955, 1960, 1982); and the number of days devoted to such major parliamentary events as the throne speech and budget and supply debates was steadily reduced (1955, 1960, 1965, 1968). Private members' bills, the main source of legislative activity in the previous century, have received increasingly short shrift in the parliamentary timetable and have lost much of their utility as a means of backbench participation in the legislative process (Cordeau, 1979).

Prior to 1965, parliamentary rules denied the existence of political parties. The fiction was abandoned in that year with the creation under the rules of an all-party business committee (Courtney, 1978). Since then, time allocation on legislation (based on Standing Orders 75A, 75B or 75C) through negotiations among the House leaders of the three parties has become an accepted feature of the parliamentary process. The rules have in many ways become political weapons in the struggle between parties; as the recent bell-ringing episodes reveal, they are not instruments of absolute control in the hands of the governing party. If the rules had not been tightened up, the legislature would have become a serious bottleneck in an era of active government. One result, however, has been to restrict the involvement of individual MPs in many aspects of the legislative process, although the growth of a more active and influential committee system has offset the trend since 1968 (Stewart, 1977, chaps. 6 and 7; Jackson and Atkinson, 1980, chap. 6).

In summary, parliamentary government has become essentially party government. Parties are essential to determining control of government and filling public offices. The governing party takes the initiative in formulating public policy, but only after the advice of powerful outside interest groups, including provincial governments, is filtered through a large and influential bureaucracy. The role of party caucuses cannot be understood in isolation from these environmental factors. The importance of caucuses as debating forums has increased because of the reduction in formal parliamentary opportunities for individual MPs to ignore party discipline.

The Origins and Development of Party Caucuses

While most contemporary observers consider it natural and perhaps inevitable that parties should take on a pre-eminent role in Parliament, this was not always the case. Parties were once a less dominant presence in Canadian parliamentary life. As the first British colony to obtain independence and to combine a cabinet-parliamentary structure with a federal division of powers, Canada had to develop a system of party organization and party solidarity without the benefit of precedents from elsewhere. Even in Britain, the term caucus came into use only in the late nineteenth century and was then used to refer to meetings devoted to election management, not parliamentary organization. Members of the governing party met on an ad hoc basis during British parliaments of the nineteenth century, but the meetings consisted of just one-way communication: party leaders would inform their supporters of decisions already taken (Norton, 1979). The beginnings of the caucus system in Canada had similar characteristics. The structures and roles of Canadian parliamentary caucuses have evolved from informal and simple events into formal bodies with regular meetings, elected officers and a system of regional caucuses and subject-matter committees.

In the first two or three decades after Confederation, the Canadian party system was not fully developed or truly national in scope. Individuals were recruited and supported in election to the House of Commons by local elites and were more responsive to them than to the national party leadership. With much smaller constituencies and electorates than occur today, MPs might well have known practically all their voters. Sectional, religious and ethnic groups identified with individual representatives in Parliament. Party discipline was weak within the House of Commons. J.D. Edgar, who served during the 1870s as the informal whip in the House of Commons for the Liberal Party, described the House as a contest of undisciplined factions, each laced through with a high proportion of members who did not take kindly to whipping (Stamp, 1964). As a result, government measures were not assured of passage, as is the case today. There were enough "loose fish," "shaky fellows" and "ministerialists" (as Prime Minister John A. Macdonald described the independents) in the Commons to make political life less predictable for the government. For example, during the first four sessions of the first Parliament, the Macdonald government was defeated six times on minor government bills, twice on government resolutions preceding bills, and twice on supply votes. At that time a more flexible definition of what constituted a government defeat meant that the Macdonald government never felt compelled by these political setbacks to give up power or to call an election.

Dissent from a party position occurred more frequently during the early parliaments. In a survey of division votes held during the first Parliament of 1867, March (1974, pp. 57–58) finds a defection rate of 20 percent; that is, on all recorded votes MPs failed to vote with the majority of their party 20 percent of the time. This contrasts with a defection rate of only 1.4 percent over two sessions of the twenty-sixth Parliament, during 1963–65 (Hoffman and Ward, 1970, p. 285). Another sign of the less structured approach prevalent in early parliaments was the significant amount of time devoted to private members' public bills. Government business did not monopolize the parliamentary agenda to nearly the same extent as is true today: relatively few bills were government-sponsored, and many dealt with local matters. This also contributed to the relaxed party discipline.

The development of national political parties and the structuring of parliamentary behaviour along strict party lines took place over many years. Thomas Hockin (1979, pp. 8–17) suggests that not until the adoption of the simultaneous and secret ballot in 1878 did all MPs agree to act as members of cohesive party teams. The secret ballot reduced intimidation of voters, while general elections made opportunistic "ministerialists" almost extinct. (These were individuals who, sensing the eventual outcome of a staggered election, would indicate their intention to support the governing party.) The gradual extension of the franchise that began in the late nineteenth century contributed to the creation of national political parties. In order to reach the wider electorate, parties began to establish organizations at the constituency level for recruiting and electing candidates. Individual candidates soon came to depend heavily upon party endorsement and organizational support for their election. An indication of this is the virtual disappearance of the independent member: between 1867 and 1888, some 72 independents were elected, but between 1921 and 1961, only eight were elected (March, 1974, pp. 18–19).

English (1977, p. 15) argues that a truly national party system emerged after 1896, thanks to the efforts of the Liberal leader, Wilfred Laurier (1896–1919), and his Conservative counterpart, Robert Borden (1901–20). These two leaders sought to overcome the local orientation of Canadian politics. Their goal was to go beyond the prevailing view of political parties as electoral instruments, consisting of individual political entrepreneurs held together for the purpose of political survival by the bond of patronage. In their opinion, parties should offer alternative definitions of the national interest and should bind their elected members to implement such broad programs once in office. To strengthen parties and to rehabilitate their image, the two leaders undertook a number of reforms. By 1900 there was a move to officially separate party financing from the position of the party leader so as to avoid the taint of corruption. Both Laurier and Borden sought to establish closer links between the national and provincial wings of their parties. They also took steps to eliminate patronage in civil service appointments, despite a campaign of resistance by many MPs who had rewarded local supporters with government jobs.

Both leaders recognized the problem posed by regionally imbalanced parliamentary caucuses and tried to overcome the problem. For example, Borden had only eight colleagues from Quebec when he assumed the party leadership in 1901, so he immediately moved to appoint a French-Canadian lieutenant. To foster federal-provincial cooperation, he cultivated close contacts with the Conservative premiers of the provinces. He also reached beyond his parliamentary caucus to recruit talent and to seek advice from the special interest groups that had become more numerous in an increasingly diversified economy.

These efforts to reorganize the parties on a national basis and to structure political debate in terms of competing visions were unsuccessful for a variety of reasons. Not the least of them was Borden's belief that brokerage politics and compromise were unacceptable. When fashioning the Unionist coalition, Borden believed he was creating an organization that would transcend local identities and would define and give expression to a clear national interest. The coalition collapsed, however, because of the resentment of the political groups that were excluded, because of French Canada's sense of outrage at the attempt to deny regional identity, and because of Borden's failure to deliver the promised goods. English (1977) draws an important lesson from this period:

> Too often modern critics forget that there was once an attempt to make vision, conflict, and "creativity" the central features of Canadian politics, and that attempt was a failure, even in the minds of its authors. Upon the party system, it left as little visible impression as a "sword cut in the water." (p. 12)

Canadians apparently preferred the non-divisive approach of Mackenzie King, who sought to muddle through controversies without alienating any significant group.

The trend toward the establishment of hegemonic national parties was slowed by the appearance of the Progressive movement during the 1920s. The Progressives harnessed western Canadian resentment against national policies and, in contrast to the older parties, directed their appeal to regional interests. Sixty-five members, most of them from western Canada, were elected to the House of Commons in 1921 (Morton, 1950, p. 127). Although the party eventually split and some of its members joined the Liberal Party, it had a permanent impact on Canadian thinking about the party system. An important argument in the Progressives' case against the existing political and economic order was that it contained a systematic bias in favour of central Canada. Western representatives in the House of Commons were restrained by party discipline from expressing regional viewpoints. Parliamentary sovereignty, it was alleged, had passed into the hands of a majority, meeting in secret in the government caucus. Within that body the views of the less populous regions were inevitably submerged by the more numerous opinions and votes at stake represented by MPs from central Canada. To restore sovereignty to Parliament and make regional views more visible, the Progressives insisted that caucus decisions should not be binding. They wanted control over nominations to be wrested from party elites by the adoption of open, public nomination meetings. In addition, the Progressives argued that election campaigns should be publicly funded. This would avoid party dependence upon powerful economic interests and would make local candidates less beholden to national party headquarters.

Morton argues that if the Progressives' attack on party government had been completely successful, it would have made bargaining, trade-offs and the potential for deadlock the outstanding features of the parliamentary process. Without guaranteed majorities, cabinets would be unable to pass the growing volume of legislation and budgetary estimates. While the impact of the Progressives fell short of this, it was nonetheless significant. According to Morton:

> The two party system did not return in its former strength. The rules and conventions of Parliament made provision for more than two parties. The electorate became more independent, indeed, to the point of political indifference. The authority of the whip became lighter, the bonds of caucus weaker, than in the old days. These were effects of the Progressive movement, and constituted its mark on Canadian political life. (p. 292)

Morton's conclusion implies that party solidarity was stressed less than in the past. It does not follow that party members, especially those on the government side of the House, were utilized more fully. The accounts of party activities during the 1930s and 1940s are skimpy and therefore provide a weak basis for sweeping generalizations. However, the memoirs of former cabinet minister Chubby Power provide a glimpse of Liberal caucus operations during the era when Mackenzie King was leader of the party. Backbenchers were expected to show "unquestioned loyalty on divisions, with little or no occasion to express our personal views or to deviate from government policy" (Ward, 1966, p. 263). The Liberals in opposition from 1930 to 1935, were initially disorganized under the cautious leadership of King, who was reluctant to challenge the powerful prime minister, R.B. Bennett. Bennett apparently dominated not only the Commons but his cabinet and caucus as well. To sharpen the Liberal attack, Chubby Power wrote at length to King about party organization and strategy within Parliament. To involve Liberal MPs more directly in the conduct of House business, Power proposed the establishment of a caucus "chief of operations" who would coordinate a series of working groups structured on both a provincial and a functional basis, each with a group captain. He stressed that these groups should be an outlet for backbenchers, a way to encourage participation and to improve morale:

> The discipline need not be strict. The main thing would be to keep the boys interested and possibly amused. Stir up a spirit of rivalry between groups and by giving every man a chance get him into active cooperation. Every now and then the boys should be given a chance to make a little obstruction, hold up estimates, block a bill, etc. The Group Captains should not be ex-ministers as a rule. (Ward, 1966, p. 271)

King accepted the proposal, as did the caucus, but Power found that implementing the plan required diplomacy and patience:

> Among backbenchers there is always resentment against others in the same category who are more active. As a result, there is a great deal of antagonism to those who might be looked upon as political climbers. . . . It was only by going ahead, and implying that the instructions emanated not from me, but from the leader or the caucus, that it was able to make much headway. But, as time went on, the members became more and more imbued with the team spirit and team play. (p. 277)

In opposition, King was prepared to entrust caucus organization to an individual like Power while he reserved his energies for the broad policy questions and the rebuilding of the party outside Parliament.

Back in office after the general election of 1935, King was less tolerant of caucus freedom. In his autobiography, Paul Martin (1983, pp. 171–77) provides a glimpse of the Liberal caucus in 1935 when he was first elected to the House of Commons. To his dismay, Martin found that the emphasis within caucus was almost entirely upon parliamentary manœuverings and party affairs rather than on the discussion of programs. The caucus arrangements put in place by Power in opposition had apparently been discarded. Martin writes:

I attribute the earlier concentration on political manoeuvre partly to the small extent to which the ordinary member had an opportunity to shape policy. When I was elected, my expectation was that I would not only represent my constituency but would also help devise responses to the great issues of the day. Committee work was much more restricted than it is now: government bills were not presented to caucus ahead of time, there were no caucus committees to investigate policies, and few backbenchers made special efforts to have government matters brought before caucus — which was basically a gripe session. (p. 171)

Caucus was a "babble" of conflicting voices, notes Martin. The members from western Canada were the most active regional grouping within caucus at that time. King was "the master of caucus," using his right as leader to summarize the discussion to great effect:

King would always speak at some length . . . taking into account every argument to weave together the threads of difference and pointing out how difficult it was to run Canada and how fortunate it was that there was a Liberal Party to take charge. We would finish with much cheering and gratitude that God Almighty had elected such a great man to be our leader. Some of King's best speeches were made in caucus; he used it to keep the party together, and powerful oratory was his instrument. (pp. 172–73)

When oratory failed to satisfy restive backbenchers, they were discouraged by the party whip and the caucus chairman (who were both selected by the leader) from speaking out, asking questions of ministers in the House, or thinking up too many new programs.

Life in the caucus of the official opposition apparently was not much more exciting than on the government side, although at least the opposition MPs had the pleasure of regularly attacking the government in public. Drawing upon the ideas about opposition organization that Chubby Power had presented earlier, the Progressive Conservatives after 1945 began to develop the notion of an organized team. After being chosen leader of the Progressive Conservatives in 1942, John Bracken, the former premier of Manitoba, elected not to seek a seat in the House of Commons immediately. His colleagues believed that this decision produced adverse publicity for the party and a deterioration in caucus morale. Dick Bell, private secretary to the two previous Conservative leaders, wrote to Bracken of the danger of the party falling back into "the same state of desuetude that confronted us six months ago."[4] "Team play," he continued, "is not easy to secure. During my experience in official capacities with the party, commencing first in 1934, it has never existed, and my great fear is that it will not exist now unless we set about to perfect the organization." Bell's detailed plan for opposition organization was not accepted until after the 1945 election, when the Conservative caucus agreed to the establishment of ten caucus committees, each with a chairman, a secretary and a membership ranging from 17 to 25 MPs. When the government introduced legislation, the bills were referred to the appropriate caucus committee for study; the chairman of each committee was expected to organize the opposition attack on the bill in the House. Chairmen of caucus committees were also responsible for ensuring scrutiny of the estimates for the departments that came within the sphere of their committees. The committee chairmen met with the party leader every Monday at noon to discuss overall party policy to ensure that the party would not speak with numerous conflicting voices.

The theoretical advantages of these arrangements were held to be numerous. Involving more MPs in the parliamentary work of the party would encourage specialization and the development of expertise. The identification and development of potential cabinet talent was another benefit. At election time, the public would view the opposition team as an alternative government-in-waiting. Involvement of members would avoid the infighting of previous Conservative caucuses.

Whatever its theoretical advantages, however, the scheme did not work well in practice. According to his biographer, Bracken was not an effective caucus leader, often failing to ensure that meetings reached agreement on a specific line of policy to be followed (Kendle, 1979, pp. 230–37). Caucus meeting attendance by Conservative MPs dropped off badly during 1946 and 1947, and the smaller CCF contingent replaced the Conservatives as the most effective opposition to the Liberals. In the summer of 1948, having learned that he no longer enjoyed the confidence of his caucus, Bracken resigned.

Reports on caucus activity during the 1950s suggest that little progress was made. Under Prime Minister Louis St. Laurent, caucus was apparently a quiet and acquiescent group. Caucus meetings were used simply to inform members about government plans and to boost morale, rather than to work out agreements on what policies should be pursued (Hoffman and Ward, 1970, pp. 161–67). The Conservative caucus under George Drew became steadily more disenchanted, mainly because of successive electoral setbacks in 1949 and 1953, but also because of the leader's habit of "confining positions of influence to a smaller inner circle," identified by critics as "the old guard" (Perlin, 1980, p. 53). The replacement of Drew by John Diefenbaker and the Conservative election victories in 1957, 1958 and 1962 gave the party a five-year respite from the frustrations of being in opposition. Although Diefenbaker insisted in his memoirs that he sought caucus involvement and debate of government policies (p. 80), this contradicts the reports of other participants, who state that as outside criticism of the government's record mounted, caucus discussion was increasingly discouraged. There was also a growing rift between Diefenbaker and the Quebec members of the caucus over their lack of representation in cabinet and other alleged slights, including the prime minister's refusal to allow them to meet as a separate regional caucus.

During the 1960s both the main parties took the first steps toward reform. According to a study done in 1965, the Liberal caucus under Prime

Minister Lester Pearson (1963–68) was more directly involved in policy making than it had been under previous leaders. Pearson sought to strengthen caucus input by encouraging his cabinet colleagues to consult with interested caucus members before introducing legislation into the House. He also instituted a pre-session meeting of caucus to allow Liberal MPs an early chance to discuss the government's legislative plans. Apparently, this practice was adopted on the recommendation of Finance Minister Walter Gordon, who was convinced that close relations should exist between cabinet and caucus. It was abandoned after a couple of years because of the opposition of other cabinet ministers. George McIlraith, then government House leader, complained to the National Liberal Federation in 1966 that caucus secrecy had broken down because MPs could not be entrusted with confidential material.[5]

When the Conservatives returned to the opposition benches in 1963, it was some time before Diefenbaker agreed to the establishment of a caucus committee system (Perlin, 1980, p. 80). Committees were few in number and met infrequently. As dissatisfaction with his leadership mounted, Diefenbaker made more and more policy decisions personally and relied upon only a few staunch loyalists for advice. The Progressive Conservative Party appeared disorganized and divided in the House of Commons as its internal problems worsened.

For a variety of reasons it was not until the late 1960s, with the accession of Pierre Trudeau and Robert Stanfield to leadership of the Liberal and Progressive Conservative parties, that truly significant reforms to caucus were accomplished. One factor was the wider scope and increased complexity of government policy, which created a need for specialization in caucus committees if government members were to contribute intelligently to the discussion of policy. The opposition developed designated critics and policy committees in response to the advantages enjoyed by cabinet ministers backed by public service expertise.[6] The desire to create the image of an alternative team, ready to take control of government once the party gained power, was another consideration for the opposition. This image making was particularly important in dealing with the mass media, which (it was hoped) would present to the voters a group of accomplished leaders prepared to assume cabinet posts. The party spokespersons would have to be ready to demonstrate, as much as possible, the facility of cabinet ministers in dealing with issues. It was also important that various party representatives not contradict one another.

The professionalization of politics as a career and the emphasis on democratic participation added to the momentum for reform during the late 1960s. By then, being an MP had become a full-time job for most members, and increased pay helped to attract better-qualified individuals from a wider range of backgrounds. These younger, abler members — lawyers, journalists, academics and business people — were often not satisfied with the minimal role traditionally assigned to the backbencher in the legislative process. Many of them were committed to a parliamentary career; they had not run to serve a brief stint in politics before returning to their full-time jobs.

Like many other institutions during the 1960s, Parliament was the target of mounting criticism, especially after the bitter and scandal-ridden sessions of the Diefenbaker-Pearson era. Beginning in 1964, the House of Commons appointed a series of committees to study parliamentary reform. After the adoption of various provisional changes to House rules, the reform process eventually culminated in the passing of major changes in December 1968 (Stewart, 1977). In particular, the standing committees of the House of Commons became more active and somewhat more influential (Thomas, 1978, 1980). Transferring work to the committees, which could meet simultaneously, allowed Parliament to deal more expeditiously with the government's growing legislative and expenditure program and heralded a breakthrough for the private member. In addition, all three opposition parties opened caucus research offices early in 1969 using financial assistance promised in the first Throne Speech of the Trudeau government (September 12, 1968).[7] Encouraged by these improvements in their position and by the talk of "participatory democracy," MPs in both main parties sought even wider involvement through changes to caucus decision making.

In June 1969 a special two-day session of the Liberal caucus was held to discuss reforms. The most innovative reform adopted was a requirement that ministers discuss the subject matter of proposed legislation with interested members before discussion of a draft bill in the appropriate cabinet committee. In addition, further consultations on the actual bill would be held before second reading took place in the House of Commons. To take advantage of this opportunity for earlier involvement in the development of legislation, the caucus established six functional committees, with terms of reference corresponding to some extent to the cabinet's subject matter committees and the standing committees of the House of Commons. Each committee consisted of a chairman, a vice-chairman (elected each session by the full caucus), a secretary, the chairmen of the parallel standing committees in the Commons, the appropriate parliamentary secretaries, a whip, and interested caucus members.

Following pressure from Liberal backbenchers, the Trudeau government agreed early in 1970 to fund a research office for the government caucus, thereby duplicating the arrangement already in place for the opposition parties.[8] Once the office was established, one of its research assistants was assigned to each caucus committee to conduct studies and to handle the housekeeping aspects of caucus operations. A national caucus executive was created, consisting of an elected chairman and vice-chairman, the chairmen of the caucus committees, the House leader, and the whips. It was responsible for staging full caucus meetings and for referring government-sponsored bills to the appropriate caucus committee. There were also regular regional caucus meetings and a place on the national caucus agenda for regional reports.

Despite these improvements, discontent persisted. Not all ministers complied with the requirement to preview their legislation with caucus committees. Time was always at a premium. Some critics considered the caucus overorganized. There were so many policy committees and regional caucuses reporting to the national caucus, along with the House leader's report and the party leader's summing up, that individual backbenchers had little time to express opinions.[9] A somewhat contradictory view held that government caucus was "still largely an ineffectual grouping of members which lacks the organization to enable it to exert a strong collective influence on the Ministry."[10] The near-defeat of the Trudeau government in the 1972 general election was partly blamed on its failure to consult MPs sufficiently in order to gauge public opinion and to use them as spokespersons for government policy. MPs resented the concentration of power in the Prime Minister's Office, particularly the establishment of regional desks in the office as sounding boards for regional opinion.

During the Liberal minority government (1972–1974), the overriding preoccupation of the government and the caucus was short-term political survival and a rebuilding of the party's fortunes. Parliamentary strategy and tactics to avoid a defeat in the House of Commons dominated caucus discussions. To ensure greater communication between the cabinet and MPs, weekly national caucus meetings became the rule, rather than the previous system of substituting caucus committee meetings every second Wednesday. The previous standing committee structure was abandoned in favour of ad hoc "legislative committees" attended by interested MPs, the minister sponsoring a particular bill, and sometimes public servants to provide explanations of particularly technical legislation. Such committees usually met during the two-hour weekday dinner break.

The reduced number of government MPs also motivated the switch to greater reliance upon full caucus. The minority position of the government made party solidarity in the Commons crucial, but as a corollary it also increased the need to persuade caucus members to accept cabinet plans. This gave caucus greater influence. Caucus blocked proposed expenditure ceilings on old age pensions and youth programs, and contributed in an important way to the decision to establish Petro-Canada. According to one perceptive journalist, the net effect of caucus strength was "to make cabinet decision making more political, more fluid, and more responsive."[11]

The system of greater use of full caucus was retained during the majority Liberal government (1974–79). Only after May 1979, when the Liberals went into opposition, was there a return to an elaborate, formalized structure of caucus. In July 1979, Trudeau announced the creation of 21 advisory groups to formulate the opposition's approaches and policies. Each group consisted of a chairman or co-chairmen, designated parliamentary critics and interested members. More than 40 members of the 114-member Liberal opposition were given caucus offices of some sort. The chairmen of the advisory groups constituted the so-called "shadow cabinet," an institution about which more will be said in a later extended analysis of opposition caucus organization. Of course, this intricate caucus structure lasted only until December 1979, when the Conservative government was defeated. The advisory groups were apparently very uneven in their performance and overall coordination. The Liberal Party was, of course, trying to recover from an electoral defeat and the loss of 12 former cabinet ministers: it was also searching, albeit briefly, for a new leader. Under these difficult circumstances, any caucus organization would be unlikely to function with great effectiveness.

When Robert Stanfield took over as Conservative leader following a bitter struggle to replace Diefenbaker, the caucus situation could hardly be described as encouraging. The Conservatives had lost the 1968 election, six former frontbenchers had retired or been defeated, and Stanfield's leadership received only grudging support from some sections of the party, particularly from the western, rural group within the caucus. A basic criticism was that control over policy had slipped out of the hands of elected MPs into the hands of appointed academic and other advisers close to the leader. Examples of the perceived downgrading of the role of elected members were the Montmorency Thinkers Conference (allegedly dominated by left-wing intellectuals) and the policy role assumed by the party's research office (directed by Professor Edwin Black and staffed by "academic amateurs").[12] Stanfield initially viewed the situation tolerantly: rather than trying to assert his leadership vigorously, he chose not to antagonize dissident members. A meeting in August 1970 of the 15-member western regional caucus, arranged by MP Jack Horner, was widely interpreted by the media as an attack on the leader. At a subsequent caucus meeting lasting four and a half hours, Stanfield accepted the explanation that the western sessions were held only to discuss agricultural problems, but he also outlined rules for future meetings. "Regional caucuses are fine — they are to be encouraged — but the leadership and the national headquarters should be kept in the picture in order to avoid the controversy and difficulty that we have had,"[13] he stated. Discipline and cohesion within caucus remained difficult to obtain, with the result, according to one commentator (Perlin, 1980, p. 53), that "Tory members remained a gaggle of private enterprisers who selfishly preferred to pursue their separate ways to the electoral gallows rather than hang together and work as a united opposition."

The problem was reflected in the operation of the caucus committee system. Twenty-three caucus committees were established in 1968; by October 1975, just before Stanfield resigned as leader, the number of committees had risen to 38. Each had a chairman selected by the party leader, and the chairmen comprised what was popularly known as the "shadow cabinet," a term Stanfield explicitly rejected because it might imply a claim on a future real cabinet post.[14] The caucus committees were intended to serve several aims. They were to develop and to harmonize the Conservative party approach to issues as they arose in Parliament. As an outlet for constructive backbench activity, they were intended to diminish tension between members and the leadership. Finally, they were seen as a training and proving ground for future cabinet ministers.

In practice, the committees never lived up to their potential. Some were sporadic in their activity, while others were constantly busy. Attendance was irregular and the memberships were very fluid, as Conservative MPs followed the shifting issues of the day and the interests of their constituents. Because of erratic attendance, the chairmen of the committees could not work out policy positions with complete confidence that all party members would defer to the designated spokesmen in the House and in Commons committees. Eventually the committees became too numerous, making it difficult to prevent overlap in their jurisdiction and to coordinate their work. An informal hierarchy developed; it was alleged that certain committees usurped the jurisdiction of others. In terms of policy development, the emphasis was almost entirely on short-term, even daily, issues rather than on medium- or long-range policy.

This brief account reveals that for most of their existence Canadian caucuses were informal and reactive institutions. They did not enjoy significant autonomy from the party leadership, who determined unilaterally the extent of caucus involvement in policy development and parliamentary planning. A recurrent complaint, regardless of which party was in power, was that the cabinet did not adequately consult the governing party's caucus. As early as the 1930s, parties in opposition recognized that organizing their caucus would strengthen and focus their challenges to the government. It was not until the 1960s, however, that significant reforms were instituted within both the government and the opposition caucuses, for a variety of reasons. Before studying each of the party caucuses in more depth, it is worth remembering that dominance by the leadership has been the historical pattern and that recent gains in terms of intraparty democracy could obviously be reversed.

The Government Caucus: The Liberals

The government caucus is obviously in a better position than the opposition caucus to influence legislation and financial planning. It must be stressed at the outset, however, that caucus is intended not for formal decision making but for communication and consultation. It is an opportunity for the party leadership to listen to the views of backbench followers on legislation and other matters and to plot parliamentary strategy. Consistent with the consultative nature of caucus operations, no meeting agenda is circulated, almost all the discussion is based upon oral reports, no votes are held, no formal announcements or press releases are ordinarily issued at the end of meetings, and it is left to the prime minister and the cabinet to determine the nature of the consensus, if any, expressed on the issues under discussion. Secrecy and frankness are considered essential to caucus discussions, although leaks do occur from time to time. The fact that the caucus does not take formal, binding decisions obviously gives cabinet some latitude in its interpretation of intraparty agreements. Yet if a majority government's caucus were given the right of formal and binding approval of legislation and spending, subsequent parliamentary debate and voting would become a mere formality. The government caucus is technically not a decision-making body; however, most Liberal MPs interviewed for this study felt that agreements reached in caucus should normally be followed in the House of Commons. This point will be examined in a later section.

Liberal MPs have comprised the government caucus for most of this century. When Parliament was in session their national caucus met in Room 308 of the West Block of the Parliament Buildings on Wednesday mornings from 10:30 a.m. to 12:30 p.m. Notices of caucus meetings were circulated to all MPs and senators by the chief government whip. Members could inquire about the topic of the day or arrange to be placed on a list of speakers by calling the caucus chairman. Cabinet ministers were expected to attend national caucus and most backbenchers made every effort to be present. At least two-thirds of the Liberal MPs and a much smaller percentage of Liberal senators were in attendance on most Wednesday mornings. Some senators abstained from attending the Liberal caucus to emphasize their independence.

At the front of the caucus room the prime minister and his cabinet, along with the officers of caucus, sat at a long table under the portraits of past party leaders. Unless they were making a presentation on a bill or program, cabinet ministers would normally just listen and respond to questions or comments. Some brought work to caucus — newspapers or documents to read, or letters to sign. This practice annoyed some of the Liberal MPs interviewed. Prime Minister Trudeau would usually listen attentively and would sometimes take notes. When 15 to 20 minutes remained in the meeting, the caucus chairman would turn the meeting over to the prime minister, who would summarize the discussion and comment on the remarks made earlier by members. While Mr. Trudeau would often debate points raised by other participants, there was no real give-and-take, since the prime minister had the last word. When his remarks were completed, the meeting was adjourned. Several Liberal MPs indicated that at the end of a caucus meeting they were often uncertain whether they had impressed the prime minister with their arguments.

Agendas for caucus meetings were set by the executive of caucus, which in June 1984, consisted of: Remi Bujold, chairman; Senator Paul Lucier, vice chairman; Carlo Rossi, treasurer; David Weatherhead, secretary; Charles Turner, chief government whip; Bob Bockstael, chairman of the western caucus; Maurice Foster, chairman of the Ontario caucus; Dennis Dawson, chairman of the Quebec caucus; and Gary McCauley, chairman of the Atlantic caucus. The executive met for lunch on Tuesdays to discuss the agenda for the caucus meeting next day.

Prior to 1969 the Liberal Party leader appointed the chairman of the caucus. Prime Minister Trudeau's agreement to permit the election of the chairman was part of the package of reforms adopted in 1969 to transform the caucus into more than a mere sounding board for cabinet ideas. In March 1970, Gerald Laniel (Beauharnois, Quebec) gave up the job of caucus chairman, to which he had been named by Mr. Trudeau after the 1968 general election. Mr. Laniel had favoured the idea of an elected chairman; because of poor health, he did not stand for the election.[15] He received no extra salary as caucus chairman but was entitled to an extra secretary, an arrangement which still prevails today.

Three individuals contested the first election, in 1970, for chairman of the Liberal caucus; Grant Deachman (Vancouver Quadra, British Columbia) emerged as the winner on a secret ballot. Mr. Deachman served as chairman of the caucus until July 1971, when he was defeated on a caucus vote by Jean Roy (Timmins, Ontario). Press speculation at the time was that Deachman was replaced because of his practice of ferreting out truant ministers to persuade them to attend caucus, as well as encouraging members to put ministers on the spot at caucus by tough questioning.[16] This interpretation does not seem entirely accurate, because most subsequent chairmen adopted Deachman's practices. It seems that Liberal members simply favour rotation of the post on a regional basis. There is low-key, informal campaigning for the job of chairman of caucus, consisting mainly of efforts to buttonhole individual MPs and senators. Regional groups of parliamentarians will occasionally campaign to support the candidacy of an individual from their region. Underlying the limited competition for all caucus positions is a recognition of the need for regional balance in the make-up of caucus offices. Furthermore, since all members can serve on any caucus policy committee, there is no great strategic advantage for an individual or a region in being on the caucus executive. In short, the position of caucus chairman is an honour and carries some influence, but is not a highly prized position.

Most MPs interviewed felt that the job was of sufficient importance to require a chairman who could stand up to the cabinet when necessary. Remi Bujold, at the time of his election as caucus chairman, expressed a desire to strengthen the link between caucus and the national Liberal Party. To this end, he arranged for the national party president to meet more frequently with the caucus executive and even at times with the full caucus. All members of the caucus executive were made members of the organizing committee for the June 1984 leadership convention, and Bujold was named co-chairman of the convention. At times the chairman was expected to communicate caucus concerns to the prime minister and other ministers.

In January 1984, for example, Bujold wrote to all ministers to express concern about four matters raised in caucus. The first related to ministerial announcements that touched upon a member's riding or region. It was "disheartening," even embarrassing, he wrote, to learn of such developments by means of a ministerial press release; he recommended that members be notified in advance and asked for advice on the content and timing of such announcements. If a public event was to be held in connection with a ministerial announcement, the elected member for the riding should be present. On a related matter, Bujold urged better consultation on policy initiatives. "Members would welcome early consultation on policies which affect their regions, or in which they have some expertise." If this were done, he concluded, "it would add a positive dimension to caucus relations." The third matter concerned ministerial staffs. Turnover and additions to ministerial staff had led to a lack of response or long delays in responding to inquiries from Liberal MPs. Finally, the letter complained that ministers travelling outside Ottawa neglected to notify the members whose ridings would be visited. Ministers were urged to meet with regional or provincial party people during such trips, if their schedules permitted. To reinforce his message, Bujold closed by indicating that he had spoken to the prime minister and his principal secretary (Tom Axworthy) about the four concerns raised in his letter. The letter highlighted the importance of both the allocation (the regional benefits) and symbolic dimensions of responsiveness, as were defined earlier. The matters raised involved perennial caucus complaints.

The weekly agenda for government caucus was determined by the executive of caucus. A typical agenda would include the following items.

- Events or caucus committee meetings were announced.
- Brief oral reports were presented by the chairmen of the four regional caucuses; these reports did not ordinarily spark debate.
- Reports on parliamentary activities from the government House were presented by the leader and the chief government whip. The House leader was responsible for the scheduling of parliamentary business and for negotiations with opposition House leaders. The whip was responsible for ensuring that the government was represented by a sufficient number of MPs when votes were held. If government members had been lax in attending House votes or committee meetings, the House leader and the whip would exhort them to do better, either by pointing to the dangers of absenteeism or by appealing to their party loyalty.
- Under the heading of miscellaneous, members were free to raise any subject they pleased. Typically, the chairman of caucus would have had

notice of six or more subjects to be raised, on each of which there might be a number of speakers. Three to five minutes were allowed for each member to voice his concerns and ministers were given a chance to reply.

- On a fairly regular basis, the miscellaneous section of caucus was replaced by a topic of the day. The topic to be discussed was usually announced beforehand in the notice of the meeting. Members could recommend topics to the caucus executive. A member who suggested a topic was given seven to ten minutues to make his presentation. Other speakers were allotted three to five minutes. If the topic involved a particular minister, he was permitted to summarize and respond to the comments at the end. In June 1984, for example, a topic of the day was quotas on textiles and shoes. The Minister of Trade introduced the topic and summed up the discussion.

- The final 15 to 20 minutes of the caucus were devoted to remarks by the prime minister. According to several respondents, Mr. Trudeau liked to enter into caucus debate and would often take a contrary position to that being expressed, just to show that there was another side to a question. The result, said one MP, was that "often you left caucus wondering exactly which way it had gone."

This last remark emphasizes the fact that on most matters before it, caucus was not a decision-making body. It met to discuss issues and attempt to influence ministerial decision making. Votes were not held in caucus except on matters that related to its internal operation. For example, the rare decision to expel a member from caucus, as occurred in 1968 with Ralph Cowan, the maverick Liberal MP from Toronto, was settled by a vote. However, most matters were decided on the basis of a consensus. Since caucus took the format of an exchange of views, it was up to the prime minister and cabinet to determine the nature of any consensus. Liberal MPs disagreed on whether the achievement of a consensus was difficult. A member with 20 years of service believed that the process of identifying a consensus was difficult because:

> It is a big country, with lots of regions. The concerns that would motivate someone from Atlantic Canada are not the same concerns that I face. So sometimes it is difficult to make everyone aware of the situation in other parts of the country. There is never perfect unanimity.

Structural arrangements were much less important to this process, according to the same MP, than the "culture of the Liberal party," which stressed the importance of "coming to terms with the forces at work within the country so as to ensure reelection."

More than just regional issues could divide the caucus. Economic and social policy questions could lead to ideological disagreements. The political centre of gravity within the cabinet and caucus on these sorts of issues could shift to the right or the left as circumstances changed and as cabinet ministers arrived or departed. During the recession of 1982, for example, a group of ten Montreal MPs — including two cabinet ministers — made public a letter to the prime minister calling for additional spending on job creation.[17] The letter caused a furor in the House and was the topic of a spirited caucus debate. Again in October 1982, after the promotion to senior economic portfolios of two cabinet ministers seen to be on the right wing of the Liberal party, there was a lengthy discussion within caucus about possible cutbacks to universal social programs.[18]

If the caucus was divided and the responsible minister was not determined to proceed, the prime minister could delay a decision until a consensus emerged. Even when a caucus seemed united on an issue, ministers did not always feel bound by such an agreement, which was often expressed imprecisely. MPs recognized that implementing caucus ideas must be left to ministers, for they often had the necessary factual background and an awareness of all the implications of a given action. The freedom of ministers to accept or reject caucus advice proved to be a valuable safeguard, according to one Liberal MP: "Even if it isn't always immediately apparent to caucus, the cabinet has often ended up being right when it rejected a caucus position, even if we only realized this months later."

Liberal MPs maintained that caucus was able to influence the content of legislation. As previously mentioned, in 1969 caucus began discussing the subject matter of proposed legislation within one of a series of standing policy committees before a bill was approved by the appropriate cabinet committee. After a bill was introduced for first reading in the House of Commons, it was again discussed in full caucus. During the minority Liberal government of 1972 to 1974, the system of standing caucus committees was abandoned in favour of greater reliance upon full caucus consultation. At this point, ministers began inviting interested members to attend meetings to discuss bills. These "pink slip" meetings (the colour of the notices) were usually sparsely attended; participants, according to one MP, were as few as half a dozen. Problems with legislation could always be raised during the miscellaneous section of national caucus and sometimes bills provided the topic of the day. Besides, MPs were busy and recognized the need to concentrate on a few topics of personal or constituency interest. In the case of highly technical legislation, the minister was sometimes accompanied by public servants who could provide factual explanations.

Cabinet ministers recognized the advantage of gaining prior caucus support for legislation as a way to forestall intraparty disagreements when a bill reached the House of Commons. "There is no way," according to one Liberal MP, "that the government will proceed if it does not have strong majority support for a piece of legislation." Caucus was regularly successful in blocking, delaying or amending proposed legislation. In 1977, for example, the government proposed to increase the prior employment period for eligibility for unemployment insurance benefits from 8 to 14 weeks. Despite warnings from the Atlantic MPs in the Liberal caucus about the hardship this would impose on their region of high unemployment, the legislation was introduced and controversy ensued. According to an Atlantic MP, caucus forced the government to reconsider:

> It was the Atlantic caucus led by myself and four other MPs who fought the government through the caucus. It went to cabinet four times as an emerging issue and eventually we won. We got the variable entrance requirement of 10 to 14 weeks across the country.

According to a Quebec Liberal, his provincial caucus was successful in blocking the recent Bill S-31, which sought to limit provincial ownership of transportation companies. In his words:

> If S-31 was left to die on the order paper, the only reason is because the Quebec caucus did everything it could to have it die. . . . The Quebec caucus said that the bill was bad politics, it was not a priority, and it was deemed to be against Quebec. There is no way that the Cabinet is going to go against a united caucus of 74 members.

Opposition to Bill S-31 from provincial governments and from the official opposition in the Commons were undoubtedly contributing factors to the success of Quebec caucus. The Liberal caucus was also reported to have been influential in causing changes to be made to the bill for amending Crow's Nest Pass freight rates for grain and to the Canada Health Act. At times ministers attempted to rally caucus support for their legislative proposals to overcome opposition within cabinet or to advance bills in the crowded legislative line-up controlled by the government House leader.

Liberal MPs were asked whether caucus influenced the level and direction of spending. Most agreed caucus pressure led to more spending rather than less. By promoting or supporting new programs, often without a clear idea of their long-term costs, caucus helped to increase expenditures. "That is part of the game," stated one MP. "If we are there to defend the interests of our constituents, we have to defend what we think they want and need." National caucus meetings were seldom used as a forum to promote projects within an MP's constituency. Such matters were more appropriately raised in private meetings with ministers or through correspondence with ministers and their officials. In addition, government MPs can frequently be seen promoting and protecting constituency and regional interests through their work on the standing committees of the House of Commons, which examine the annual spending plans of the government. MPs from areas of high unemployment, for example, were anxious to serve on the regional development committee of the Commons to ensure that their constituents would benefit from whatever job creation money was available.

In 1969 the Liberal caucus was divided into six policy committees, each with an elected chairman and a voluntary membership. This system proved unworkable because many committee meetings were held simultaneously (during the 6 to 8 p.m. dinner hour), which made it impossible for MPs to follow all their interests. Many MPs were not prepared to put in the effort needed to make the committees work successfully. Since the committees met over dinner, more of a social than a business atmosphere prevailed. The chairmen of the committees brought varying levels of drive and skill to their leadership activities. With the greatly reduced number of government members in the twenty-ninth Parliament (1972–74), the system of standing committees was disbanded.

It was replaced by an arrangement of ad hoc policy committees open to all members. Chairmen of the policy committees were selected by the caucus executive from a list of volunteers. Members who indicated an interest in a topic would usually be asked to chair a policy committee. As busy as MPs were, few were looking for extra work and being chairman of a policy committee seemed to involve more burdens than rewards for many MPs. The policy committees were transitory bodies, so it was difficult to ascertain exactly how many were active at a given time. In recent years committees have been established on agriculture, youth unemployment, tariffs and trade, forestry, social policy and economic policy. The forestry committee, for example, met for several months, prepared two reports, and then arranged for the subject to be the topic of the day at a national caucus.

Four to six weeks prior to the presentation of a budget, the Liberal caucus established an economic policy committee. Members showed a great deal of interest in its work. A series of meetings were held and a preliminary and a final report were brought to caucus. By prior arrangement the chairman of caucus made the reports the first topic on the agenda for two caucus meetings. Caucus input was important in shaping most recent budgets, according to MPs. It was hoped that the minister of finance would find the economic policy committee a useful source of broad, political advice on the budget. A more common occurrence was for him to use well-informed MPs as part of the general effort to get the political message of the budget out to the country. To this end, MPs were supplied with a "budget kit" containing information to rebut opposition criticism, a list of groups consulted on the budget, sample questions and answers, model radio and television speeches, a summary of media commentaries, and a set of "good news" economic indicators. Committee meetings continued with officials from the Department of Finance and ministerial advisors to provide an explanation of technical matters after the budget had been presented to Parliament. The same opportunity for a briefing was offered in recent years to opposition caucuses on the condition that the parliamentary secretary to the minister of finance accompany public servants as a precaution against their entanglement in partisan controversies.

In addition to the ad hoc policy committees, the Liberal caucus also operated a series of regional caucuses. The distribution of Liberal party seats in the House of Commons in the last Parliament meant there were four regional caucuses: Atlantic (19 MPs); Quebec (74 MPs); Ontario (52 MPs); and the West (2 MPs). Senators were eligible to attend regional caucuses, but many did not, and in any case their political credibility was less because of their appointed status. The regional composition of the government caucus, based on the House of Commons, was: Atlantic, 12.9 percent; Quebec, 50.3 percent; Ontario, 35.4 percent; and the West, 1.4 percent. Rather than being a recent phenomenon, the regional imbalance within the government caucus appears to have been a fairly persistent pattern throughout Canadian history, as shown in Table 2-1, presented by Professor Robert Jackson to the Special Joint Committee of the Senate and House of Commons on Senate Reform reveals. Apart from the early years of Confederation, only rarely has the national government been backed by well-balanced regional caucuses. In other words, it is wise to question the conventional wisdom that there was an earlier extended period when the system permitted interregional compromises to be hammered out in the frank but congenial atmosphere of a one-party caucus. The so-called "crisis in representation" about which so much was said and written after the 1979 and 1980 general elections appears to have existed, at least at the level of House of Commons representation, for many years. This point must be borne in mind before Canadians endorse sweeping constitutional or institutional reforms.

Regional caucuses met regularly on Wednesday mornings for an hour (9:30 to 10:30 a.m.) before national caucus. The meetings focussed on the implications of national policies for specific areas and on provincial or local matters. As mentioned earlier, the regional caucuses presented brief reports on their meetings during national caucus, and if a regional caucus felt particularly strongly about an issue, its chairman could request that other representatives from the region be allowed to speak. Sometimes matters mentioned in a regional report would be brought up again during the miscellaneous section of the caucus agenda.

Regional caucuses obviously varied in size, level of activity, cohesion and quality of membership. The Quebec Liberal caucus in the last Parliament, with 74 MPs, included half the total Liberal caucus membership. Quebec members had a strong sense of having been sent to Ottawa to represent their province and their culture in national politics, where they are a minority, and this contributed to regional solidarity. The presence of several powerful cabinet ministers, including the prime minister, added to the strength of the Quebec caucus. Unlike the Ontario caucus, according to one Quebec MP, there was a definite hierarchy among Quebec ministers that gave unity and direction to the caucus. Most Quebec MPs attended the provincial caucus. There was also a series of subregional caucuses — Montreal, Quebec City, Gaspé, and the South Shore. Each

TABLE 2-1 Regional Composition of Government Caucus and House of Commons, Canadian General Elections, 1867–1980

Election	Governing Party	Regional Composition of Government Caucus				Regional Composition of House of Commons			
		West	Ont.	Que.	Atl.	West	Ont.	Que.	Atl.
1867	CONS	—	45.5	44.6	9.9	—	45.3	35.9	18.8
1872	CONS	8.7	36.9	36.9	17.5	5.0	44.0	32.5	18.5
1874	LIB	1.5	48.1	24.8	25.6	4.9	42.7	31.6	20.9
1878	CONS	6.6	43.1	32.8	17.5	4.9	42.7	31.6	20.9
1882	CONS	5.8	38.8	34.5	20.9	5.2	43.3	31.0	20.5
1887	CONS	11.4	42.3	26.8	19.5	7.0	42.8	30.2	20.0
1891	CONS	11.4	39.0	24.4	25.2	7.0	42.8	30.2	20.0
1896	LIB	6.8	36.8	41.9	14.5	8.0	43.2	30.5	18.3
1900	LIB	9.1	27.3	43.2	20.5	8.0	43.2	30.5	18.3
1904	LIB	15.1	27.3	38.8	18.7	13.1	40.2	30.4	16.4
1908	LIB	13.5	27.1	39.8	19.5	15.8	38.9	29.4	15.8
1911	CONS	13.5	54.1	20.3	12.0	15.8	38.9	29.4	15.8
1917	UNIONIST(CONS)	35.9	48.4	2.0	13.7	24.3	34.9	27.7	13.2
1921	Lib	4.3	18.1	56.0	21.6	24.3	3.9	27.7	13.2
1925	Lib	23.2	11.1	59.6	6.1	28.2	33.5	26.5	11.8
1926	Lib	20.7	19.8	51.7	7.8	28.2	33.5	26.5	11.8
1930	CONS	22.6	43.1	17.5	16.8	28.2	33.5	26.5	11.8
1935	LIB	20.5	32.7	32.2	14.6	29.4	33.5	26.5	10.6
1940	LIB	24.2	30.9	34.2	10.7	29.4	33.5	26.5	10.6
1945	LIB	15.2	27.2	43.2	14.4	29.4	33.5	26.5	10.6
1949	LIB	22.6	29.5	34.7	13.1	27.5	31.7	27.9	13.0
1953	LIB	15.9	29.4	38.8	15.9	27.5	32.1	28.3	12.5
1957	Prog. Cons.	18.8	54.5	8.0	18.8	27.2	32.1	28.3	12.5
1958	PROG. CONS.	31.7	32.2	24.0	12.0	27.2	32.1	28.3	12.5

Election	Governing Party	Regional Composition of Government Caucus				Regional Composition of House of Commons			
		West	Ont.	Que.	Atl.	West	Ont.	Que.	Atl.
1962	Prog. Cons.	42.2	30.2	12.1	15.5	27.2	32.1	28.3	12.5
1963	Lib	7.8	40.3	36.4	15.5	27.2	32.1	28.3	12.5
1965	Lib	6.9	38.9	42.7	11.5	27.2	32.1	28.3	12.5
1968	LIB	18.1	41.3	36.1	4.5	26.5	33.3	28.0	12.1
1972	Lib	6.4	33.0	51.4	9.2	26.5	33.3	28.0	12.1
1974	LIB	9.2	39.0	42.6	9.2	26.5	33.3	28.0	12.1
1979	Prog. Cons.	43.4	41.9	1.5	13.2	28.4	33.7	26.6	11.3
1980	LIB	1.4	35.4	50.3	12.9	28.4	33.7	26.6	11.3

Source: Special Joint Committee of the Senate and House of Commons on Senate Reform, *Minutes of Evidence and Proceedings*, June 28, 1983, p. 10A3.
Notes: LIB/PROG. CONS. = Majority Government Lib/Prog. Cons. = Minority Government
N.B. Rows may not add up to 100.0% due to rounding.

was linked to a designated minister. Unlike other regional caucuses, Quebec often held special meetings lasting three or four days following a parliamentary break or before the opening of a new Parliament.

Only MPs and senators were invited to national and regional caucuses; outsiders and parliamentary staff were normally excluded. Quebec opened up its caucus by inviting representatives from the Prime Minister's Office, the communications group of the Liberal Party, and the Liberal caucus research bureau. In addition, an MP served as executive secretary to the caucus to keep records of decisions reached. Unlike other caucuses, the Quebec caucus issued press releases to publicize its positions on issues. In the opinion of two Quebec MPs interviewed for this study, these arrangements improved the quality of work being done in the Quebec caucus. As in other regional caucuses, the chairman of the Quebec caucus was elected by a secret ballot of its members, but the election process was more competitive than in other caucuses. "To be chairman of the Quebec caucus," one MP stated, "you have to be from a riding where you can risk alienating the regional minister occasionally." In November 1980, Jacques Olivier (Longueuil) defeated the incumbent, Maurice Dupras (Labelle), by a vote of 36 to 33. This was seen as a victory of the younger, reform wing of the Quebec caucus over the party establishment.

The Quebec caucus influenced many decisions reached within the national Liberal caucus. MP Celine Hervieux-Payette spoke of the power of the Quebec caucus: "Once we've put our act together at the regional level, there is no need to have a fight at national caucus. It's understood that if we know what we want, we'll get it because the others are not necessarily concerned about it."[19] Another Quebec MP described the influence of his regional caucus on legislation:

> If you have a good argument, if you can get the Quebec caucus to say that it wants a bill amended in a certain way, then nine times out of ten you are going to win at national caucus. So I go there [to Quebec caucus] all the time because I know that it has been successful for me. If more MPs were to use caucus in the way that it is supposed to be used, it would be a more productive institution.

Examples of the influence of the Quebec caucus on legislation were cited earlier. The Quebec caucus has also been influential in expanding relations with la Francophonie, increasing foreign aid, and protecting such Quebec-based industries as textiles and footwear.

Campaigns for the allocation of benefits to the province have not always been behind the scenes and low-key. In 1980, when the fighter aircraft procurement decision was being made, Quebec MPs lobbied extensively; they openly used the media to make the case for the General Dynamics F-16. While the other aircraft, the F-18, was eventually chosen, Quebec MPs did not lose out entirely, as Dobell (1981) writes:

Chief among these was Jacques Oliver, who articulately represented the interests of his constituency company, Pratt and Whitney, one of the two Quebec Partner companies of General Dynamics. Pratt and Whitney shortly thereafter (the announcement of the F–18 contract) was chosen as one of the two finalists for the new naval frigate contract. Canadair, the other General Dynamics partner, was encouraged to bid on sub-contracting for the F–18, and later was awarded the forward nose barrel contract. Beyond that, other sub-contracts were moved to Quebec that would otherwise have been awarded to Ontario. The political manoeuvring had a real impact on the placing of sub-contracts, if not in reversing the order of the victorious and of the successful aircraft. (p. 11)

The need to publicize caucus dealings with the government was made necessary by the lack of opposition representation from the province. In the case of Ontario, which was represented by Conservatives and New Democrats as well as 52 Liberal MPs, the natural processes of the House brought out opposition to government policies. In Quebec's case, Liberal MPs had to reflect this opposition through caucus, since they could not regularly ask questions in the House, make parliamentary speeches against the government, or vote against it. This created a perceptual problem for Quebec MPs: "We are seen in Quebec as always supporting the government. Yet we are basically the strongest lobbying group in Ottawa."

To publicize the success of their lobbying, Quebec MPs arranged for the Canadian Unity Information Office (CUIO) to produce (at public expense) pamphlets for each of the four regions of the province. The pamphlets, which were circulated to all households, outlined the spending done by the federal government in each area and contained pictures of all local MPs as well as profiles of their ridings. The publication for the South Shore area, titled "The Government of Canada: An Active Partner on the South Shore," began with a greeting from Labour Minister André Ouellet, who was described as "the minister responsible for the eight South Shore ridings."[20] He extolled the virtues of the eight local MPs: "Each made extraordinary efforts in handling the multitude of requests from their respective ridings." Originally, the CUIO was located in the Department of the Secretary of State (and its director was a member of the federal-provincial relations branch in the Privy Council Office). The office became part of the Department of Justice several years ago. It was the local MPs, however, who approved the content of the pamphlets. A similar publication for Saskatchewan, which elected no Liberal MPs in 1980, contained no pictures of MPs.

The second largest regional caucus was Ontario. It was divided into three subcaucuses: metropolitan Toronto, southern Ontario, and northwestern Ontario. The chairman of the Ontario caucus was elected annually by a secret ballot. Ontario, according to several MPs, was not as successful in getting its "act together recently." The overall political minister for

Ontario was Herb Gray (Windsor), but he was forced to compete with several Toronto ministers for overall leadership of the caucus. As a result, Ontario lacked the kind of unified direction that Marc Lalonde provided to the Quebec caucus. One interviewee suggested that Ontario MPs did not consider themselves "provincial ambassadors" as did their Quebec colleagues. The interests of Ontario tended to be equated with the national interest.

METPAC was a group of 17 Toronto-area MPs, including four cabinet ministers, who met on a regular basis. They played an important role in identifying the types of issues that appeared on the agenda of the provincial caucus. Since Toronto served as the main battleground during recent elections, it would be surprising if METPAC concerns did not also figure prominently in national caucus discussions. Limited information on the influence of METPAC was obtained during the research for this paper. The group dealt with political matters and appointments involving the Toronto area. Periodically, it produced a newsletter for Toronto-area Liberals. The *Toronto Star*, in an 1981 editorial dealing with the housing crisis in the city, expressed disappointment with the Liberal delegation:

> It's time for METPAC to become more than a casual koffeeklatch. It should be a vigorous advocate of the interests of the people of Toronto and a force within the Liberal Party. . . . The Metro 17 should realize that when they go to a Liberal caucus meeting in Ottawa as they did this week, the voters back in Toronto expect some results. From all reports, it sounds as though the local Liberals did at least let the cabinet know that the people in Toronto are getting very angry.[21]

Liberals from other regions of Ontario felt that Toronto concerns dominated provincial caucus. A northwestern Ontario MP indicated that he had reduced his attendance at provincial caucus because "METPAC issues tended to dominate and when northern Ontario issues were raised it tended to be as a token." He also expressed disappointment with the northwestern Ontario caucus:

> It was once very active, but in the last few years, since 1980, it has become quite divisive. At one time we were highly united around a very competent cabinet minister called Robert Andras. He was the single regional minister. Since 1980 there have been two ministers. One of those ministers came directly from the election into cabinet. He was inexperienced. The end result of all this is that the group is fragmented.

The twelve constituencies of northwestern Ontario were divided between the two cabinet ministers, and the MP noted that he regularly discussed local projects with the minister responsible for his constituency. A harbour project was initiated as a result of his joint efforts with another area MP.

Bud Cullen, a former cabinet minister, enjoyed similar success working through the southwestern Ontario caucus:

Regional caucus has been very effective for me on the problem of petrochemicals, for example, where the subject went from the southwestern Ontario caucus to Ontario caucus to a special committee. If used properly regional caucus can be very effective.[22]

An interesting innovation by the northwestern Ontario caucus was to hold public information and discussion meetings on relevant topics at points throughout the region. These meetings began after the 1980 election, which returned a number of new MPs. The topics included forestry, economic development, tourism, and parliamentary redistribution. When a Conservative MP was returned from the region in a 1982 by-election, he asked to participate in these meetings and the Liberal MPs agreed. Previously, when there were NDP members from the region, the sense of political competition was too strong for such interparty cooperation to occur.

The Atlantic caucus within the Liberal party had only 19 members and they recognized the exigency of presenting a united stand before national caucus. Size is very important but it is not the only determinant of the influence of regional caucuses. If the Atlantic caucus was united and felt strongly about an issue, other regional caucuses would often heed its wishes. A New Brunswick MP maintained that "this country has always been very sensitive to minority and regional concerns. This has been the case not only within our party." The strength of regional cabinet ministers, the timing in moving a regional issue to the national agenda and the quality of the arguments affected whether proposals would be adopted.

The Liberal caucus was less successful as a vehicle for regional accommodation in relation to western Canada. With only two elected MPs from the region, there was a real danger that western interests would receive short shrift. Even during the twenty-eighth Parliament (1968–72), when there were 27 Liberal MPs from western Canada, the Trudeau government produced policies that were rejected by the region, such as the grains policy (Lower Inventories for Tomorrow) and bilingualism. In 1983, Edmund Osler, who served as a Manitoba Liberal MP during the first Trudeau government, told the Special Joint Committee of the Senate and the House of Commons on Senate Reform of his perception of why the West's concerns were ignored within the Liberal caucus:

Everybody was always very polite and nice to you in caucus, and it was very democratic. You could say any damn thing you liked. But the fact remained that there were sixty-odd members from three cities within a couple of hundred miles from where you were sitting, and in the end what you thought was not going to make any difference to anybody when a thing was decided by a definite vote. There were other things on which you could make great contributions.[23]

The reference to votes must have been a slip, since they were not held in caucus, but the attitude expressed was widely shared in western Canada.

Another part of the explanation was the absence at that time of a strong regional minister. The presence in the cabinet of a powerful regional minister, Lloyd Axworthy from Winnipeg, may have been reassuring to Manitobans, who clearly benefited from federal largesse, but voters in the other western provinces may not have seen him as a true spokesman for their needs.

The party tried a number of approaches to ensure that some input from the West was incorporated into caucus. Three western senators were appointed to the Liberal cabinet. This may have produced some additional benefits for the region, but in terms of public relations it backfired, according to a not-entirely-objective source, a western Conservative MP: "The Liberals may have had no choice but to use senators, but to the voters in my region this was just another symbol of our status as a political colony." Western Liberal senators performed party functions that normally would be the responsibility of MPs, but they were not seen by the electorate as legitimate regional spokespersons (Standing Committee on Legal and Constitutional Affairs, 1980, p. 41).

Another approach to the problem of underrepresentation was the "twinning of ridings," whereby Liberal MPs from other parts of the country volunteered to maintain contact with a western riding. The approach had limited success: few MPs agreed to participate, and their riding contact was infrequent and mainly with Liberal riding associations. MPs were disinclined to lobby as vigorously for their adopted ridings as they would for their own, especially if there was regional competition for government benefits.

After the 1980 election, a western affairs committee of cabinet was established but it, too, was a disappointment. Even the much-heralded Western Development Fund, the original amount of which seemed to have shrunk considerably since its establishment, was controlled by another committee of cabinet.

The government caucus did play an important role in the governing process. Working through regional and then national caucus, individual MPs had influence in delaying, blocking or modifying legislation. The impact of caucus on financial decisions was seen mainly in terms of the distribution of benefits and increases in spending. For example, the cabinet would decide to build four new frigates, but the caucus would advise the responsible ministers to split their construction between different shipyards. Or, in relation to the recent special capital recovery projects, regional ministers would be given a total budget and lists of possible projects compiled by government departments, the distribution of which was then subject to negotiation with other ministers from the region and with the regional caucus. Regional caucuses were also usually consulted by their regional minister about government appointments from their province.

The principal constraints on the government caucus are time and information. Extended discussions about policy are not often practical because ministers, and to a lesser extent MPs, simply do not have the time. Ministers have a somewhat ambivalent attitude toward caucus. Occasionally the consultation requirement seems like a nuisance, since their time is scarce and the advice being rendered by MPs is necessarily less "expert" than that received from the bureaucracy or pressure groups. Yet, for ministers who face a blizzard of paper and endless meetings, caucus represents a valuable, though indirect, contact with public opinion. The caucus plays an important role in highlighting issues of public concern and providing feedback to harried ministers on how policies are being accepted. The caucus helps to identify issues for the political agenda of the government, but it lacks the time and expertise to explore them in depth.

The information needs of government MPs were better provided for in the past few years; each had one or two personal research assistants. In addition, since 1970 the Liberal caucus research bureau existed to assist MPs. In June 1984, the bureau had a staff of only three researchers and five support staff, but it was undergoing reorganization and at one time employed up to eight researchers.[24] Originally, the bureau emphasized medium- and long-term policy research in support of the standing policy committees of caucus, which existed between 1969 and 1972. There was growing pressure to give the bureau more of a communications function, assisting backbench MPs in their defence of government policies. The bureau found itself responding increasingly to requests for material for immediate use in the House of Commons, the caucus, or in the MPs' constituencies. According to a former cabinet minister, there were sometimes mistakes in the information supplied by the bureau.

Additional support to caucus members was provided by the Liberal communications group, which was of a similar size to the research bureau. It provided Liberal MPs with material for speeches and newsletters, operated a press clipping service and ran a speakers bureau. The emphasis within the group was on using MPs and senators to increase public knowledge and support for government policies. For example, in July 1983 Liberal members were sent on their summer holidays with a sales kit to be used in the selling of the "six-and-five" restraint program and the recent budget.[25] The kit consisted of a plastic suitcase that contained a 45 rpm recording, a series of prepared speeches, and a paper titled "Recovery Canada: A Strategy for Members of Parliament." MPs were instructed to take "the initiative and adopt a hands-on approach" to the selling of the recovery program in their region. They were told they should be "exploiting and seeking out media and speaking opportunities solely for the selling of the recovery."[26] MPs were to meet once every two weeks with the designated minister for their region to provide feedback on the acceptance of the program and each minister was to hold a regional caucus of riding executives to improve communication of the program, especially in ridings not held by Liberals. A recovery tabloid featuring "good news" indicators and articles on government programs was to be published every second week. Efforts to mobilize public support in this way have always been carried out by governments, though probably MPs have never before been equipped as systematically to serve as travelling salesmen complete with bulging suitcases.

The eight Liberal MPs interviewed for this study were satisfied with the structures and procedures of the government caucus. Several emphasized that caucus was basically a responsive, humane institution. Attempts to structure it greatly would detract from its flexibility and weaken its human relations functions. In the words of a New Brunswick MP:

> A caucus has very little or nothing to do with structure, it is all a question of mood and of the psychology of the group. . . . When the mood is good, caucus can be very effective.

This message about the importance of the human factor to the role of caucus as an organization should be remembered when possible reforms are discussed in the final section.

The Official Opposition Caucus: The Progressive Conservatives

In his excellent study, *The Tory Syndrome: Leadership Politics in the Progressive Conservative Party*, George Perlin (1980, p. 1) begins by noting that the party has been subject to recurring crises because of conflict over leadership. The leader of the Progressive Conservative Party owes a dual accountability to the national association and the parliamentary caucus. The problems this creates are compounded by the fact that the extra-parliamentary party has been dominated by provincial elites and provincialist attitudes; thus the leader has had less leverage in relation to this part of the party. In opposition, the leader has controlled such patronage as the appointment of party spokespersons, the assignment of prominent seats in the House, and the approval of the party's memberships on House of Commons committees. He also has appointed the party House leader, the whips and, until recently, the chairman of caucus. Theoretically, these appointments were made by the caucus based upon the recommendation of the leader; in fact, the leader's list was simply presented to caucus and was not discussed or voted on. The leader also had the right to declare policy unilaterally and was responsible for determining the sense of caucus discussions. Therefore, in formal constitutional terms the parliamentary party was leader-dominated, but in practice the relationship between the party leader and his parliamentary followers was more complicated. The structural bias in favour of the party leader contributed to tension and discord within caucus.

Unlike the leader of a party in office, an opposition leader has far fewer tangible rewards to bestow. The leader can make symbolic appointments that might hold the promise of tangible fulfillment should the party achieve power, but these do not have the same impact as actual cabinet appointments. In opposition, conflict within the party, though never welcome, is regarded less seriously because there is not the need for cohesion to obtain the passage of government programs through Parliament. An opposition leader appoints office staff, chooses the national director of the party to oversee headquarters staff, and also names the director of the party's research office. These resources, however, do not come close to matching the personal staff and public service resources available to the leader of the governing party. The relative information advantage that an opposition leader enjoys in relation to his backbench followers will never be as great as that enjoyed by a prime minister in relation to his caucus.

The orientation of the opposition caucus is naturally different from the government caucus, since the prime minister and the cabinet are not there to hear the views expressed. "When opposition members meet in caucus — if they are not distracted by internecine strife — they are chiefly concerned to conspire against the ministry" (Stewart, 1977, pp. 18–19). The emphasis within the opposition is on the daily and weekly routines of parliamentary business: what reactions will be taken to government initiatives, what topics will be used for opposition "supply days," what ministers will be challenged in question period, when important votes will be held, and what impact the party's activities are having on the electorate. The longer-term problems of governing the country necessarily take second place to these strategic issues, because there is nothing an opposition party can do in the immediate future. Moreover, frontbench opposition spokesmen (so-called shadow cabinet ministers) have no first-hand contact with the work of government and lack the public service resources that provide ministers in a government caucus with an advantage in relation to backbenchers. There is less chance, in other words, of some inner circle completely dominating caucus decision making.

The development of the Progressive Conservative caucus up to 1976, when Joe Clark took over as leader, was traced in an earlier section. Clark set out to change the fractious and ragged image of the parliamentary party. His relations with caucus never went smoothly, with the possible exception of the period from May to December 1979 when the party was in office. Not surprisingly, caucus relations deteriorated after the government lost the crucial budget vote in December 1979 and the subsequent general election of February 1980. By 1982 there were serious challenges to Clark's leadership both from within caucus and outside. In that year, with Clark's consent, a committee chaired by MP Frank Oberle was established to study the caucus structure, identify problems and suggest reforms. After a series of discussion meetings and several drafts, the committee presented a final report to caucus in August 1983. The chairman wrote a brief article summarizing his findings and recommendations

(Oberle, 1983, 1984). The full report was not made public, but a copy was obtained during the course of this study.[27] The Oberle report made a total of eleven recommendations, many but not all of which were accepted by Mulroney and his caucus.

The report observed that "no leader, under the present structure, can secure the contentment of all the caucus and the extra-parliamentary party, because the leader is made the focal point of all disputes and target of virtually all resentment" (Oberle, 1983, p. 1). Members of caucus wished to share both the burdens and the privileges of power. More specifically, the report identified four goals of the reforms it was proposing (p. 2):

- improvement of morale in caucus and the perception of unity;
- the efficient utilization of time in caucus and its committees;
- the enhancement of the role of private members and better utilization of their talents and industry, particularly in the process of policy formation; and
- the establishment of a system of accountability for frontbench party members.

In the past, the policy work done by various caucus committees had often been ignored while the party placed its faith in "technical experts to fashion policy in accordance with transient public opinion." Conservative MPs came to feel, the report stated, that "the party is more prone to follow public sentiments than to lead with well-conceived policies" (p. 21).

While the Orberle report characterized the Progressive Conservative caucus as "underdeveloped," it actually resembled, on paper at least, an elaborate bureaucratic structure. In June 1984 there were ten positions directly involved with the full national caucus. There were also 34 designated spokesmen who monitored the performance of a government minister. Each of the spokesmen was assigned a deputy. There were also nine caucus committees, each with a chairman and a vice-chairman and eight regional caucuses, each with an elected chairman. Three Conservative MPs served as opposition chairmen of Commons or joint standing committees. In total, close to 90 of the 101 Conservative MPs held jobs within caucus. A number of coordinating bodies were established to ensure direction and consistency throughout this far-flung structure. The multitude of caucus jobs seemed designed to avoid any appearance of a dominating elite and to combat potential restiveness among members.

When Clark was leader, several bodies were created to ensure coherence in the party's approaches. First, there was the national caucus executive composed of the party leader, the chairman of the national caucus, the House leader, two deputy House leaders, the secretary of caucus, and three caucus representatives. There was also a steering committee with a somewhat broader membership and it, in effect, subsumed the role of the executive. The steering committee was composed of the leader, the chairman of the caucus, the House leader and the deputy House leader (committees), the chairman of the committee of chairmen, and the chairmen of the subject-area committees. The chairman of the committee of policy chairmen chaired the steering committee. Its role was to plan House strategy and discuss party discipline and morale. Steering committee deliberations and activities were communicated to the full caucus by the House leader and the chief opposition whip.

On September 8, 1983, Brian Mulroney announced the chairmen of the nine caucus committees and the members of a planning and priorities committee of caucus.[28] Chaired by the leader, all but one of the twelve members of the priorities and planning committee were former members of the cabinet during the Clark government. The press release announcing these appointments offered no description of the role of the new committee. It was unclear whether it replaced the steering committee. Under Mulroney, the opposition caucus committees were apparently given the difficult and time-consuming task of reviewing the government's spending envelopes and fitting the party's proposed policies within the financial resources of the envelopes. The priorities and planning committee took the work of the individual policy committees and sought to fit their analyses into an overall fiscal framework. The entire analysis was then reviewed by a special committee of outside experts and selected frontbenchers. Eventually, the whole caucus held a two-day meeting at Mont St. Marie, Quebec, to discuss the final results of this complicated process of policy development. These developments did not override the short-term tactical preoccupations that normally dominated caucus discussions. However, they represented the furthest extension to date of the policy development role of an opposition caucus and brought more Conservative MPs than ever before into contact with senior public servants, who had been given permission by the Liberal government to offer factual background information on government operations.

In addition to caucus committees, there was also a daily question period strategy meeting attended by the party leader (when he was available), the House leader, the deputy House leader (question period), the whips and the director of the research office. The main purpose of the meeting was to reach agreement on which matters were most urgent and which should be the basis for the lead-off question at the start of question period. One of two deputy House leaders was responsible for orchestrating question period activity, assisted by a staff member (called a policy coordinator) from the research office. This individual prepared a brief "morning document" that summarized major overnight news stories, the latest statistics on unemployment, and so on. The director of research, who was present at the morning strategy meeting, followed up assignments made at the meeting. Just before the Commons opened for the day, the deputy House leader met with all those caucus members who wished to raise questions. At that point, new questions might have arisen because of government news releases or research done by individual MPs or the research office.

A list of MPs who were to ask questions was then submitted to the speaker. The trend toward a more organized and coherent approach to the use of question period created some tension between the role of the party and the needs of individual members to raise matters of concern to them or their constituents. An informal division of question time was followed, with the first 20 minutes allotted to the frontbenchers and the other half available to individual backbenchers.

Prior to February 1982 the party leader appointed the chairman of the national caucus and three caucus representatives to serve on the national executive. Joe Clark, who was then leader of the party, agreed to secret-ballot elections to fill these positions, although there was media speculation that he was forced to accept the change after he announced his opposition to an early party vote on a leadership convention.[29] Those elected were believed to favour an early convention.

The first elected chairman of national caucus was Ron Huntington (British Columbia). Also elected were Elmer MacKay (Nova Scotia), Allan Lawrence (Ontario), and Peter Elzinga (Alberta). Bill McKnight, who had previously been appointed chairman by Clark, was defeated by Huntington. Clark said that he could have arranged for a slate of his own appointments to be elected but did not because he believed in caucus democracy.

By the end of 1982 media speculation was rife about demands within caucus for a leadership review. In December 1982 Huntington threatened to resign as chairman of caucus after reports of what had been said in caucus appeared in the media.[30] In January 1983, at a party convention in Winnipeg, Clark stepped down as leader and announced he would run for a renewed mandate as leader. The annual elections for caucus executive were held in February 1983 and Huntington, who had been criticized for campaigning openly for a leadership convention, decided not to run again for the post of caucus chairman. Another MP from British Columbia, Benno Friesen, was elected chairman. The three caucus members on the national executive were also changed. When Mulroney took over the party after the June 1983 convention, Friesen was reappointed (not elected) to serve as chairman.

The weekly meeting of full caucus on Wednesday from 9:30 to noon followed a regular format:

- call to order;
- health of caucus — reports on illnesses and deaths of interest to caucus members;
- whips' remarks on attendance at votes and in the House and committees;
- leader's report and reports from regional caucuses and from caucus committee chairmen, with the leader's remarks lasting approximately ten to fifteen minutes;
- House leader's report, dealing with forthcoming House business and arrangements agreed to with the government House leader;

- open forum; and
- leader's summation.

No formal agenda was printed for national caucus meetings. Speeches by members were limited to three to five minutes, except those introducing major agenda items for discussion. The time limit also applied to regional caucus reports.

From time to time the Conservative caucus held special sessions outside the national capital. The practice began in 1973 when Stanfield was leader, and the first meeting was held in a Vancouver hotel.[31] In addition to MPs, party candidates for British Columbia ridings and other local party officials attended the closed, two-day caucus. Invited specialists spoke on western issues such as seaport development, forestry, fisheries and mining. "Immersion visits" to study regional problems were subsequently held in other cities. The logistics of bringing a caucus of 101 MPs and 24 senators, plus the pressures of parliamentary business in Ottawa, prevented such mobile caucuses from becoming a regular event.

As government activity has grown in complexity, the official opposition has been forced to introduce specialization among its members if they are to serve as intelligent critics of ministers and their departments. This has led to the development of the so-called "shadow cabinet" — individuals assigned specific responsibilities for scrutinizing departments, questioning ministers in Parliament, and coordinating the study of subject areas within caucus committees (see Ort, 1979). While the term enjoys wide usage in the media, successive opposition leaders have avoided its use in public statements preferring instead to use the terms "caucus spokesman" or "designated critic" to describe the arrangements for frontbench opposition. The term "shadow cabinet" has been avoided to prevent giving the impression of an inner circle and to convey the message that appointment to one of these posts does not imply a commitment to a cabinet post in the event of the party forming a government.

Selection of caucus spokesmen is essentially the prerogative of the party leader. Leaders usually consult with their own staff and certain caucus members on their choices, and eventually the lists are presented to caucus for its approval. Principles of regional representation similar to those that condition appointments to actual cabinet posts are followed in constructing shadow cabinets. An opposition leader may use appointments as a way to placate disgruntled groups, to advance certain policy positions in caucus deliberations, or to promote the careers of promising younger MPs. The practice has been to rotate shadow cabinet positions frequently (Ort, 1979, pp. 55–57). The size of the shadow cabinet has increased over the years; it rose to 45 members under Clark in 1978. In June 1984, there were 34 spokesmen and an equal number of deputies. A number of the spokesmen served as chairmen and vice-chairmen of nine caucus committees. The party spokesmen were expected to prepare recommendations on government bills for approval in the appropriate caucus committee and eventually by full caucus. They were expected to lead the debate on such bills in the House and arrange for other speakers through consultation with the House leader and the whip. They were also expected to organize and lead the opposition's examinations of bills and estimates within the standing committees of the House of Commons. Often they took the lead in questioning ministers during question period. They also served as contact points for the media and outside groups. Each of the policy coordinators employed by the party's research office was assigned to several specific areas of public policy and was expected to work closely with individual critics and caucus committees for that area.

The 1983 Oberle report noted that "an overwhelming majority" of caucus favoured the adoption of a formal shadow cabinet system. Such a system would have to include the assumption that the shadow minister would become the minister of that portfolio when the party assumed office. "Only such an understanding," it was argued, "justified the time he/she will spend learning about the operations of that ministry" (Oberle, 1983, p. 12). In order to give caucus some input into the leader's selection of spokespersons, a secret rating sheet would be used to allow members to evaluate annually the performance of shadow ministers and other caucus officers appointed by the leader. Twenty-five percent of the caucus could request a review of performance at any time. The leader's response to ratings would be at his discretion. The committee also urged measures to reward members on a seniority basis so as to ensure them a continuing role. Despite the assertion of majority support, the rating system was seen as "too provocative a measure and was replaced with an assurance of frequent consultation and additional personnel assigned to caucus liaison" (Oberle, 1983, p. 43).

By June 1984 there were nine caucus committees: agriculture, federal-provincial relations and constitutional reform, cultural affairs, justice and legal affairs, energy and resources, fisheries, economic development and job creation, social affairs, and external affairs and defence. Membership on these policy committees was by interest; anyone could serve, and usually the membership paralleled the party's contingent on the corresponding House of Commons committees. While full caucus was closed to staff from the party's research office and to the research assistants of individual MPs, such individuals were allowed to attend caucus committee meetings. A policy coordinator from the research office served with each caucus committee. Outside witnesses, including public servants, periodically attended policy committees to provide expert advice. Prior clearance from the minister was necessary before public servants appeared in such settings and it was understood that their contribution would be strictly factual in nature.

Party policy positions were to be worked out initially in the caucus committees, sent to the priorities and planning committee, and eventually adopted by the full caucus. According to the Oberle report, the committees should be "the cornerstone" of the policy development process, the forum where "the experience and intellectual capital" of members can be drawn upon. Into these committees, it was suggested, "flow the letters of ordinary Canadians, the research work and recommendations of research institutes and academics, and the testimony of experts in many fields" (Oberle, 1983, p. 22). Policy papers adopted by caucus should receive wide distribution within the extra-parliamentary wing of the party, should be the subject of regional policy seminars, and eventually should be approved by a national policy convention of the party.

It was recognized that the model entailed some compromise of the leader's traditional right to declare policy unilaterally. Oberle noted, "Caucus members feel strongly that a system can be created in which the authority of the leader is protected, but the responsibility for policy development shared among a larger body" (p. 22). The Oberle report argued further that "an extension of the policy formation process will stimulate interest in both the party and the specific policies, while encouraging early working compromises between ideological wings of the party currently forced to capture the favour of a single individual" (p. 23).

There was a strong element of optimism in these forecasts of the benefits from the new approach. On the matter of the autonomy of the leader, Mulroney made several policy statements during his leadership campaign and shortly after his victory that conflicted with existing caucus policy. For example, he said that he would tear up the Kirby report on the Atlantic fisheries, while the caucus position was that the report did not go far enough in supplying help to the ailing industry. He said that a Conservative government would not compensate financially a separatist Parti Québécois government that opted out of certain shared-cost, federal-provincial programs. The caucus had been on record since 1981 as favouring compensation.[32]

Caucus committees have been used for many years to bridge ideological and regional disagreements, but at times the cleavages have simply been too wide. When Clark was leader, western and Ontario MPs clashed over energy policy and the party never succeeded in developing a coherent and politically salable energy policy. The controversial plan to dismantle Petro-Canada, which apparently hurt the party electorally, "reflected the views of those who happened to occupy the key shadow cabinet positions" (Simpson, 1980, p. 159). More recently, a split in the party's external affairs committee was revealed when MP Doug Roche (Edmonton South) wrote in a financial newspaper that the "new right" approach to foreign policy was achieving predominance.[33] He described this "school of thought" as espousing massive military spending, cuts in foreign aid, support for military dictatorships and confrontation with the Soviet Union. This was contrasted with the traditional Canadian approach, which emphasized foreign aid, disarmament, improved relations with the Soviets, and cooperation but not necessarily agreement with the United States. Both the party leader and the external affairs critic (Sinclair Stevens) glossed over the apparent differences, arguing that the party was not irrevocably divided.[34] Subsequently, Roche announced his plans to retire from political life. It was not the first time that his views represented a minority opinion in caucus.

In other fields, the policy committees worked very successfully. In agriculture and transportation, where the party benefited from having numerous members with direct, practical experience, the committees produced interesting and innovative policy blueprints. In April 1983, for example, the party released a ten-point agricultural policy statement directed mainly at the problem of crippling interest rates.[35] Contrary to media reports that it was an instant election gimmick, the Conservatives' mortgage interest deductibility scheme presented during the 1979 federal election was in fact a product of a lengthy process of discussion with a caucus committee and full caucus.

The Conservatives have also experimented with the use of caucus task forces for policy development. A number of these were appointed during Joe Clark's tenure as party leader; for example, a caucus task force was used to consult widely on the 1982 budget. In September 1983, Brian Mulroney announced the formation of five task forces, dealing with youth unemployment, accountability of Crown corporations, productivity enhancement in the public and private sector, tax simplification, and technological displacement and manpower retraining. Each of the task forces was co-chaired by an MP and a senator. When a Conservative task force completed cross-country hearings on the tax collection practices of Revenue Canada, it issued a report and the chairman (Perrin Beatty) was granted an opportunity to review the recommendations with the Minister of National Revenue. Task forces appear to have been a useful innovation to bring together parliamentarians from all regions, to make greater use of senators, and to allow the party to respond to emerging issues.

When in opposition, the Progressive Conservative caucus operated eight regional caucuses: Atlantic, 13 MPs; Quebec, one MP; Ontario, 38 MPs; Manitoba, 5 MPs; Saskatchewan, 7 MPs; Alberta, 21 MPs; British Columbia, 16 MPs; and the Yukon and Northwest Territories, 2 MPs. To these totals must be added the party's senators from each of the provinces and territories, although not all senators were active in party caucuses. As it was not possible to gather information on each of the regional caucuses, the impressions described below must necessarily be selective.

Most regional caucuses met weekly, usually on Tuesdays, but the smaller ones only met as business required. Two or three weeks sometimes would pass between meetings of the Atlantic caucus. In the case of Saskatchewan, the chairman of the provincial caucus canvassed MPs on Mondays and Tuesdays to determine whether there were any problems that would require a meeting. A regular meeting had been tried previously but it was difficult to find a time convenient to all members. Chairmen of regional caucuses were elected annually, but in the smaller caucuses the process was very informal. As one MP explained, "I was 'railroaded' into the job of regional caucus chairman when I first came down here. Nobody really wants the job."

Announcements of regional caucus meetings usually indicated the topics to be discussed and any speakers who had been invited to attend. During the interview stage of this study, the Ontario caucus heard a presentation from the Association of Francophones Outside of Quebec and had recently held a joint federal and provincial caucus meeting in Toronto. An MP described the meeting: "We got together with our provincial colleagues to discuss five main issues which we felt might come up in the next eighteen months, and we wanted to be, if not 'singing from the same song sheet,' at least aware of the provincial party's position." This was the first time such a meeting had been held in Ontario, but federal-provincial caucus meetings had been held in Alberta in the past. The topics that surfaced in regional and provincial caucuses tended to be local matters or concerns arising from the impact of national policies. The Atlantic caucus discussed such problems as the upkeep of wharves, the reduction of the salmon season, the level of freight rate subsidies on feed grain, Via Rail service, Canada Post service, or Eastern Provincial Airlines schedule difficulties. Crown corporation and department officials occasionally attended such meetings to answer questions.

Not surprisingly, the regional caucuses were uneven in their quality and effectiveness. Their influence was not dependent solely, or even mainly, upon the size of their membership. The type of issue at stake and the quality of regional representatives were also important, according to MPs. An Atlantic MP who had ceased to attend his regional caucus on a regular basis explained why:

> The Atlantic caucus is weak. There are too many prima donnas and too much focus on constituency problems. The quality of MPs from the Atlantic region is not high, much less high than it once was with towering figures like Robert Stanfield, Gordon Fairweather and David McDonald.

Ontario, with the largest membership, was regarded by the MPs interviewed as the most effective caucus. According to one Ontario MP, members of the provincial caucus were conscious of the dangers of imposing their will upon national caucus:

> On the Crow's Nest Pass issue, for example, I think the western members played a very important role in making Ontario members more aware of all aspects of the issue. . . . The crucial factor is the way members handle themselves in presenting a regional issue. If you are going to lobby, you have to be diplomatic and political in what you are trying to do.

A western Conservative still sensed an underlying bias in favour of central Canada:

> Let's face it. When you are a political party the name of the game is to win and you have to do those things that will gain the party seats in an election. When Ontario and Quebec have the majority of seats, that fact colours the thinking of the leader and the caucus. You can have the best policies in the world, but if you cannot win, they are no good to you or to anyone else.

Very little time at national caucus was normally spent on regional caucus reports unless a matter was regarded as urgent or very important. During the 1983 leadership campaign, regional caucuses met less frequently. They have never returned to their previous level of activity.

The Conservative MPs questioned agreed that achievement of a consensus in national caucus was sometimes difficult. Ideological disagreements on such issues as energy have placed regional caucuses in conflict. Since votes were not held in caucus, the role of the leader was important in forging a consensus. One MP praised Clark's role as a conciliator:

> Mr. Clark was a superb debater in caucus. He was very incisive and more effective in caucus than in any other forum. He was a first-class assimilator of ideas. He made a practice of listening attentively to individuals and then weaving together all the different points of view within caucus.

Another MP suggested that during the initial "honeymoon" period the caucus granted Mulroney considerable latitude in interpreting the nature of the caucus consensus. MPs agreed that a leader could exercise moral suasion with the caucus by "tipping his hand" as to the direction he felt things should go.

The weakness of the Progressive Conservative caucus as a vehicle for regional accommodation was based on the lack of elected Quebec members. Several approaches were used to try to ensure Quebec input. An advisor on Quebec was appointed to the leader's office, and several bilingual MPs from other provinces worked with the lone Quebec MP, the five Conservative senators from Quebec, and staff people to form a "quasi-caucus" for the province. In addition, efforts were made to ensure that at least one Quebec representative sat on the party's task forces.

The main staff support to all caucus activities was provided through the research office.[36] The office's staff complement consisted of a director, an administrative assistant, twelve policy coordinators, two clerical staff, and two librarians. Each policy coordinator was assigned to specific areas of public policy and worked with the appropriate caucus committee and party spokesmen. The research office prepared a précis of every government bill, drafted amendments and motions, supplied background material for use in budget debates and in opposition "supply day" debates, operated a press clipping service and historical files, and produced longer detailed reports on current issues. In addition, most MPs employed researchers, although some chose to use their staff budgets for staff that were largely secretarial and clerical. The presence of researchers in members' offices reduced the workload of the research office but not its basic worth, since the office enabled the development of expertise and continuity when the designated spokesmen changed duties.

The eight Conservative MPs interviewed for this study were satisfied in most respects with the structure and procedure of their caucus. They felt that the caucus had adjusted to the change in leadership and to structural changes. It would not be surprising to find dissatisfaction with certain aspects of caucus operations. Prolonged periods in opposition and a recent, short-lived government were bound to produce frustrations that would be directed at the leader and the caucus process. Still, all the MPs saw caucus as essential and as an important opportunity to exert influence within the party.

The New Democratic Party Caucus

The NDP, and the CCF before it, has always prided itself on the calibre of its parliamentary caucus and the positive nature of its contribution to the policy process (Young, 1969, chap. 5). Part of the reason for its strong reputation has been the general ethos of the party, which assigns a high value to free debate and the careful preparation of policy positions. Successive party leaders have encouraged collective decision making on policy and tactical issues. While the freedom granted to caucus members has led on occasion to well-publicized and painful splits within the party, in general it has served to bolster party solidarity.

Because of the smaller size of its parliamentary group, the NDP has not employed caucus committees to the same extent as the major parties. Instead, policy approaches and strategies have more often been worked out in full caucus. The party's designated critics chair policy committees that come into existence in response to parliamentary business. Any interested member can serve on a committee. The party leader chooses the designated critics: he asks party members to state their preferences and then prepares a list of party spokesmen that is voted on by full caucus.

NDP critics are expected to monitor the activities of government agencies in their field, to lead debates on bills, and to take the lead in question period. In addition, they are expected to act as party spokesmen outside the Commons, including, of course, the media. Each critic is supported by a researcher from the party's research office, although with 31 MPs and only 7 researchers most critics are obliged to share staff members. They can, of course, draw upon their own office staff.

The chairman of the national caucus has always been elected, as are the chairmen of regional caucuses. Unlike the caucuses of the two main parties, the NDP caucus circulates an agenda for national caucus and holds formal votes. Agreement on policy is usually easy to obtain, but well-publicized disagreements do occur, such as Lorne Nystrom's opposition to the party's stand in support of the 1982 constitutional package.

In an earlier period the NDP caucus was weighted in favour of Ontario, but in the last Parliament 24 of its 31 members were from western Canada. On paper there were four regional caucuses — Ontario with six MPs, Manitoba with seven, Saskatchewan with seven, and British Columbia with eleven — but only the British Columbia caucus met regularly. The others met periodically, depending upon the issues that arose. Outside groups occasionally addressed regional caucuses and on rare occasions public servants attended. The Saskatchewan caucus, for example, met with a Via Rail official to talk about discontinuance of passenger service. The regional weakness of the NDP in Quebec and the Atlantic provinces is a long-standing problem. At its 1983 policy convention in Regina only five of the 1,433 registered delegates were from Quebec. Not counting party officials, the four Atlantic provinces were represented by only a dozen rank-and-file delegates.[37] A party that purportedly bases its appeal upon class considerations might not regard such regional underrepresentation as seriously as the other parties, which see themselves as "honest brokers" among different regions and interests.

NDP caucus officers (chairman, vice-chairman, secretary and treasurer) are elected annually. Along with the House leader, his deputy, the whip and the party leader, they form the executive committee of caucus. It meets daily to plan the strategy for question period. The weekly caucus meetings include reports from the party leader, the House leader, and the whip. Unlike the case of the other parties, non-parliamentarians regularly attend the NDP caucus, including staff from the leader's office, some members of the caucus research office, and a representative from the Canadian Labour Congress.

An Overview of Caucus Operations and Some Directions for Possible Reforms

In testifying before the 1982 Special Committee on Standing Orders and Procedure, Douglas Fisher, a former MP and advisor to the Canadian Bar Association's committee on parliamentary reform, noted that

> MPs spend between nine to twelve hours a week in caucus. Now caucus is the great unknown. . . . It seems to me one of the real problems is that so much energy and some of the best efforts of MPs of all parties go into caucus work and get, in a public sense, no recognition at all. But it is also apparent that in many ways an awful lot of what you do, attitudes, the whole thing is congealed in caucus. I suggest that this is one of the things that you really have to take a look at, the operation of the caucus system, just for this one thing, to get it out in the open.[38]

It is true that most Canadians are either unaware of the existence of caucus or deeply suspicious about its impact on their elected representatives. An editorial expressed the negative image of caucus and party discipline:[39]

It turns honest men into rogues, under the unholy pretext of being good team men and party regulars. This is the essential factor in our parliamentary procedure which has to be changed if we are to find good men and honest men to represent us in Ottawa.

This study disagrees with such sweeping negative assessments of caucus. Caucus is an essential element of the parliamentary system. Caucus meetings serve a variety of purposes: they allow for the frank, private exchange of information and opinion on parliamentary, partisan and other matters. When a party is in office, caucus represents an opportunity to influence legislation, spending and the administration of programs. Since caucus discussions are secret, it is impossible to document the actual influence of caucus. However, the testimony collected from cabinet ministers and government MPs makes it clear that caucus is able to block, delay, and modify the legislative proposals presented by ministers. Responsibility for legislation and spending does not rest with caucus: it resides with ministers who answer to Parliament. Government caucus represents an opportunity for MPs to attempt privately to convince ministers to introduce legislative changes, spend funds, or change the way programs operate. While the government caucus usually reacts to cabinet initiatives, it is also a factor in the planning of legislation. Ministers, even public servants, anticipate caucus reactions to legislation. Since the opposition parties can almost always be counted upon to be critical and vote against legislation, but cannot block it in a majority government situation, ministers see their main legislative task as convincing a majority of their own supporters to go along with their plans. In this way, caucus helps to set the parameters of what legislation is judged to be politically acceptable.

Caucuses also play a role in devising the parliamentary strategy and tactics to be employed by their parties. However, contrary to the results of an earlier study, this was not found to be a major part of caucus deliberations (Kornberg, 1967; Kornberg and Mishler, 1976). In this respect the government and opposition caucuses differed, as was indicated earlier. The opposition caucus spent more time on tactical issues, because they did not have the initiative in terms of policy making and were expected to respond, often on short notice, to government plans. The main staple of opposition contributions to the parliamentary process is rhetoric and criticism.

Opposition parties have a vested interest in highlighting disagreements with government proposals, since they can then argue that the government is not acting on the basis of a consensus. This often leads opposition parties to stress defects in the process of policy making (such as the failure by governments to consult affected groups) more than substantive disagreements. The information advantage enjoyed by the government because of the backing of the public service also accounts for this pattern. Parliamentary delay is one way in which opposition parties seek to extract concessions from government. Delay requires knowledge of the rules, and here the party House leaders enjoy an enormous advantage over most MPs, who regard parliamentary procedure as an arcane, technical and difficult matter. Usually MPs defer, therefore, to the expertise of their House leaders. This tendency is less strong in the opposition caucuses. In the government caucus, members recognize that the House leader has the difficult job of making all the pieces of the legislative jigsaw puzzle fit together and obtaining the passage of the maximum possible amount of legislation during the crowded parliamentary timetable.

Caucus meetings contribute in several ways to party solidarity and unity. They permit intraparty agreements to be hammered out behind closed doors. The caucus has been likened to a "huddle" and a half-time "pep talk" in football. It is in the secrecy of the huddle that the plays are called. It is in caucus that the "coaches" give rousing speeches about "team play" in order to boost the morale of the players, particularly those who are "riding the bench" and will not see much action. Silent and disgruntled MPs could instigate public and politically damaging splits within the party. Caucus represents a safety valve for discontent, a "gripe session" and an opportunity "to let off steam."

In the competitive arena of Parliament, political parties could not settle their policy disagreements and plan their strategy in the open, because their opponents would exploit divisions in their ranks. The oral tradition of the caucuses of the two leading parties — no printed agendas, no minutes, no recorded votes, and no press releases — reflects in part the parties' desire to preserve the confidentiality of caucus deliberations. It also reflects the search for consensus, since the casting of votes and issuance of formal announcements would hinder parties from taking refuge in ambiguity when agreement is hard to reach. As discussed earlier, caucus also allows party leaders to rally support for party policies and positions. It is tempting to dismiss such sales pitches as manipulation or "boosterism." Caucus plays an educative role, alerting MPs to implications they might not have foreseen. Moreover, the importance of group dynamics and collegiality to the success of political parties in the performance of their parliamentary roles should not be underestimated.

Politics is not simply a matter of debating and adopting party policies. Equally important are party loyalty, morale, seeing the party through the rough spots, enthusiasm and camaraderie. The maintenance of party discipline and unity is far more a function of such social-psychological considerations than of coercive sanctions or rewards. The advantages of party cohesion are not seen by most MPs in personal terms, i.e., as advancing their own careers. Rather, party unity is seen as a necessity within the adversarial system of Parliament. For MPs who do not aspire to leadership positions — and such individuals do exist — the parties must offer rewards other than advancement: a sense of participation in important events, opportunities for personal development, some measure of public recognition, and a sense of belonging. Furthermore the communication that flows within caucus is not one way, with leaders telling followers what they should do. Leaders feel obliged to listen to caucus and they benefit from doing so. Leaders who neglect the opinions of their MPs soon find themselves out of touch not only with their parties, but also with the country as a whole.

Party caucuses have the potential for facilitating regional input into party discussions. The regional imbalances evident in the party representation in the last Parliament detracted from the role of caucuses as sounding boards of regional opinion. Quebec concerns were represented predominantly by Liberal MPs, while the West was represented predominantly by opposition MPs. As noted earlier, this situation was not unprecedented; in fact, past governments have often lacked breadth of support across the country. Still, there are several reasons why such imbalances could be judged undesirable.

First, a region like the West, which historically has placed the majority of its MPs on the opposition benches, may be at a real disadvantage in competing for policies favourable to the region and other government benefits. Governments respond to sectional and other pressures, and a region may suffer when it fails to place members within the government caucus. It may lose, in other words, in terms of allocation and policy responsiveness.

Such a region may also lose in terms of symbolic responsiveness. Regional justice may not be seen to be done, regardless of how fair the actual distribution of tangible benefits is, when a particular region lacks a credible presence within the government caucus. Appearances matter in politics; if a governing party lacks broad support, the policies adopted by Parliament will not have complete legitimacy. Having a disproportionately small number of government MPs from a given region will create the suspicion that the needs of that region will be neglected.

It is more difficult to determine whether service responsiveness declines for the citizens of a region that fails to elect government MPs. Answering the question would require knowledge of what advantages, if any, government MPs enjoy in intervening with ministers and public servants on behalf of their constituents. Members from all parties regard constituency service as important, so it seems unlikely that government MPs make any extra effort in this regard. The government MPs interviewed for this study indicated that caucus meetings were not an appropriate place to contact ministers about constituency problems. Private meetings and correspondence with ministers are the normal ways of handling such cases. Such routes are also open to opposition MPs, and ministers will frequently seek to avoid an embarrassing question in the House by ensuring that prompt attention is paid to such queries. Furthermore, ministers are usually approached only after an MP has failed to get a satisfactory answer from the bureaucracy. The first approach with a constituent's problem is to look for assistance within the complex maze of departments and agencies. Given that the bureaucracy operates programs and applies regulations impartially, according to universalistic criteria, there should be no favouritism shown toward the cases brought to the attention of public servants by government MPs. Much more research needs to be done on the extent and importance of the role of MPs as intermediaries with the federal bureaucracy.

When party representation is skewed, issues that might otherwise be debated in functional terms are transformed into regional policy debates. The parties are not capable of resolving such debates internally; instead, they spill over onto the floor of Parliament when contending regional blocs face each other across the aisles. All these problems might be offset if the parties alternated regularly in forming the government, but this has not occurred with great frequency.

The parties have recognized the importance of regional factors in Canadian politics by establishing regional party caucuses. On the government side, these regional caucuses are linked in important ways to regional ministers within cabinet. Regional ministers are expected to play a lead role in organizing their regional caucuses. They are expected to ensure that there is regional understanding and support for government policies. They play a large role in supervising party organization and party affairs for their region. They are expected to keep in touch with regional opinion leaders in various fields. They lobby with other ministers to obtain financial benefits for their areas. As they are also consulted on the distribution of patronage, there is a tendency to deny the existence of powerful regional ministers, with the result that few members of the public are aware of their role within government and party operations. To be underrepresented within the government caucus is not necessarily to be underrepresented in cabinet, if a regional grouping is led by a powerful minister.

The influence of regional caucuses within national caucus is determined by several factors. Size is obviously important, but it is not the determining factor in most cases of interregional conflict. All parties recognize the importance of heeding legitimate regional concerns. The quality of regional spokespersons is very important. A regional caucus can enjoy influence disproportionate to its size if its members are experienced, knowledgeable, articulate, persistent and persuasive in influencing party leaders. As a former MP stated:

> This numbers business is a mirage. I think that Jack Pickersgill was worth 30 members from his region. Today, I think that Allan MacEachen is worth 40 members. It is the quality of the people you send, not just send them once but send them back again and again so that they become key people.

The unity and clear sense of political direction of a regional caucus enhances its chances of success. Another factor is the willingness of cabinet ministers or the opposition party leader to be persuaded. The level of activity and the quality of representation achieved by regional caucus will fluctuate over time.

The Liberal and Progressive Conservative parties' experience of being mainly in office and in opposition, respectively, has helped to shape what might be called the internal culture of the parliamentary wing of each party. By force of circumstance, the Liberals have been compelled to search more frequently and comprehensively for a working definition of "the national interest." The national perspective adopted by the federal caucus sometimes brings it into conflict with the provincial wings of the party. Provincial Liberal parties have found it politically advantageous, as well as proper in terms of their electoral role, to maintain some policy distance between themselves and their partisan colleagues at the federal level. Wider trends in electoral competition, party organization, financing and ideology, as well as personality factors have also encouraged policy divisions between the federal and provincial wings of the party. With more or less conviction, Liberal MPs have propagated the notion that there is one party rather than semi-autonomous federal and provincial wings. The fact that the Liberals have not been in office at the provincial level in recent years has reduced the level of intraparty conflict. The provincial wings of the party may have seen the national connection as an asset in terms of patronage and a window into on-going intergovernmental relations. Overall, the long period of officeholding at the national level has probably contributed to a widening of the gap between the two wings of the Liberal Party.

In contrast, the Progressive Conservative caucus in the recent past has been more provincial in outlook. A national party that has been in opposition for prolonged periods attracts to its ranks individuals who resent national policies. If the party is in office provincially, as has been the case recently with seven provincial Progressive Conservative governments, the national party becomes dependent to some extent upon the provincial wings. Not only can the provincial parties be an important source of financial and organizational support, they can also serve as a source of policy analysis and criticism to be used by Conservative members of the federal Parliament. Two of the eight Conservative MPs interviewed for this study described their role in part as agents in Ottawa acting on behalf of their provincial government.

The usefulness of the national caucus of a party to its provincial counterpart in office was illustrated by the most recent round of constitutional negotiations (1980–82). The Conservative premiers of both Ontario and Alberta sought to influence the respective provincial caucuses of their national party (Cairns, 1985). The national party in Parliament justified its highly critical posture and parliamentary tactics of obstruction by citing the lack of broad national support for the Liberal constitutional plan, and its position was reinforced by the presence of influential allies outside Parliament. The absence of elected federal Liberals from west of Manitoba required that the Trudeau government, at least for reasons of public symbolism, seek the support of the NDP caucus in Parliament. The eventual decision by the national NDP to go along with the Liberal plan provoked deep splits within the national caucus and between the national party and the only NDP provincial government at that time (Saskatchewan). Even the NDP, united to a greater extent by a shared ideology, could not escape the force of regional cleavages.

Disagreements among the Conservative provincial governments in the Atlantic region surfaced within the regional parliamentary caucus of the party (McKinley, 1981, pp. 110–12). For example, during the brief Clark government, the federal Fisheries Minister, James McGrath from Newfoundland, authorized the use of freezer trawlers in the Atlantic fishery. This action was opposed by the Conservative premier of Newfoundland, Brian Peckford, and had been rejected by the former Liberal minister of fisheries. It has been speculated that McGrath found himself caught in cross pressures and seemed to have yielded to the demands of the Nova Scotia contingent, which then dominated the Atlantic caucus. Conversely, in 1978, the Atlantic Conservative caucus was unified in its opposition to a Liberal government plan to tighten the unemployment insurance regulations, a step opposed by the Conservative provincial governments in the region. The majority in the national caucus favoured the clampdown but was persuaded to change its position, vote against the bill, and accept the principle of variable entrance requirements for UI eligibility as a way to avoid economic hardship for the Atlantic region.

Regional caucus reports do not normally take up a great deal of time at national caucus. This reflects the fact that most issues do not polarize regions against one another. All MPs interviewed for this study indicated that they regarded regional representation as an important part of their role, but most of the examples they cited could just as accurately be described as specific concerns of a functional nature. The reduction of the salmon fishing season on the East Coast or the discontinuance of Via Rail passenger service in the West are typical examples. The problems are important to a region but do not pit regions against each other. A former Atlantic MP suggested that there may be a generalized sense of discontent in western Canada but his region did not feel it had done so badly. There was not the same suspicion of the tyranny of caucus as was found in the West. He went on to suggest that regional representation was so vague an expression as to be almost useless. In his words, "It is better to talk about the real political issues rather than regionalism per se, which is as vaporous as clouds on a summer afternoon." While it is going too far to dismiss regionalism as wisps of nebulosity, this comment reiterates the difficulty of defining the nature of regional issues. In the real world, regional and party considerations overlap and intermingle. Yet there is little doubt that regional sentiments, at least in terms of feeling closer to provincial governments than to the national government, are on the increase among Canadians.

Could any caucus reforms be instituted to deal with growing regionalism? A simple answer would be that political parties should make whatever policy and organizational changes are necessary to appeal effectively to regions where they currently lack support. According to this view, parties should be forced to work at their electoral problems rather than have them solved or alleviated through such constitutional changes as the adoption of proportional representation for the House of Commons or an elected Senate.

A brief word is required on the implications of such reforms for the role of caucus. This study has confirmed that caucus is an important institution within the parliamentary process and that its policy formulation role has been upgraded in recent years. Given the important role of caucus, particularly in the case of the governing party, it should for two reasons be as representative as possible of the regions. First, regional balance would assist the parties in demonstrating policy responsiveness to regional concerns, although it would not guarantee that regional demands would always be met. Second, greater representativeness within caucus, particularly on the government side, would enhance the legitimacy of actions taken by the federal government, and government MPs from a region could serve as spokespersons within their regions on behalf of national policies that are the target of criticism by opposition parties and provincial governments. After the 1980 election, the Trudeau government promised in its Throne Speech to appoint a parliamentary committee that would examine ways to alter the electoral system so as to achieve a higher degree of representativeness and confidence in parliamentary institutions.[40] The aim of the proposal was not just to elect Liberal MPs from Alberta, for example (where none had been elected in 1980), as a way to ensure sensitivity to provincial concerns within the government caucus, but also to have Alberta MPs capable of defending national policies against provincial attacks. The proposal was based upon acceptance of the idea of electoral reform among all parties; it was eventually dropped when conversations among the party leaders revealed that no agreement was possible.[41]

An elected Senate might be another approach to curing regional imbalances within caucuses. Any such plan is fraught with difficulties in a system of responsible cabinet government, and there are good grounds for questioning the political acceptability of such an idea in the foreseeable future. To avoid creating a mirror image of existing party representation within the House of Commons, an elected Senate would have to be based upon some system of proportional representation; otherwise little would be done to alleviate the problem supposedly being addressed.

The remainder of this paper concentrates on more limited changes to the parliamentary caucus. But first, a brief comment: the way caucus operates at present is not accidental. Caucus has evolved over many years into its present structure and approach. It reflects the constitutional order as well as surrounding political forces. The trends that have given the cabinet important advantages and led to a politics centred around leaders have affected the role of caucus. Improvements to the caucus system made during the last decade represent efforts to counteract its ostensible decline, and such changes must win the acceptance of party leaders. The feasibility of any proposed reforms is an essential factor in their potential acceptability.

Proposals for Change

A number of internal reforms to party caucuses could be made without great difficulty. For example, major reports from regional caucuses or policy committees of caucus could be printed and circulated to all members before their discussion in caucus. Members would then have a chance to digest and reflect upon the ideas being presented before going to caucus. Extended caucus sessions could be arranged to allow enough time for serious discussion of substantive reports.

The Progressive Conservative Party's experimentation with task forces, paid for out of party funds, appears to have worked successfully. Such task forces should travel to regions where the party is underrepresented. Well-publicized itineraries should be announced in advance. Contact should be made with journalists in the region to obtain coverage of such tours. Interest groups should be invited to present briefs. The emphasis in task force meetings should be on consultation and dialogue, not on making political speeches. Task force reports should be published and made available to interested Canadians.

Greater use should be made of public servants as a source of background information for caucus policy development. Guidelines would have to be developed to govern appearances before caucus committees or task forces. Prior ministerial approval and a prohibition on policy debate would be necessary. In Australia, public servants regularly appear before party committees, and the result has not been destructive to the neutrality of the public service. The aim is to improve the quality of the partisanship by making MPs from all parties better informed about the background to policy choices.

Improved links to the provincial wings of the party (where these exist) and to the party organization outside Parliament could be valuable. In July 1984, the Liberal Party of Canada examined the creation of a western council to revitalize the party in western Canada, where not a single Liberal sat in a provincial legislature and there were only two MPs.[42] The plan was for the council to consist of provincial party presidents and leaders, Liberal MPs and MLAs (if any), national executive members from the region, and between two and five constituency presidents from each province — about 50 people in all. The council would be disbanded when the party elected a significant number of MPs from the region.

In other situations, where there are members of the party in the provincial legislature, joint federal-provincial caucus meetings should be held periodically to ensure adequate communication between the two levels of the party. The goal should not necessarily be to work out common policy questions, since the members have different electoral mandates.

An innovation introduced by the Liberal caucus was to have sitting MPs from other parts of the country twinned with western ridings to compensate for lack of government representation from the West. Several Liberal MPs interviewed for this study were part of a twinning arrangement. The scheme had not been entirely successful. Some MPs treated their responsibilities for keeping in touch with their adopted riding more seriously than others. Most of the contact was made with local Liberals. Since the twinning plan was set up at the time of the National Energy Program controversy and the constitutional crisis, a Liberal MP suggested that it smacked of "paternalism and arrogance." A Conservative MP related that the visit of a Quebec MP to his twinned Saskatchewan riding was dismissed cynically or humorously by most of the constituents. The benefits of twinning, always seen to be a second- or third-best solution, would appear to be marginal.

Another suggestion has been the establishment of all-party regional caucuses (Standing Committee on Legal and Constitutional Affairs, 1980, p. 41). Such bodies would identify regional needs and aspirations and would monitor the attitudes of provincial governments and legislatures toward federal legislation and programs. Such all-party committees have operated within the British Parliament since the 1930s, and their number increased rapidly during the 1950s (Morgan, 1982). Their popularity reflected the fact that until recently the British House of Commons (unlike the Canadian situation) did not operate a series of standing committees specialized by policy fields and responsible for the review of legislation, spending and program administration. British all-party committees seek to influence government by developing a consensus among backbench MPs on more technical questions, not issues involving deep partisan divisions. Only two of approximately 150 such committees have an explicit regional focus (the Isle of Man group and the Welsh group), but certain functional committees examine issues of greater importance to particular parts of Britain. The committees serve an educative role for members. Though only advisory, they have influenced the technical content of legislation and the implementation of programs.

MPs were questioned about the idea of all-party regional caucuses. Most had not heard of the idea before and felt that it would not work. They felt that partisanship was too entrenched an aspect of Parliament's operation for it to be put aside, even temporarily, in order to pursue a cooperative approach. In their view, the party leadership would not accept all-party regional caucuses because they would diminish the partisan spirit, which would then have to be restored by the next election. There has been limited experimentation with all-party cooperation, for example in the northwestern Ontario region and to a lesser extent in the Atlantic caucus, but there will always be the inhibiting factor of partisanship.

The reaction of MPs was also sought to the concept of a standing House of Commons or joint Senate–House of Commons committee on regional affairs. The committee would identify regional problems, calling to the attention of provincial governments legislation that would affect regional interests and inviting them to present their views either to that committee or to other parliamentary committees. The committee would be mobile, holding hearings across the country. Such a committee for the Senate had been proposed in a 1980 report on Senate reform (Standing Committee on Legal and Constitutional Affairs, 1980, p. 41). The former government leader in the Senate, Ray Perrault, related his disappointment that the idea had not been acceptable to the Liberal government:

> I regard my inability to persuade my Cabinet colleagues that we should establish a standing Senate committee on regional affairs and aspirations as one of the failures of my time as Senate leader; a committee to meet Canadians in the regions, to hear their ideas, to hear their grievances, to meet with economic groups and minority groups . . . with that Senate committee reporting to Parliament its finding and recommendations. Frankly, there was resistance to the ideas by some members of the other place who were apprehensive about any plan to allow a non-elected body to provide Canadians with this substantial opportunity to be heard.[43]

Few MPs had thought about the idea but most agreed that it was worth exploring. Part of the plan might be to make the role of the regional minister less of a clandestine operation. Regional ministers in cabinet would be identified publicly and would appear before the committee to discuss federal programs directed at the region and federal-provincial relations.

MPs agreed that the secrecy surrounding caucus deliberations contributes to the impression that regional interests are being ignored. None offered any solution to this dilemma. The essence of caucus is external secrecy and internal frankness. The institution would not work effectively if it were open to publicity. Even the practice of the Quebec Liberal caucus in issuing press releases was resented by some Liberal MPs because it risked the appearance of internal disagreement when the media and the public had come to expect solidarity.

In Australia and New Zealand, the respective Labour parties require that the cabinet be elected by caucus, but the party leader is permitted to assign portfolios. Such a system would obviously give caucus greater control but would clearly be unacceptable to Canadian party leaders, who have always enjoyed the prerogative of appointment. It is not clear either whether elections would produce norms that now apply to cabinet making. A less dramatic step would be to provide for the presence of the whip in the cabinet's membership, as is the case in Great Britain. This would have perhaps two contradictory effects in terms of caucus autonomy. It would improve communication links between cabinet and caucus, since the whip would be responsible for monitoring backbench opinion. On the other hand, the whip would enjoy additional leverage with caucus colleagues because of his cabinet position.

Various types of procedural reforms within the House of Commons could affect party caucuses. Some of these can be discussed here. Recently, there has been considerable talk about the desirability of allowing more free votes on legislation. Presumably this would allow MPs to act as true regional spokespersons, with greater freedom from party discipline. The reputation of the institution of Parliament might be enhanced if the public saw more voting take place on an individual basis.

Several brief comments on this line of argument are in order. First, nearly all votes in the Commons are already free votes in a technical sense. Presumably a government could indicate in advance that a vote on a particular bill does not involve "confidence," and MPs are therefore free to vote as they please. What is to prevent a government, however, from designating a free vote in public while still pressuring MPs in private to support their position? There might be tactical advantages in doing this. The sources of party cohesion are more psychological than political sanctions. MPs see party voting as natural in a parliamentary system. They believe that the media and the electorate expect party unity. They recognize that voters have not taken favourably to independent mavericks. A system of free votes, however that phrase is interpreted, would not be likely to produce widespread cross-party voting on the floor of the Commons. It would, however, put much greater pressure on the party leadership to persuade their followers in the secret confines of caucus to follow the party line. Free votes would also produce more lobbying efforts directed at individual MPs, more internal caucus bargaining and trade-offs, and further public exposure of the internal disagreements faced by all parties.

Caucus has been a flexible and creative institution. It responds well to changing political forces. There is no neat "organizational fix" to solve the problems of reaching a consensus in a diversified country. There is only so much time, energy and capacity available to caucus. Not all MPs aspire to be policy entrepreneurs; many accept the role of ombudsman on behalf of constituents and loyal supporter of their party leader. Caucus will never find the time and the resources to operate high-level policy seminars that are intellectually satisfying to all its members or to outside observers. The role of caucus is to create understanding of problems and to mobilize support for satisfactory solutions to difficult problems, not to find the perfect answer to every issue.

Notes

This study was completed in October 1984. The author would like to acknowledge the excellent research assistance provided by Ernest Keenes, Political Science, Carleton University, Ottawa. He would also like to thank the Members of Parliament who shared their knowledge and opinion on the operation of party caucuses. Without their cooperation, this study would not have been possible.

1. The most recent proposal is contained in the report of the Special Joint Committee of the Senate and the House of Commons on Senate Reform (Canada, 1984). The proceedings of this committee were consulted for references to the role of parties as "brokers" of regional interests.

2. Secondary sources on party caucuses are very limited. See *Parliamentary Government* 4 (1) (1983) on this topic. See also Cheverette (1981), Oberle (1984) and Pelletier (1981).

3. There is not a great deal written about the operation of the party caucuses. Also, the secrecy surrounding caucus operations compounds the problem of constructing sound generalizations. Accordingly, interviews were conducted with individuals with caucus experience. Included in the group of interviews were several cabinet ministers or former ministers, so that some impression could be gained of the impact of caucus deliberations on individual ministers and the government as a whole. A total of twenty interviews were held: eight Liberals, eight Progressive Conservatives and four New Democratic MPs. The interviewees were selected on the basis of positions occupied in party caucuses and a demonstrated interest in questions of parliamentary reform.

   The interviews were based upon prepared questions but took more the character of a discussion than a straight question-and-answer format. This approach was more consistent with the exploratory nature of the research and the desire to record the perceptions of participants without forcing responses into a highly structured questionnaire. The interviews were conducted by the principal investigator and a research assistant (Ernie Keenes), and lasted approximately 45 minutes on average. Unless the respondent objected, the interviews were tape-recorded and transcribed later. Otherwise, notes were taken and the interview was reconstructed immediately following. In both cases, respondents were promised anonymity, with the hope that this would engender greater frankness.

   In addition to the interviews, contact was made with the research branch of the Library of Parliament to determine whether papers on the subject of caucus had been prepared. The directors of the research offices of each of the three party caucuses were contacted to obtain information on how their operations supported the activities of caucus. The literature on parliamentary caucuses in Canada and in a number of other parliamentary democracies was reviewed, as were the more general works on Canadian politics.

4. Cited in Kendle (1979), p. 229. I am indebted to Professor Kendle for providing me with memoranda from the Bracken papers dealing with caucus organization.

5. See Arthur Blakely, "It Is Precedent Shattering," *Montreal Gazette*, September 19, 1969. The charge was countered by backbencher Pauline Jewett, who claimed that the leaks from cabinet were massive; see Jewett (1968).

6. An excellent discussion of the development of the shadow cabinet within the Progressive Conservative Party is found in Ort (1979).

7. See the remarks of Prime Minister Trudeau, House of Commons, *Debates*, November 15, 1968, p. 2791.

8. House of Commons, *Debates*, February 6, 1970, p. 3295. See also Black (1972).

9. Mark MacGuigan, MP, "The Government Caucus," *Windsor Star*, July 2, 1969, p. 13.

10. John Roberts, MP, "Methods of Giving MPs Independence and Power," *Globe and Mail*, November 21, 1970, p. 7.

11. Richard Gwyn, "Liberal Caucus Has Become a New Power Block in Ottawa," *Ottawa Journal*, April 16, 1974. See also Geoffrey Stevens, "A Changed Caucus," *Globe and Mail*, November 1, 1974.

12. Richard Jackson, "P.C. Caucus Triumphs over Backroom Boys and Eggheads," *Telegraph Journal*, November 24, 1969.

13. Donald Newman, "Confident Stanfield Claims Support of All 70 Tory MPs," *Globe and Mail*, September 10, 1970; and Arthur Blakely, "The Tories Got Around to Quebec . . . But Only Just," *Montreal Gazette*, September 11, 1970.

14. John Rolfe, "Committee Spokesmen Not 'Shadow Cabinet,' Stanfield Makes Clear," *Globe and Mail*, November 17, 1972. See also Caplan (1979).

15. "Open First Free Vote for Caucus Chairman," *Globe and Mail*, March 26, 1970.

16. Canadian Press, "Caucus Chairmanship Cause of Speculation," *Ottawa Citizen*, July 5, 1971.

17. Iain Hunter, "Liberal MPs Upset about Budget Ordered to Keep Criticism Secret," *Ottawa Citizen*, February 11, 1982; Keri Sweetman, "Opposition Gloats over Liberal Dissidents," *Ottawa Citizen*, May 26, 1982; and Andrew Szende, "Action Plan for Economy on Way: PM," *Toronto Star*, June 17, 1982.

18. David Vienneau, "Some Liberals Fear Spending Cuts Will Affect Welfare System," *Toronto Star*, October 6, 1982.

19. Cited in Rivington (1983), p. 5.

20. James Rusk, "Liberal 'Profiles' Carry $158,000 Price," *Globe and Mail*, April 25, 1984.

21. Editorial, "Liberal MPs on the Spot," *Toronto Star*, September 18, 1981.

22. Cited in Rivington (1983), p. 5.

23. Special Joint Committee of the Senate and the House of Commons on Senate Reform, *Minutes of Proceedings and Evidence*, November 3, 1983, p. 14.

24. Correspondence from the Liberal caucus research director, June 28, 1984.

25. Thomas Walkom, "How to Hustle Policy Part of MPs Sales Kit," *Globe and Mail*, July 20, 1983.

26. "Recovery Canada: A Strategy for Members of Parliament," July 1983, p. 3.

27. See also Michael Valpy, "New Ways to Policy," *Globe and Mail*, September 12, 1983.

28. Office of the Leader of the Opposition, News Release, September 8, 1983.

29. Robert MacDonald, "Clark's Foes Win Caucus Top Jobs," *Toronto Sun*, February 18, 1982.

30. Keri Sweetman, "Angry PC Caucus Chairman Threatens to Quit," *Ottawa Citizen*, December 3, 1982.

31. Carl Mollins, "Conservative MPs to Hold Caucus outside of Ottawa for the First Time," *Toronto Star*, October 19, 1973.

32. Michael Valpy, "Dealing with Caucus," *Globe and Mail*, June 15, 1983.

33. Douglas Roche, "A Humanitarian Foreign Policy," *Financial Post*, August 17, 1983.

34. "Foreign Policy Views of 'New Right' Dominate Mulroney Caucus, MP Says," *Toronto Star*, August 18, 1983.

35. "PCs Submit 10-Point Farm Plan," *London Free Press*, April 14, 1983.

36. Correspondence from Geoff Norquay, director, Progressive Conservative research office, May 23, 1984.

37. Don Smith, "A Touch of Irony behind the NDP Compromise Plan," *Toronto Star*, July 4, 1983.

38. See Canada (1983), p. 19.

39. Leslie Roberts, "On the Reform of Parliament," *Montrealer*, November 1965, p. 19.

40. House of Commons, *Debates*, April 14, 1980, p. 6.

41. Ibid., June 9, 1983, p. 26,232.

42. Edward Greenspon, "Westerners Will Call in IOUs and Demand Active Role in National Decision-Making," *Financial Post*, June 21, 1984.

43. See Canada (1984), p. 72.

Bibliography

Aiken, Gordon. 1974. *The Backbencher. Trials and Tribulations of a Member of Parliament*. Toronto: McClelland and Stewart.

Black, Edwin. 1972. "Opposition Research: Some Theories and Practice." *Canadian Public Administration* 15 (1): 24–41.

Cairns, Alan C. 1985. "The Politics of Constitutional Renewal." In *Redesigning the State: The Politics of Constitutional Change*, edited by R. Simeon and Keith Banting. Toronto: University of Toronto Press. Forthcoming.

Canada. Parliament. House of Commons. 1984. Special Joint Committee of the Senate and the House of Commons on the Constitution of Canada. 1972. *Final Report*. Ottawa: Information Canada.

Canada. Parliament. House of Commons. Task Force on Canadian Unity. 1979. *Coming to Terms: The Words of the Debate*. Ottawa: Minister of Supply and Services Canada.

Canada. Parliament. The Senate. 1980. Standing Committee on Legal and Constitutional Affairs. *Report on Certain Aspects of the Canadian Constitution*. Ottawa: Minister of Supply and Services Canada.

Canada. Parliament. House of Commons. Special Committee on Standing Orders and Procedures. 1983. *Tenth Report*. September 30. Ottawa: Minister of Supply and Services Canada.

Canada. Parliament. House of Commons. Special Joint Committee of the Senate and the House of Commons on Senate Reform. 1984. *Report*. Ottawa: Minister of Supply and Services Canada.

Caplan, Gary Michael. 1979. "The Dynamics of Opposition: The Conservative Front Bench, an Analysis and a Proposal." In *The Canadian House of Commons Observed*, edited by Jean-Pierre Gaboury and James Ross Hurley, pp. 239–56. Ottawa: University of Ottawa Press.

Cheverette, G. 1981. "The Government Member: His Relationship with Caucus and Cabinet." *Canadian Parliamentary Review* 4: 5–8.

Clarke, Harold D., Colin Campbell, F.Q. Quo, and Arthur Goddard, eds. 1980. *Parliament, Policy and Representation*. Toronto: Methuen.

Cordeau, Marie. 1979. "Private Members' Hours in the Canadian House of Commons." In *The Canadian House of Commons Observed*, edited by Jean-Pierre Gaboury and James Ross Hurley, pp. 57–68. Ottawa: University of Ottawa Press.

Courtney, J.C. 1978. "Recognition of Canadian Political Parties in Parliament and in Law." *Canadian Journal of Political Science* 11 (1): 33–60.

———. 1980. "Reflections on Reforming the Canadian Electoral System." *Canadian Public Administration* 23 (3): 427–57.

Dahl, Robert A. 1980. *After the Revolution? Authority in a Good Society*. New Haven: Yale University Press.

Dobell, W.M. 1981. "Parliament's Role in Choosing the New Fighter Aircraft." *International Perspectives* (September-October): 9–12.

Elton, David, and Roger Gibbins. 1980. "Electoral Reform: The Need is Pressing, the Time is Now." Report prepared for the Canada West Foundation, Calgary.

English, John. 1977. *The Decline of Politics: The Conservatives and the Party System 1901–1920*. Toronto: University of Toronto Press.

Eulau, Heinz, and Paul D. Karps. 1977. "The Puzzle of Representation: Specifying Components of Responsiveness." *Legislative Studies* 11 (3): 233–54.

Eulau, Heinz, and John Wahlke. 1978. *The Politics of Representation*. Beverly Hills: Sage.

Forsey, Eugene. 1974. *Freedom and Order: Collected Essays*. Toronto: McClelland and Stewart.

Fraser, A. 1969. "Crisis in the House of Commons." *The Table* 38: 59–63.

Gaboury, Jean-Pierre, and James Ross Hurley, eds. 1979. *The Canadian House of Commons Observed*. Ottawa: University of Ottawa Press.

Goodin, Robert E. 1984. "Symbolic Rewards: Being Bought Off Cheaply." *Political Studies* 25 (3): 383–96.

Granatstein, J.L. 1967. *The Politics of Survival: The Conservative Party of Canada, 1939–1945*. Toronto: University of Toronto Press.

Gregory, Roy. "Executive Power and Constituency Representation in United Kingdom Politics." *Political Studies* 27: 63–83.

Hockin, Thomas, ed. 1977. *Apex of Power: The Prime Minister and Political Leadership in Canada*. 2d ed. Scarborough: Prentice Hall.

———. 1979. "Flexible and Structured Parliamentarism: From 1848 to Contemporary Party Government." *Journal of Canadian Studies* 14 (2): 8–17.

Hoffman, David, and Norman Ward. 1970. *Bilingualism and Biculturalism in the Canadian House of Commons*. Ottawa: Queen's Printer.

Irvine, W.P. 1979. *Does Canada Need a New Electoral System*? Kingston: Queen's University, Institute of Intergovernmental Relations.

———. 1982. "Does the Candidate Make a Difference? The Macro-Politics Micro-Politics of Getting Elected." *Canadian Journal of Political Science* 15(4): 755–83.

Jackson, Robert J., and Michael M. Atkinson. 1980. *The Canadian Legislative System: Politicians and Policymaking*. 2d ed. Toronto: Macmillan.

Jewett, Pauline. 1968. "The Reform of Parliament." *Journal of Canadian Studies* : 11–16.

Kendle, John. 1979. *John Bracken: A Political Biography*. Toronto: University of Toronto Press.

King, Anthony. 1969. "Political Parties in Western Democracies." *Polity 2 (2)*: 111–41.

Kornberg, Alan. 1967. *Canadian Legislative Behavior*. New York: Holt Rinehart and Winston.

Kornberg, Alan, and William Mishler. 1976. *Influence in Parliament: Canada*. Durham: Duke University Press.

LaMarsh, Judy. 1969. *Memoirs of a Bird in a Gilded Cage*. Toronto: McClelland and Stewart.

Lyon, Vaughan. 1983. "The Future of Parties — Inevitable — Obsolete?" *Journal of Canadian Studies* 18: 108–31.

MacGuigan, M. 1977. "Backbenchers: The New Committee System and the Caucus." In *Politics: Canada*, edited by Paul Fox, pp. 431–38. 4th ed. Toronto: McGraw-Hill.

March, Roman. 1974. *The Myth of Parliament*. Scarborough: Prentice Hall.

Martin, Paul. 1983. *A Very Public Life, Volume One: Far From Home*. Ottawa: Deneau Publishers.

McCormick, Peter. 1983. "Is the Liberal Party Declining? Liberals, Conservatives, and Provincial Politics 1867–1980." *Journal of Canadian Studies* 18: 88–107.

McCormick, Peter, Ernest C. Manning, and Gordon Gibson. 1981. *Regional Representation*. Calgary: Canada West Foundation.

McKinley, Cindy. 1981. "A Study of the Atlantic Caucuses of the Liberal and the Progressive Conservative Parties." Master of Arts thesis, Queen's University, Kingston.

Mitchell, Austin. 1968. "Caucus: The New Zealand Parliamentary Parties." *Journal of Commonwealth Political Studies* 6: (1) 3–33.

Morgan, G. 1982. "All Party Committees in the House of Commons." *Parliamentary Affairs* 35: 56–65.

Morton, W.L. 1950. *The Progressive Party in Canada*. Toronto: University of Toronto Press.

Munroe, Ronald. 1977. "The Member of Parliament as Representative: The View from the Constituency." *Political Studies* 25 (December): 577–87.

Neilson, W.A.W., and J.C. MacPherson. 1978. *The Legislative Process in Canada: The Need for Reform*. Toronto: Butterworth.

Norton, Philip. 1979. "The Organization of Parliamentary Parties." In *The House of Commons in the Twentieth Century*, edited by S.A. Walkland, pp. 7–68. Oxford: Clarendon Press.

———. 1983. "Party Committees in the House of Commons." *Parliamentary Affairs* 36: 7–27.

Oberle, Frank, MP. 1983. "Caucus Reform: Update August, 1983." Ottawa.

———. 1984. "Caucus Reform in the Canadian Conservative Party." *The Parliamentarian* 16: 39–43.

Ort, Karen M. 1979. "The Role of the Shadow Cabinet in the 30th Parliament." Paper presented to the Canadian Parliamentary Internship Program, June, Ottawa.

Pelletier, Serge. 1981. "Parliamentary Caucuses in the Old Commonwealth Countries: Roles, Structures and Operations." Ottawa: Research Branch, Library of Parliament.

Perlin, George C. 1980. *The Tory Syndrome: Leadership Politics in the Progressive Conservative Party*. Montreal: McGill–Queen's University Press.

Pitkin, Hanna F. 1967. *The Concept of Representation*. Berkeley: University of California Press.

Pross, Paul. 1982. "Space, Function and Interest: The Problem of Legitimacy in the Canadian State." In *The Administrative State in Canada*, edited by O.P. Dwivedi, pp. 107–30. Toronto: University of Toronto Press.

Punnett, R.M. 1977. *The Prime Minister in Canadian Government and Politics*. Toronto: Macmillan.

———. 1984. "Regional Partisanship and the Legitimacy of British Governments 1868–1983." *Parliamentary Affairs* 37: 141–59.

Rivington, Lynda. 1983. "Sanctum/Sanctorum: The Role of Caucus." *Parliamentary Government* 4 (1): 2–7.

Roche, Douglas. 1976. *The Human Side of Politics*. Toronto: Clarke, Irwin.

Rose, Richard. 1980. *Do Parties Make a Difference?* Chatham, N.J.: Chatham House.

———. 1983. "Still the Era of Party Government." *Parliamentary Affairs* 36: 282–95.

Simpson, Jeffrey. 1980. *Discipline of Power: The Conservative Interlude and the Liberal Restoration*. Toronto: Personal Library.

Stamp, Robert M. 1964. "J.D. Edgar and the Liberal Party: 1867–1896." *Canadian Historical Review* 44 (June): 93–105.

Stanfield, Robert. 1984. "The Role of National Parties." *Policy Options* 5: 6–10.

Stewart, John. 1977. *The Canadian House of Commons: Procedure and Reform*. Montreal: McGill–Queen's University Press.

Thomas, Paul G. 1978. "The Influence of Standing Committees of Parliament on Government Legislation." *Legislative Studies* 3 (4): 691–99.

———. 1980. "Parliament and the Purse Strings." In *Parliament, Policy and Representation*, edited by Harold D. Clarke, Colin Campbell, F.Q. Quo and Arthur Goddard, pp. 160–80. Toronto: Methuen.

———. 1982. "The Role of House Leader in the Canadian House of Commons." *Canadian Journal of Political Science* 15: 127–44.

Walkland, S.A., ed. 1979. *The House of Commons in the Twentieth Century*. Oxford: Clarendon Press.

Ward, Norman. 1952. "The Formative Years of the House of Commons, 1867–1871." *Canadian Journal of Economics and Political Science* 18 (4): 431–51.

———. 1966. *A Party Politician: The Memoirs of Chubby Power*. Toronto: Macmillan.

Young, Walter D. 1969. *The Anatomy of a Party: The National CCF, 1932–1961*. Toronto: University of Toronto Press.

3

Regionalism, Party and National Government

PETER AUCOIN

Introduction

In the original design of Canada's institutions of national government, the founding fathers sought to ensure that regional interests would be represented at the centre of political decision making but accommodated within the confines of party government. Party government, it was acknowledged, constituted the foundation of "responsible government," which is the basic constitutional convention of parliamentary government. Although less developed then than it is today, the basic dynamic of party government was well understood at the time of Confederation. Party government would provide the legislative majority in the elected House of Commons to sustain effective executive power in the cabinet and enable national and regional interests to be reconciled within the cabinet at the apex of party government. In this way, party government would provide the critical link between the political forces of regionalism then extant in the new Dominion and the constitutional requirements of parliamentary government as the principal form of government.

Precisely because of these political forces of regionalism, however, the Confederation settlement also required the adoption of a federal form of government. But the ways in which our founding fathers sought to combine parliamentary and federal government demonstrated clearly that the parliamentary form was to take precedence over the federal principle. Indeed, a foremost student of comparative federal constitutions, K.C. Wheare, describes our original constitutional design as merely "quasi-federal." Wheare means that the central government had the power to intervene in certain areas of provincial jurisdiction. The federal-provincial division of powers could be overridden by certain instruments of the national cabinet, despite the division of powers as spelled out so precisely in the British North America Act.[1]

The Fathers of Confederation were confident that both this design and the operation of party government would secure a system of strong central or national government, a system strong enough to overcome the regional or sectional divisions of the new Dominion.

Since 1867, changes in the constitutional and political systems of Canada have altered a number of the assumptions upon which our original design was predicated. Only rarely, if at all, have the conditions which the founding fathers hoped would prevail actually prevailed. With precious little in the way of formal constitutional change, our "quasi-federal" constitutional framework gave way to a de facto system of federal government. Our party system, once a two-party system, became not only a multi-party system with strong regional party preferences but also one in which legislative majorities were not always achieved in the House of Commons. Finally, party government itself could ensure neither that regional interests were adequately accommodated within the cabinet nor that the cabinet had adequate control over the administration of national public affairs.

It is the thesis of this paper that our original constitutional design has proved to be ineffective in its capacity to ensure that our national institutions of government represent and respond to regional interests in ways that reconcile them with national interests. In the sections that follow, the basic elements of this design are outlined. Its deficiencies are then analyzed, with particular emphasis given to the practice of party government, which was meant to provide the mechanism whereby regional interests would be represented and reconciled with national interests in the formulation and administration of national policy. The paper concludes with an assessment of what is required in terms of a redesign of our institutions to accommodate regionalism.

The Constitutional Design of National Government

The combination of parliamentary and federal government that comprised the constitutional arrangement of 1867 was an attempt by the founding fathers to achieve a compromise between those who favoured a strong "legislative union" for governing the new Dominion and those who insisted on some measure of local control over their public affairs. Parliamentary government was adopted to give the Dominion, as the British North America Act stated, "a constitution similar in principle to that of the United Kingdom." At the same time, however, the BNA Act created two orders or levels of jurisdiction: national and provincial. In this respect, our constitution was not "similar in principle" to that of the United Kingdom.

However, for several reasons, the constitutional design of 1867 did not give equal weight to each of these two principles of government. First, the legislative powers given to the Dominion Parliament were meant to establish the national government as the principal order of government insofar as the political economy of the time was concerned. Second, the general legislative powers of Parliament for "the peace, order and good government" of Canada, as well as the significant executive powers vested in the national government, were also meant to establish the dominance of the national government in the constitutional arrangement. Third, the inclusion of the Senate as the second chamber of Parliament meant that "both the less populous provinces and the predominantly French-speaking province of Quebec were . . . given some protection against the wishes of a simple majority of Canada's population, as represented by the decisions of the House of Commons."[2] But this was little more than a token recognition of the federalist principle in the design of the national government, since the Senate was to be appointed by the Crown, in fact by the prime minister, on the basis of party.

The paramountcy of the parliamentary principle was the result of the prevailing opinion among the founding fathers that the new Dominion should have a national government based upon the "unity principle" or "majoritarianism." This view rejected the American system of checks and balances within the national government, as well as the federalist basis of the national institutions of government. As Jennifer Smith puts it:

> The Canadian fathers described parliamentary government in the following manner: undemocratic yet popularly responsive; animated by the principle of unity of action; capable of great strength, vigour and speed; authoritative, possibly because of the monarchial element; majoritarian.[3]

The Canadian Senate was the price paid by those founding fathers who favoured a strong legislative union governed by majoritarianism in order to secure the Confederation settlement. But it was a small price. Party government was sufficiently well established as the basis of responsible government to assure that effective power was based upon legislative majorities in the House of Commons. In this sense, and especially insofar as the institutions of national government were concerned, the British form took complete precedence over the American form.

The British view prevailed sufficiently to lead to establishment of a national government that was predominant over the provincial order of government and was essentially parliamentary in form, but there was also political recognition of the need to represent and accommodate regional or sectional interests within the national government and national policy. Party government was not only preferred but was seen as the ideal political mechanism to serve this purpose. It provided the opportunity for coherent policy, legislative majorities, executive control over administration, and disciplined parliamentary representation. These arrangements were to enable national and regional interests to be reconciled in an efficient yet reasonable manner.

Party Government as National Government

The use of party government as the principal mechanism for linking the political forces of regionalism and the constitutional requirements of national government meant that a number of conditions had to be met in whole or in part. The basic assumptions were that:

- the national government would be dominant over the provincial governments;
- the governing parties would be national in terms of representation and policy;
- the cabinet would exercise tight control over the administration of national public affairs; and
- the legislative parties in the House of Commons, however disciplined for the purposes of responsible government, would provide the forum for regional interests to be represented in party caucus and, in the case of the governing party, in cabinet.

A number of developments since Confederation have affected these conditions in ways which have undermined the capacity of party government to provide effective national government. Among the most important of these are: the federal system, the party system, the electoral system, the executive system, and the legislative system. Although these systems constitute only parts of a total system, each will be considered separately and then their interrelationships will be discussed.

The Federal System

Despite the high hopes of the founding fathers for assuring the paramountcy of the national government within Confederation, which they believed they had secured in the British North America Act of 1867, their fundamental assumptions have not been realized in actual political experience. The regional political forces which necessitated adoption of the federal form of government in 1867 did not abate in the immediate post-Confederation period. Rather, these forces were transformed into the political bases upon which provincial governments asserted their jurisdictional claims against the Dominion government. These claims, moreover, were supported in large measure by judicial decisions on constitutional disputes between the two orders of government — decisions which have transformed the federal constitution. In the process, the national government has come to operate in a "federal" system as opposed to the "quasi-federal" system instituted at the outset.[4] Party government at the national level was unable to check these forces of regionalism within the federal system.

This transformation of our constitutional system of federal government has clearly affected the capacity of party government to provide the kind of national government the founding fathers desired. It is not necessary here to detail all the constitutional or political ramifications of this change.[5] A complex array of formal and ad hoc institutional arrangements has developed for intergovernmental relations, and well-established political norms have evolved in support of both the autonomy and interdependence of the two orders of government. The result is a pattern of "intergovernmental governing" that has elevated the provincial order of government to a level of importance beyond what the founding fathers considered appropriate.

An important consequence of federalism which has become very pronounced in recent decades has been its extension to the major national political parties. This is discussed in the study by David Smith in this volume. There is no simple cause-and-effect relationship between our constitutional and party structures. However, the basic patterns of our constitutional system, with the jurisdictional independence of our two orders of government, have created a significant degree of organizational separation between the national and provincial wings of the major parties. This separation has diminished the capacity of national party leaders to assert the national objectives of their party over the provincial objectives of their partisan colleagues, and conversely has diminished the capacity of national party leaders to assert their claims to be the principal party representatives for their province or region in national politics. This makes the national parties less effective instruments for the reconciliation of national and regional interests, because provincial parties claim to represent regional interests. In this sense, the operation of party government at both national and provincial levels of government has dictated a competition within as well as between parties.

The Party System

Other developments in our party system have also had important consequences for our system of party government at the national level. The most obvious and important change in the party system in Canada since 1867 is the development of a multi-party system. Having more than two parties increases the likelihood that the governing party will be unable to represent or respond to regional interests adequately, as it may have few or no elected members from some regions of the country. The multi-party system has not only fostered regional party preferences but also has weakened the ability of the parties to act as unifying forces within the national political system. The electoral system, to be considered below, has contributed to the problem, but it is not the only factor.

Ideological reasons relating to political philosophy on the role of the state have also accounted for the most important of our "new" parties. But although regionalism per se has not been the only determinant of the rise of new parties, especially not in the case of the Co-operative Commonwealth Federation/New Democratic Party or the Social Credit Party, socio-economic, ethnic and political factors have led certain regions to favour one or two parties over the others. Consequently, the very multiplicity of parties has served in some critical ways to further regionalize our party system.

The Electoral System

Our use of the "first-past-the-post" or simple plurality electoral system has meant that party representation in the House of Commons, either nationally or regionally, need not be in accord with the national or regional level of popular support a party receives. Rather, a party can be either over-represented or under-represented, given the workings of our electoral system. Since regional party preferences have constituted an important determinant of electoral outcomes, our parties have found themselves subject to regional voting patterns that cut across a region and thus encompass more than a single constituency. When these patterns favour a party, it will be over-represented in the region in terms of the number of seats it obtains relative to its share of the region's popular vote. When these patterns do not favour a party, it will be under-represented. The consequences are well known: our major parties at times have been "regionalized" and indeed our party system has included what can only be described as "regional parties." These electoral issues are examined in the paper by William Irvine in *Institutional Reform for Representative Government*, volume 38 in the Commission's research series.

When the governing party is subject to this "regionalized" effect, then its legislative caucus in the House of Commons is drawn primarily or only from certain regions and its cabinet will have few or no elected representatives from the other regions. In such circumstances, the instrument of party government is deficient on the political criterion of regional representation.

Although the incidence of this deficiency has varied over time, it has occurred often since the Second World War. In some respects, the massive national majorities of 1958, 1968 and 1984 may constitute a reaction of sorts to this phenomenon. In any event, it is well to remember that highly regionalized electoral outcomes, in both cases producing minority governments, followed the 1958 and 1968 landslides. Moreover, the increased incidence of regionalized electoral outcomes has accompanied the significant growth of the state, making the deficiencies of party government with respect to regional representation even more serious than in earlier periods. Accordingly, it is not surprising that changes to the electoral system have been on the reform agenda for the past several years.

What is most instructive about the character of the many electoral reform proposals offered over the past decade or more is their focus on the need to provide a greater degree of national or cross-regional representation in the legislative parties. The assumption of course is that party government cannot be an effective basis for national government if the major parties, and especially the governing party, do not contain elected representatives from all regions of the country. The present electoral system is viewed as deficient on this criterion because it does not reasonably ensure balanced regional representation. The electoral outcomes of 1958, 1968 and 1984 are therefore the exceptions to the more likely outcome.

The Executive System

Party government as the vehicle for responsible government is predicated upon the assumption that the prime minister and cabinet have effective control over the formulation and implementation of public policy. It also assumes, of course, that regional interests will be represented and accommodated in these processes.

From the outset, regional representation has been an important factor in the composition and operation of the cabinet. More than one prime minister has had to face the problem of constructing a cabinet representing all regions when the party representatives in the House of Commons did not represent all regions of the country. A number of other developments have also diminished the capacity of cabinet and of party government to link regional and national interests. Among the most important of these are:

- the organization of our modern "administrative state";
- the significant role played by Crown corporations and regulatory agencies; and
- the structures and processes of the cabinet itself.

These developments are discussed in papers by Kenneth Kernaghan and by Herman Bakvis and myself, in *Regional Responsiveness and the National Administrative State*, volume 37 in the Commission's research series.

The organization of our modern administrative state has been designed primarily to manage the highly differentiated functions now undertaken by the national government. The result is a structure that is functional and not regional in its orientation.[6] This was true at the time of Confederation and the development of the modern administrative state has not altered this orientation. Rather, it has been reinforced by the institution of the merit system in the national public service, by priority in staffing given to technical expertise and by the close and mutually supportive relationships between the public service and its functionally organized clientele.

This functional orientation, as well as the size and complexity of the contemporary bureaucracy, present a challenge to ministers who wish to represent regional interests in the formulation and implementation of public policy. In order to do so, these ministers must introduce a regional perspective on national policy within a bureaucratic structure that is focussed instead on functional considerations.

The success of ministers in this regard is mixed at best, especially in the postwar period which witnessed the full flowering of the modern administrative state. On the one hand, a number of ministers, especially those with clearly identified responsibility for representing regional interests, have managed to assert their authority in order to accommodate these interests. On the other hand, with a few important exceptions, the administrative machinery of government at the bureaucratic level is structured in ways that do not facilitate, let alone promote, administrative responsiveness to spatial or regional interests. Hence, ministers who succeed in introducing a regional perspective on national policy must do so in spite of the bureaucratic organization.

The role of Crown corporations and regulatory agencies within the executive system has been significant from the perspective of party government because these organizations have been delegated a degree of autonomy from cabinet direction and control that puts them at "arm's length" from the operations of party government.[7] Although there is considerable variation in the autonomy granted each of these organizations, the general result has been that a major part of government policy and administration is not under direct cabinet management.

The need for regional representation within Crown corporations and regulatory agencies is recognized in appointments made to their boards. But such representation is one step removed from the centre of elected regional representation in the political executive. Moreover, these organizations themselves are functionally oriented in the same way as government departments, and there is little evidence that they are any more sensitive to regional interests than are government departments. If anything, their relative autonomy may make them even less sensitive.

The third major development within the executive system that has affected the capacity of party government to represent and accommodate regional interests within national government involves changes to the structures and processes of cabinet itself. There are two contradictory developments. On the one hand, there has been increased recognition within government, beginning with the Diefenbaker government in the late 1950s, that the regional dimension of national policy should be given high priority and that this should be reflected in the structures and processes of the cabinet. The ultimate reflection of this recognition occurred in 1982, when a major committee of cabinet was reorganized as the Cabinet Committee on Economic and Regional Development, with the expressed intent that all ministers who were members of this committee become responsible for the recognition of regional interests in national economic development policy. On the other hand, the growing dominance of the prime minister over the cabinet and governing party and the establishment of a more functionally structured cabinet have reduced the capacity of ministers individually and collectively to represent and accommodate regional interests in cabinet decision making.

Taken together, these contradictory developments represent the organizational dilemma for party government in seeking to accommodate both spatially oriented regional interests and national interests which are functionally oriented. These two orientations overlap in certain sectors of public policy such as fisheries or agriculture, and this has minimized somewhat the organizational dilemma in that certain portfolios can be assigned to ministers from certain regions. But the growth and complexity of state intervention over the past four decades have further complicated the efforts of successive national governments to cope with this dilemma. Since the late 1960s, television has personalized national politics, and this has strengthened the position of the prime minister. In addition, the agencies that serve the prime minister have been strengthened. At the same time, cabinet decision making has become both more hierarchical and decentralized.[8]

While this personalization of politics has not increased the powers of the prime minister, it has given him a greater degree of independence from cabinet and caucus. A prime minister cannot ignore the regional dimensions of national politics or public policy, but he now is less dependent upon cabinet colleagues for regional political support. Television and the entire mass media have given the prime minister a national constituency. It is the prime minister rather than regional party leaders who garners the support of the electorate in each region. Regional ministers are not eliminated by virtue of this development, but their status now is much more dependent on the personal style and disposition of the prime minister.

At the same time, in order to cope with the demands on the government decision-making system, the Prime Minister's Office and the Privy Council Office have been strengthened. The former serves the prime minister as party leader and the latter serves him as the chief executive officer of the government. The Privy Council Office also doubles as a cabinet office to serve other ministers in their roles as members of a collective executive. These two "central agencies" have used their control over the information system to strengthen the position of prime minister and to manage the central elements of cabinet decision making.

This centralization has also led to the creation of a functional if not official "inner cabinet" that has introduced a formal hierarchical principle to the decision-making system. As a result, the burden of representing regional interests with respect to the cabinet's major priorities now falls on the dozen or so senior ministers who comprise the Planning and Priorities Committee, including of course the prime minister, who chairs the committee. This concentration of power within the "inner cabinet" is balanced by the decentralization of decision-making authority to committees organized by function or sector, such as the Treasury Board or the economic and regional development and social development committees. While this decentralization of authority is significant, the representation of regional interests is dispersed among the ministers who sit on these committees. Thus, the full cabinet no longer constitutes the forum wherein regional interests are represented and accommodated in government policy making. To be effective, regional ministers now must not only convince the prime minister and their cabinet colleagues of the need to accommodate the regional interests which they represent, but must accomplish this within a decision-making system that has become more formal, structured and complex.

The Legislative System

An essential feature of responsible party government is that the cabinet — the political executive — must have the confidence of a majority in the House of Commons — the elected legislature. The basic dynamic in our operation of this kind of party government is "party discipline." This dimension of party government is often misunderstood as nothing more than the exercise of power by legislative party leaders over their party members. Although it is usually recognized that any exercise of power involves positive incentives as well as negative sanctions, this focus on "power" more often than not misses what is perhaps the essential element of party discipline. Party discipline is first and foremost a consequence of the pursuit and maintenance of political power, a discipline that is accepted by leaders and followers alike as a prerequisite to success in party competition. The positive incentives and negative sanctions available to party leaders, especially but not exclusively to the leaders of the party in power, are not insignificant but generally have the acceptance of the party members. They have rarely been effective when this general acceptance was lacking. When a common partisanship has not been sufficient to maintain unity within a legislative party, discord and thus independence have soon appeared.

At the same time, however, at least two features of Canadian politics and government have given rise in recent decades to an increase in the need for party discipline. These features include party leadership and the mass media.

The selection of party leaders by national party conventions has increased the extent to which the party leader has a national constituency, particularly because of the attention focussed on leadership conventions by the mass media. The media now treat national elections as contests between party leaders whether or not the parties themselves engage in such campaigns. These developments have not only strengthened the role of the leader in determining party policy, but also increased the need for party discipline. Party leaders are now less obligated to accommodate all factions and interests within their party as they play to their national constituency, and the need to project a strong leadership image has made party discipline even more necessary.

The mass media have affected the need for party discipline in a second way. The media, particularly television, have become the principal means for government and parties to communicate with the general public and electorate. The media's demand for drama, conflict and controversy has tended to promote partisanship between the parties. The media's search for news and politicians' search for exposure have led to an escalation of party competition, even on a daily basis: the bearpit of "question period" says it all.

The media are often critical of party discipline, primarily because it restricts their access to conflicts and controversies within parties, especially within the governing party. In fact, the persistence of the media in pursuing all signs and indications of breaches in party discipline or unity, and their ability to present them on an instantaneous and national basis on television and radio (as opposed to presenting reports by journalists of what was allegedly said by a minister or MP), have led parties to pay strict attention to party discipline in all conceivable public forums to which the electronic press have access. Insofar as parties are concerned, "1984" arrived with the advent of political reporting by the electronic media.

Partly in response to these developments, the party caucus has become a more important institution of party government, as noted in the study by Paul Thomas in this volume. The privacy of this unofficial forum enables parties to consider, more fully and directly (and more frankly) than it can in public, those interests which it cannot always accommodate in party policy or, in the case of the governing party, in government policy. In this sense, the caucus is more than simply a safety valve for the expression of discontent with party policy. It is the mechanism whereby the members of caucus can seek to consolidate their position within the party decision-making process. Efforts towards this ideal over the past two decades have been greater than was previously the case.

The party caucus has also been used to offset the functional and sectoral orientation of the legislature itself. Just as the cabinet has become more formally structured along functional and sectoral lines, so has the House of Commons, particularly with regard to its system of standing committees. Private members have had to find ways to assert their responsibilities for the representation of regional interests, as have ministers. The device which has been developed to serve this purpose is the regional caucus, which allows regional groupings of MPs to ensure that the regional dimensions of party policy are discussed and articulated first within the regional caucus and then in the full caucus. Although this device appears to have proved itself useful to the major parties on many occasions, it is noteworthy that it has been primarily a corrective device deployed as a last resort in party decision making.

An Overview of Party Government

Constant change in the political environment makes it difficult to assess an organizational design for government over a long period of time. It is clear, however, that a number of the assumptions of the founding fathers that were incorporated in their design for party government no longer obtain. This is especially true with respect to the design of party government as the mechanism to link the representation of regional interests to the requirements of national government. The national government and the national party leaders no longer dominate public affairs as the founding fathers assumed they would. Not only is the provincial order of government more important, but also provincial political leaders have assumed positions as representatives of regional interests in debate on national policy. In so doing, they have challenged both the right and status of national party leaders to speak on behalf of the regions at the national level. The fragmentation of the party system regionally, caused in part by the demise of the two-party system, has further diminished its ability to accommodate regional interests within national government as the founding fathers intended. This has been reinforced by the electoral system, even if the effect was unexpected and unintended. In some years, the government party has been shut out electorally in some regions, which has virtually eliminated legislative representation in the governing party from those regions.

Institutional arrangements are only partly responsible, of course. Political, governmental and judicial decisions, at various levels and over time, have also influenced these changes, especially those made at the party level. When parties have failed to represent certain socio-economic or regional interests, they have found themselves without sufficient political support in these areas, and new parties have been formed. These circumstances have been sufficient to derail our system of party government in some important respects.

Accordingly, the institutions of national government are judged harshly for their failure to reconcile regional and national interests. They are regarded as obstacles to the reconciliation process. In light of political experience, the Canadian system of party government on this score has been deficient. This same political experience, moreover, indicates clearly that election of a governing party with support from all regions of Canada is insufficient. Institutional change is also required.

Principles of Institutional Design

The founding fathers originally designed the Senate as a second chamber of Parliament. They also were willing to allocate seats in the Senate to regions in a way that favoured the less populous regions (and provinces). But because the Senate was to be a second house of Parliament, with members appointed by the Crown, in effect by the prime minister, it was clear at the outset that the Senate would not be able to check the House of Commons. Despite the regional composition of the Senate, representation by region was not to check representation by population; the federalist principle was not truly present in our institution of national government. It was to be found only in the division of powers between the national and provincial orders of government and even here it was (or was thought to be) compromised to a considerable extent.

The attempt to base legislative majorities on representation by population ignored the federal principle insofar as our national institutions were concerned. The assumption that these majorities would be representative of all regions has not always obtained. Whether party has tempered the dominance of the more populous regions is more difficult to establish, given the lack of quantitative evidence and evaluation. The less populous regions and provinces often complain that the interests of Quebec and Ontario are too often equated with the national interest. From the National Policy of Sir John A. Macdonald to the National Energy Policy of Pierre Trudeau, the less populous, peripheral provinces have argued that their regional interests have been overwhelmed by the more populous central provinces.

For many years prior to the 1984 election, the distinction between electoral balance based on regional representation or on popular vote was blurred or confused. The Liberal Party, for example, was weak in the West, which was also a less populated region. The Conservatives, on the other hand, were weak in the populous province of Quebec. Since the critical political issue was one of regional representation per se, would-be institutional reformers tended to look either to change in the electoral system of the House of Commons or to an elected Senate or to both to resolve this general imbalance. Those who viewed the problem in terms of representation of regions with very different population structures tended to favour the construction of a second chamber, either a reformed Senate or a brand-new body, wherein provincial governments or legislatures would appoint "regional representatives" to check the House of Commons, at least on certain matters. Proposals along these lines, because they provided a role for provincial governments or legislatures in the institutions of national government, naturally muddied the waters even further.[9]

The Conservative sweep of 1984 has taken the urgency out of institutional reform. Long political experience, including long periods of one-party dominance, suggests, however, that even a strong majority government — the model of party government desired by the founding fathers — does not necessarily constitute an ideal institutional arrangement for national government.

I would argue on the basis of my analysis in this section that:

- the federal basis of our political system is now so well established that only incremental changes can be expected in the relations between the two orders of government;

- party government will continue to be the norm for our system of responsible parliamentary government; and
- Canada is not likely to dismantle its modern administrative state.

Within these bounds, what institutional changes would bring about a more appropriate design to link the political forces of regionalism to the requirements of national government? In my view the most suitable sites for reform are the Senate, the executive/administrative branch of government, and the parliamentary process, in that order.

Senate Reform

In Canada, the reconciliation of regional and national interests depends on the willingness to provide greater institutional weight to certain regions. The specific regional characteristics of our socio-economic order as well as the federal structure of our political system demand that the federalist principle be inserted into the design of our national institutions of government.

Senate reform constitutes the critical link to accommodate the forces of regionalism and the requirements of national government. It is only by way of the Senate, as a second chamber of Parliament, that we can institute representation by region to check representation by population, as instituted in the House of Commons. The Senate not only provides a more explicit form of regional representation than the House of Commons, but also elevates the regional criterion above the population criterion. Therefore, in the Senate, the regional interests of the less populous provinces seem to have a proportionately greater weight than the regional interests of the more populous provinces.

Senate reform is preferable to alternative reforms of institutional deficiencies. The alternative reform most often proposed is reform to the electoral system of the House of Commons to ensure that the governing party, if not all major parties, would represent all regions in the House of Commons. While desirable, electoral reform is not sufficient in itself. A legislative majority with adequate representation from all regions does not necessarily achieve a reconciliation of national and regional interests, particularly from the perspective of the less populous provinces. This reconciliation is more likely to arise under strong leadership representing the less populous regions, be they prime ministers like John Diefenbaker, regional ministers like Allan MacEachen, or provincial premiers like Robert Stanfield.

This shows that the institutions of national government should be structured in ways that use the framework of party government to represent regional interests on a firmer basis. Representation by region, which necessarily gives greater weight to the less populous regions, should become a central element in the institutional design. What is needed is a system of national government that combines a reduced dependence on the personal preferences of the prime minister or the individual capacities of regional ministers to accommodate regional interests, and a greater responsiveness to regional interests as represented within the institutions of national government. In short, regional interests are best advanced by including representation by region as a check on representation by population.

Incorporating representation by region into the institutional design while maintaining the principle of representation by population requires two fundamental changes. First, the Senate must become an elected house of Parliament. Neither appointment by provincial governments nor indirect election by provincial legislatures is a satisfactory alternative to direct election, for each would subject national policy to partisan considerations outside the established parties. This is acceptable in the American political system only because Congressional government is not based upon our understanding of party government. It is also acceptable in the West German political system only because its federal system is radically different from Canada's. Finally, the present Senate design, like that of the Crown, is separate from the political principles and practice of representative government. If the Senate is to be constituted on the basis of representation by region, then it must be part of representative government. This demands election.

Second, Senate powers must be restricted to a check on the House of Commons and must not constitute a veto on the House to which the cabinet is alone "responsible." This means a reduction of its formal powers, as established at the outset in the British North America Act of 1867 (now the Constitution Act, 1867). The logic here is based simply on the need for greater representation by region within our institutions of national government; the Senate need not be equal in powers to the House of Commons. The "power to delay," as set forth by the recent report of the Special Joint Committee of the Senate and House of Commons on Senate Reform, is sufficient to provide the required check.[10]

Similarly, in the composition of a reformed Senate, all regions (or provinces) need not be given an equal number of representatives. The federalist principle only requires that the composition of the Senate provide a weighting in favour of regions against population. In this respect, the Special Joint Committee's recommendation to adjust marginally the present provincial allocation of seats in the existing Senate accords more appropriately with the existing regional structure of our federal system without giving equal representation to all provinces.[11]

Given the requirements of party government as responsible government, what kind of electoral system should be used to elect such a reformed Senate? There are those who argue that party discipline will compromise the representation of regional interests by senators if the method and timing of Senate elections and the terms and tenure of office are dominated by partisanship to the same degree as in the House of Commons. Others are concerned that a Senate that is not elected according to the same system used for the House of Commons will be balkanized among regional parties.

Each of these concerns overlooks the role of party as the essential political feature of our system of parliamentary government. There is absolutely no reason to presume that partisanship and party discipline could be made less critical in the Senate simply by adopting a different electoral system (including any of the features noted above). Parties would have every incentive to contest Senate elections and to discipline senatorial behaviour, even if the Senate did not participate in the confidence convention of responsible government. Partisanship and party discipline are based not only on the shared interests of party members in having their party in power but also on the shared interests of party members in having their party's policies adopted as legislation; each requires that party members do whatever is necessary to ensure that legislative majorities are formed and maintained. Although the possible challenge to national parties from regional parties cannot be totally dismissed, experience indicates that new parties are successful because of perceived failures of the existing parties, rather than because of institutional factors per se.

Assuming the Senate will operate within our system of representative party government, what electoral system should be used? The basic alternatives are essentially two: the first-past-the-post system now used for election to the House of Commons or some system of proportional representation. The first alternative does not ensure that the major parties will have representatives from all regions of the country even when their share of popular support is significant in all regions. If this electoral system were applied to a legislative chamber with an even smaller number of seats, this characteristic would likely be magnified. If the governing party were not adequately represented in all regions in both the House of Commons and the Senate, then the check of the latter on the former would assume an excessively partisan character.

The second alternative, namely a proportional representation electoral system, would likely ensure some reasonable measure of representation from all regions in the Senate for the governing party, whether the required multi-member constituencies encompassed the entire province or (preferably) regions within each province. Equally important, such an electoral outcome would ensure that senators from all regions played an important role within party caucuses, especially in that of the governing party. In this way, representatives elected on the basis of representation by region would check those elected on the basis of representation by population. For these fundamental reasons, it is clear that an electoral system of proportional representation must be the preferred system for an elected Senate.

A Senate elected on this basis may rob the governing party of a legislative majority in the Senate, if past experience with party competition is an accurate basis for prediction. But since the Senate would not participate in the confidence convention of responsible government, and since past minority governments have generally been able to carry out their programs with the support of minor parties, major alterations in the practice of party government will probably not be required. Moreover, since party government clearly has suffered from an excess of executive dominance of the legislature, the demands of the upper chamber for greater cabinet responsiveness may actually improve the overall system.

With respect to the trade-off between executive control of the legislature and executive responsiveness to the legislature, the former clearly has the upper hand. It is hardly likely that a Senate elected on the basis of proportional representation would reverse this balance. What such a Senate would likely do is temper what has been an excess in the direction of executive dominance. Indeed, perhaps the ultimate litmus test of an elected Senate in putting a check on the House, on both an intraparty and interparty basis, will be its ability to temper the dominance of Parliament by the cabinet. Unless the institutional design promotes this, the reconciliation of national and regional interests in national policy will depend largely, if not entirely, on the discretion and personal dispositions of the party leaders.

Executive-Administrative Reform

A Senate elected along these lines would likely enhance the capacity of party government to incorporate regional interests in executive-administrative structures. Since any governing party would probably elect representatives from all provinces to the Senate, the ideal of cabinet representation from all regions would invariably be met. The selection of senators to serve in the cabinet would in no way diminish the role of an elected Senate under the Canadian system of party government; on the contrary, precisely because partisanship and party government would encompass the Senate, the appointment of Senators to the cabinet would enhance its role. In fact, this could be extended so that the cabinet included at least one senator from each province, especially if past growth trends of the cabinet continue. A cabinet including a number of senators should serve to reinforce not just the form but the substance of the original purpose of regional representation in the cabinet.

The Senate could also serve a useful function with respect to the regional responsiveness of Crown corporations and regulatory agencies if appointments to their governing boards required Senate approval. This is not to suggest that the representation of regional interests should constitute the sole criterion for assessing those nominated by the prime minister, but rather that at least increased attention should be paid to regional considerations. Such a process would also serve to alert appointees to these semi-autonomous corporations and agencies that they should be more responsive to the regional dimensions of their operations.

The obstacles to regional responsiveness found in the cabinet are also found in the governing boards of these corporations and agencies, perhaps to an even greater extent. While line departments as well as Crown corporations and regulatory agencies may vary in the design of their organizational capacities to be regionally responsive, the usual centralization for the purposes of policy planning and development remains, despite the apparent dispersal of their operational activities across the country. This centralization is often defended on the grounds of ministerial responsibility and public accountability, especially in line departments. But this excuse has served to create a bureaucracy in Ottawa which not only lacks regional or field experience, especially among middle and senior professional levels, but also possesses a deprecatory view of regional interests that are to be tolerated only when forced on them by their "political masters." These views, more often than not, are reinforced by their sectorally oriented clientele constituencies.

Not surprisingly, there is a good deal of resistance to the idea of invoking regional responsiveness as a criterion for organizational design on the part of those departments, corporations and agencies which have conformed to the highly centralized model of policy planning and development. They usually view demands to become more regionally responsive as intrusions on what ought to be considered their central objectives or missions. Insofar as regional interests are considered "intrusions," the most notable instance of this is the case of regional development policy, as noted in the Aucoin-Bakvis paper. Here the record is one of very gradual organizational change on the part of line departments, for example, to respond to the stated objectives of successive governments. Nonetheless, there has been some change and what there has been suggests that two elements of organizational design are important.

The first element is the need to single out a responsibility structure for the regional dimension of an organization's role or activities. If responsibility for the regional dimension is not identified and differentiated, or if the organization as a whole has only a diffuse responsibility for it, then its emphasis will in most instances be lost as an operating priority. Moreover, even external pressures are unlikely to produce the desired results. In short, some unit within the organization must have the responsibility for ensuring that the regional dimension is taken into account, especially in policy planning and development. There is no one best way to organize for this requirement that applies to all departments, corporations and agencies, but it must be present in some way.

The second element is equally critical and concerns the need for each organization to place some measure of its policy planning and development on a decentralized or regionalized basis, that is, decentralized to regional offices. Notwithstanding the ease with which information and personnel can now be communicated and transported, policy research and intelligence gathering on regional views, needs and opportunities remain functions which still require personnel in the field on a permanent basis. If this is not done, the organization's capacity for regional responsiveness will be limited accordingly. Few organizations meet this requirement. Most relegate regional officials to line management and operation of regional services.

These two organizational requirements are unlikely to be met, however, unless the cabinet itself adopts the regional dimension as a major goal. A reformed Senate could become a constant force for ensuring regional representation in both party government and cabinet decision making. At the same time, the design of the machinery for cabinet decision making and policy coordination also affects its capacity to accommodate regional interests in national policy and administration. The personal preferences of the prime minister for cabinet design are therefore crucial, given his responsibility for cabinet structure and organization. However, a good deal of experience with various management systems at this level has been developed over recent decades and a number of lessons have been learned.

The first lesson is that a highly structured cabinet, with an inner cabinet for setting the priorities for general government policy, which is supported by functional and sectoral committees having delegated powers for specific areas, is essential for maintaining the scope and magnitude of the national government's role in public affairs. A reduction in the role of the national government on the order required to simplify the cabinet structure is not likely. Some increase in the discretionary powers of individual ministers is clearly not out of the question. However, there are strong political forces, namely the need for the prime minister to be involved in critical decisions as they relate to a wide range of portfolios as well as the need for ministers to formulate government policy on a collective basis and to ensure that individual ministerial autonomy is kept within limits. Finally, it is most unlikely that increased discretion for officials in line departments or semi-autonomous organizations would be considered an acceptable alternative to the complex structures of cabinet decision making now in place. If anything, there will be greater efforts to rein in the discretion and autonomy of both officials in line departments and the governing boards of Crown corporations and regulatory agencies.

Recent cabinets, because they exceed the size usually considered practical for collective discussion of complex matters, present obvious difficulties for executive control and coordination. However, the managerial principles of hierarchy, specialization and delegation of complex structures enable them to cope better with complex functions. Therefore, the size of recent cabinets is not out of line with the functions they must perform. In fact, greater political control and coordination of the administrative state probably requires an even larger cabinet. The obvious and most appropriate way for enlarging the cabinet is by making greater use of "junior ministers" or, more formally, "ministers of state" to assist departmental ministers. This could serve to introduce a greater degree of coherence to the hierarchical structure of cabinet, a more effective span of control over complex policy portfolios, and a more politically responsive arrangement of staff-line relationships at the ministerial level. In so doing, the regional dimension could be inserted or reinforced within major portfolios beyond the administrative and organizational changes suggested above, because more than one minister would become involved.

The second lesson is that the central agency apparatus which supports cabinet decision making, especially in the inner cabinet, must be organized in ways that make ministers, including the prime minister, more open to expression of regional interests. In this regard, the brief experience of the decentralized Ministry of State for Economic and Regional Development (MSERD), with its regional offices in each of the provinces, is instructive. MSERD served both the minister responsible and the cabinet committee which he chaired. Each of its regional offices was headed by a coordinator who also participated in the central management committee of the ministry, and this provided a mechanism for incorporating the regional dimensions in national economic policy. The experience with this particular mechanism was short-lived and faced resistance to regional input from some officials at MSERD headquarters in Ottawa. The regional ministers, however, seem to have found this new approach very useful and productive, especially the interaction with the ministry's regional coordinators, which gave ministers in this policy sector generally better briefings on the regional dimensions of national policy. In addition, the regional offices of MSERD facilitated the communication of cabinet policy to the regions and the coordination of policy implementation within the regions.

Although the regional coordinators of MSERD survived the subsequent elimination of MSERD, their transfer to the portfolio of a line minister, even if this minister chairs a sectoral cabinet committee, means that the cabinet is not briefed by a secretariat organized to provide advice on the basis of professional input from regional officials. This deficiency is especially critical for the inner cabinet, given its function of establishing the general priorities for national policies — policies which must accommodate national and regional interests.

These lessons can be used for improving the design of an executive-administrative system that more effectively accommodates regional interests in the determination and implementation of national policy. Aside from the personal dispositions of the prime minister and powerful regional ministers, however, there are few political forces to promote this kind of design. Thus, an elected Senate, to provide for representation by region as a check on representation by population, constitutes an essential catalyst for reform to the executive-administrative system. Under the system of party government, a change in the dynamics of party caucuses is required to promote the institutional incentive for change.

Parliamentary Reform

Party government has clearly, indeed intentionally, restricted the institutional capacity of Parliament to reconcile national and regional interests in the formulation and administration of national policy. Not only has it virtually excluded the Senate from any role in representing regional interests, but also it has more generally confined the accommodation of regional interests within the arenas of caucus and cabinet. Opposition parties may object to government policies or those of semi-autonomous administrative organizations that are perceived to ignore or override regional interests. But in such cases, the opposition usually is — and is seen to be — inspired by partisan considerations. Only rarely does it induce government to reconsider its policies in order to accommodate the regional interests in question.

A Senate reformed along these lines could alter the traditional practice of party government, to make it more responsive to regional interests in at least three ways. First, the regional representation within the caucuses of the major parties, especially that of the governing party, would have an obvious effect on the full caucus and would facilitate the operation of a system of regional caucuses even if some regions were shut out of representation in the House of Commons. Second, representation of the interests of the less populous provinces would invariably be enhanced, as a result of the different weight in representation afforded these provinces in the Senate compared with that in the House of Commons. Third, the party caucuses would be able to strengthen their positions within the party hierarchies, in part because of the previous two factors. Even for the governing party, this would likely occur because a larger cabinet — if it were enlarged along the lines mentioned above — would meet less frequently as a full body. The experience of the past decade and more has shown caucuses to be a growing force within party government; an elected Senate would add to the momentum of this development.

Many of the factors leading to caucus reform in recent years have also led to changes in the public processes of parliamentary government and to demands for more change. The most notable of these involve the development of the existing standing committee system of the House of Commons and, more recently, the creation of ad hoc or special parliamentary task forces. Although standing committees and task forces differ in their functions, the differences in design enable private members of Parliament to contribute to policy debate in a forum wherein the dictates of party policy and thus the constraints of party discipline are relaxed, if not entirely absent.

The positive response of private members to the use of parliamentary task forces reflects in part their dissatisfaction with the existing system of standing committees, as noted in the study by Peter Dobell in *Institutional Reform for Representative Government*, volume 38 of the Commission's research series. These committees serve three purposes: legislative review, expenditure scrutiny, and investigation. Legislative review is the function most subject to party discipline, since it is government legislation which is under review, following its approval in principle in the Commons. The function of expenditure scrutiny is performed in an equally partisan manner, especially when ministers are present to defend their portfolio expenditures, although perhaps greater opportunity exists for members to obtain information on government policy and its implementation. The third function, which committees share with task forces, has the most obvious appeal to private members because it provides a measure of independence for members from party discipline.

The committee system of the House of Commons would benefit from recent developments and suggestions for continued change to enlarge its capacity to accommodate regional interests. Task forces also would afford private members more time to concern themselves with subjects touching on regional interests. The proposal to have ad hoc committees rather than standing committees review each bill, as is the practice in the British Parliament, would have the same effect. In short, a more flexible parliamentary process cannot but provide private members with greater opportunities for representing regional interests. Reinforced with a more significant parliamentary role for an elected Senate, the committee system would benefit by having both more special joint Senate-Commons committees and more attention paid to regional interests as a result of the anticipated greater priority given by Senators generally to the regional dimension of national policies.

These changes will give MPs political incentive to pay closer attention to the regional dimension of national policy in their party caucuses and in Parliament. Their desire for greater autonomy from the excessive strictures of party discipline, in both appearance and fact, and their anticipated future conflict with senators for the attention of their distinct but overlapping constituencies, will inevitably sharpen their responsiveness to regional concerns. This will be the case especially when the governing party does not possess a majority in the Senate; a "minority government" in the House of Commons as well would no doubt induce an even greater responsiveness to regional interests.

Conclusions

To be truly national, the national system of parliamentary government in Canada requires more than a simple majority in the House of Commons for passing legislation constituted on the basis of the principle of representation by population. National policy must accommodate and be seen to accommodate regional interests as well. Party government, the traditional mechanism for the accommodation of regional interests in national policy making, has too often been found wanting in this role.

Not only was its design fundamentally flawed in conception, but also the conditions required to enable it to be reasonably effective no longer obtain in some important respects, and only rarely in others. The institutional shortcomings of this mechanism have been overcome at times through astute and responsive political leadership at the level of national politics and through cooperative relations between national and provincial governments. But since our institutions of national government are not neutral in their effect on national policy, regional interests are accommodated in an effective manner only when political leaders are willing and able to act in ways that counter the built-in institutional bias of our present systems.

In order to offset the weight of these biases within our structures of parliamentary government, it is necessary that the basic dynamic of party government be altered in favour of the representation of regional interests. Clearly the most effective way to achieve this is by providing a check on the manner in which legislative majorities now determine national public policy. This is the logic for a reformed Senate, elected on the basis of representation by regions, as an essential part of parliamentary government. Such a change would temper the present balance in Parliament by giving greater weight to the less populous provinces. In so doing, it would modify but not distort the practice of party government. Party caucuses should be better able to reconcile regional interests with national interest in party policy and this in turn should serve to make our executive-administrative systems more sensitive to the regional requirements in the management of national public affairs. At the same time, party discipline within the legislative processes would likely be subject to greater restrictions as MPs and senators in the caucuses sought to be, and to be seen as, more responsive to the regional interests they represent in the Commons and Senate.

In short, a reformed Senate would be a catalyst for change in the several structures and processes that constitute party government. Consequently, party would be re-established as the crucial link between the political forces of regionalism and the political requirements of national government. The practice of party government would thus ensure that parliamentary government remained a suitable form for the institutions of national government within the federal system of government.

Notes

This paper was completed in January 1985.

1. K.C. Wheare, *Federal Government*, 4th ed. (London: Oxford University Press, 1963).
2. Special Joint Committee of the Senate and of the House of Commons on Senate Reform, *Report* (Ottawa: Minister of Supply and Services Canada, 1984), p. 7.
3. Jennifer Smith, "Intrastate Federalism and Confederation," in *Political Thought in Canada*, edited by Stephen Brooks (Toronto: Irwin Publishing, 1984), p. 274.
4. See Alan C. Cairns, "The Governments and Societies of Canadian Federalism," *Canadian Journal of Political Science* 10 (1977): 695–726.
5. See Donald V. Smiley and Ronald L. Watts, *The Reform of Federal Institutions: Intrastate Federalism in Canada*, volume 39 of the research studies prepared for the Royal Commission on the Economic Union and Development Prospects for Canada (Toronto: University of Toronto Press, 1985).
6. See A. Paul Pross, "Space, Function and Interest: The Problem of Legitimacy in the Canadian State," in *The Administrative State in Canada*, edited by O.P. Dwivedi (Toronto: University of Toronto Press, 1982), pp. 107–30.
7. See G. Bruce Doern, "Regulatory Processes and Regulatory Agencies," and John Langford, "Crown Corporations as Instruments of Policy," in *Public Policy in Canada*, edited by G. Bruce Doern and Peter Aucoin (Toronto: Macmillan, 1979), pp. 158–89 and 239–74.
8. See Richard French, *How Ottawa Decides*, 2d ed. (Toronto: James Lorimer, 1984).
9. For an outline of these various reform proposals see Donald V. Smiley and Ronald Watts, *The Reform of Federal Institutions*, and the paper by William P. Irvine in *Institutional Reforms for Representative Government*, volumes 38 and 39 of the research studies prepared for the Royal Commission on the Economic Union and Development Prospects for Canada (Toronto: University of Toronto Press, 1985).
10. Special Joint Committee, *Report*, pp. 29–31.
11. Ibid., pp. 28–29.

Peter Aucoin is Director of the School of Public Administration and Professor in the Department of Political Science at Dalhousie University, Halifax. He is Research Coordinator for the Representative Institutions section of the Politics and Institutions of Government Research Area, Royal Commission on the Economic Union and Development Prospects for Canada.

David E. Smith is Professor in the Department of Economics and Political Science, University of Saskatchewan, Saskatoon.

Paul G. Thomas is Associate Professor of Political Studies, University of Manitoba, Winnipeg.

THE COLLECTED RESEARCH STUDIES

Royal Commission on the Economic Union and Development Prospects for Canada

ECONOMICS

Income Distribution and Economic Security in Canada (Vol.1), *François Vaillancourt, Research Coordinator*

Industrial Structure (Vols. 2-8), *Donald G. McFetridge, Research Coordinator*

International Trade (Vols. 9-14), *John Whalley, Research Coordinator*

Labour Markets and Labour Relations (Vols. 15-18), *Craig Riddell, Research Coordinator*

Macroeconomics (Vols. 19-25), *John Sargent, Research Coordinator*

Economic Ideas and Social Issues (Vols. 26 and 27), *David Laidler, Research Coordinator*

---

* (C) denotes a Collection of studies by various authors coordinated by the person named.
   (M) denotes a Monograph.

POLITICS AND INSTITUTIONS OF GOVERNMENT

Canada and the International Political Economy (Vols. 28-30), *Denis Stairs and Gilbert R. Winham, Research Coordinators*

Vol. 28 Canada and the International Political/Economic Environment, *D. Stairs and G.R. Winham* (C)
Vol. 29 The Politics of Canada's Economic Relationship with the United States, *D. Stairs and G.R. Winham* (C)
Vol. 30 Selected Problems in Formulating Foreign Economic Policy, *D. Stairs and G.R. Winham* (C)

State and Society in the Modern Era (Vols. 31 and 32), *Keith Banting, Research Coordinator*

Vol. 31 State and Society: Canada in Comparative Perspective, *K. Banting* (C)
Vol. 32 The State and Economic Interests, *K. Banting* (C)

Constitutionalism, Citizenship and Society (Vols. 33-35), *Alan Cairns and Cynthia Williams, Research Coordinators*

Vol. 33 Constitutionalism, Citizenship and Society in Canada, *A. Cairns and C. Williams* (C)
Vol. 34 The Politics of Gender, Ethnicity and Language in Canada, *A. Cairns and C. Williams* (C)
Vol. 35 Public Opinion and Public Policy in Canada, *R. Johnston* (M)

Representative Institutions (Vols. 36-39), *Peter Aucoin, Research Coordinator*

Vol. 36 Party Government and Regional Representation in Canada, *P. Aucoin* (C)
Vol. 37 Regional Responsiveness and the National Administrative State, *P. Aucoin* (C)
Vol. 38 Institutional Reforms for Representative Government, *P. Aucoin* (C)
Vol. 39 Intrastate Federalism in Canada, *D.V. Smiley and R.L. Watts* (M)

The Politics of Economic Policy (Vols. 40-43), *G. Bruce Doern, Research Coordinator*

Vol. 40 The Politics of Economic Policy, *G.B. Doern* (C)
Vol. 41 Federal and Provincial Budgeting, *A.M. Maslove, M.J. Prince and G.B. Doern* (M)
Vol. 42 Economic Regulation and the Federal System, *R. Schultz and A. Alexandroff* (M)
Vol. 43 Bureaucracy in Canada: Control and Reform, *S.L. Sutherland and G.B. Doern* (M)

Industrial Policy (Vols. 44 and 45), *André Blais, Research Coordinator*

Vol. 44 Canadian Industrial Policy, *A. Blais* (C)
Vol. 45 The Political Sociology of Industrial Policy, *A. Blais* (M)

LAW AND CONSTITUTIONAL ISSUES

Law, Society and the Economy (Vols. 46-51), *Ivan Bernier and Andrée Lajoie, Research Coordinators*

Vol. 46 Law, Society and the Economy, *I. Bernier and A. Lajoie* (C)
Vol. 47 The Supreme Court of Canada as an Instrument of Political Change, *I. Bernier and A. Lajoie* (C)
Vol. 48 Regulations, Crown Corporations and Administrative Tribunals, *I. Bernier and A. Lajoie* (C)
Vol. 49 Family Law and Social Welfare Legislation in Canada, *I. Bernier and A. Lajoie* (C)
Vol. 50 Consumer Protection, Environmental Law and Corporate Power, *I. Bernier and A. Lajoie* (C)
Vol. 51 Labour Law and Urban Law in Canada, *I. Bernier and A. Lajoie* (C)

The International Legal Environment (Vols. 52-54), *John Quinn, Research Coordinator*

Vol. 52 The International Legal Environment, *J. Quinn* (C)
Vol. 53 Canadian Economic Development and the International Trading System, *M.M. Hart* (M)
Vol. 54 Canada and the New International Law of the Sea, *D.M. Johnston* (M)

Harmonization of Laws in Canada (Vols. 55 and 56), *Ronald C.C. Cuming, Research Coordinator*

Vol. 55 Perspectives on the Harmonization of Law in Canada, *R. Cuming* (C)
Vol. 56 Harmonization of Business Law in Canada, *R. Cuming* (C)

Institutional and Constitutional Arrangements (Vols. 57 and 58), *Clare F. Beckton and A. Wayne MacKay, Research Coordinators*

Vol. 57 Recurring Issues in Canadian Federalism, *C.F. Beckton and A.W. MacKay* (C)
Vol. 58 The Courts and The Charter, *C.F. Beckton and A.W. MacKay* (C)

FEDERALISM AND THE ECONOMIC UNION

Federalism and The Economic Union (Vols. 58-72), *Mark Krasnick, Kenneth Norrie and Richard Simeon, Research Coordinators*

Vol. 59 Federalism and Economic Union in Canada, *K. Norrie, R. Simeon and M. Krasnick* (M)
Vol. 60 Perspectives on the Canadian Economic Union, *M. Krasnick* (C)
Vol. 61 Division of Powers and Public Policy, *R. Simeon* (C)
Vol. 62 Case Studies in the Division of Powers, *M. Krasnick* (C)
Vol. 63 Intergovernmental Relations, *R. Simeon* (C)
Vol. 64 Disparities and Interregional Adjustment, *K. Norrie* (C)
Vol. 65 Fiscal Federalism, *M. Krasnick* (C)
Vol. 66 Mobility of Capital in the Canadian Economic Union, *N. Roy* (M)
Vol. 67 Economic Management and the Division of Powers, *T.J. Courchene* (M)
Vol. 68 Regional Aspects of Confederation, *J. Whalley* (M)
Vol. 69 Interest Groups in the Canadian Federal System, *H.G. Thorburn* (M)
Vol. 70 Canada and Quebec, Past and Future: An Essay, *D. Latouche* (M)
Vol. 71 The Political Economy of Canadian Federalism: 1940–1984, *R. Simeon* (M)

THE NORTH

Vol. 72 The North, *Michael S. Whittington, Coordinator* (C)

COMMISSION ORGANIZATION

Chairman

Donald S. Macdonald

Commissioners

Clarence L. Barber	William M. Hamilton	Daryl K. Seaman
Albert Breton	John R. Messer	Thomas K. Shoyama
M. Angela Cantwell Peters	Laurent Picard	Jean Casselman-Wadds
E. Gérard Docquier	Michel Robert	Catherine T. Wallace

Senior Officers

Executive Director
J. Gerald Godsoe

Director of Policy	*Senior Advisors*	*Directors of Research*
Alan Nymark	David Ablett	Ivan Bernier
	Victor Clarke	Alan Cairns
Secretary	Carl Goldenberg	David C. Smith
Michel Rochon	Harry Stewart	
Director of Administration	*Director of Publishing*	*Co-Directors of Research*
Sheila-Marie Cook	Ed Matheson	Kenneth Norrie
		John Sargent

Research Program Organization

Economics	Politics and the Institutions of Government	Law and Constitutional Issues
Research Director	*Research Director*	*Research Director*
David C. Smith	Alan Cairns	Ivan Bernier
Executive Assistant & Assistant Director (Research Services)	*Executive Assistant*	*Executive Assistant & Research Program Administrator*
I. Lilla Connidis	Karen Jackson	Jacques J.M. Shore
Coordinators	*Coordinators*	*Coordinators*
David Laidler	Peter Aucoin	Clare F. Beckton
Donald G. McFetridge	Keith Banting	Ronald C.C. Cuming
Kenneth Norrie*	André Blais	Mark Krasnick
Craig Riddell	Bruce Doern	Andrée Lajoie
John Sargent*	Richard Simeon	A. Wayne MacKay
François Vaillancourt	Denis Stairs	John J. Quinn
John Whalley	Cynthia Williams	
	Gilbert R. Winham	
Research Analysts	*Research Analysts*	*Administrative and Research Assistant*
Caroline Digby	Claude Desranleau	Nicolas Roy
Mireille Ethier	Ian Robinson	
Judith Gold		
Douglas S. Green	*Office Administration*	*Research Analyst*
Colleen Hamilton	Donna Stebbing	Nola Silzer
Roderick Hill		
Joyce Martin		

*Kenneth Norrie and John Sargent co-directed the final phase of Economics Research with David Smith

· AARON BLABEY ·

los TiPOS MALOS

SCHOLASTIC INC.

en

EL CONEJILLO CONTRAATACA